Spoils of War

Spoils of War

Women of Color, Cultures, and Revolutions

EDITED BY
T. DENEAN SHARPLEY-WHITING
AND
RENÉE T. WHITE

FOREWORD BY CHELA SANDOVAL

ROWMAN & LITTLEFIELD PUBLISHERS, INC.
Lanham • Boulder • New York • Oxford

ROWMAN & LITTLEFIELD PUBLISHERS, INC.

Published in the United States of America
by Rowman & Littlefield Publishers, Inc.
4720 Boston Way, Lanham, Maryland 20706

12 Hid's Copse Road
Cummor Hill, Oxford OX 9JJ, England

British Library Cataloging in Publication Information Available

Library of Congress Cataloging-in-Publication Data

Sharpley-Whiting, T. Denean.
    Spoils of war : women of color, cultures, and revolutions / T.
Denean Sharpley-Whiting and Renée T. White.
        p. cm.
    Includes bibliographical references and index.
    ISBN 0–8476–8604-3 (cloth : alk. paper).—ISBN 0–8476–8605–1
(pbk. : alk. paper)
        1. Minority women—Social conditions. 2. Afro-American women—
Social conditions. 3. Women, Black—Social conditions. 4. Women—
Arab countries—Social conditions. 5. Women and war. 6. Women—
Crimes against. 7. Patriarch. I. White, Renée T. II. Title
HP1161.S53 1997
305.42—dc21   97-10161
                                                                CIP
ISBN 0-8476-8604-3 (cloth : alk. paper)
ISBN 0-8476-8605-1 (pbk. : alk. paper)

Printed in the United States of America

⊚™ The paper used in this publication meets the minimum requirements of American National Standard for Information Sciences—Permanence of Paper for Printed
Library Materials, ANSI Z39.48-1984.

Contents

Acknowledgments

We would like to thank the Departments of Foreign Languages and Literatures, Sociology and Anthropology, and the programs in Women's Studies and African American Studies for their support of the Spoils of War symposium in the spring of 1995 at Purdue University. The Dean's Office in the School of Liberal Arts was equally gracious in their support of our effort.

And last but certainly not least, we would like to extend the greatest appreciation to the contributors in this volume and the editors at Rowman & Littlefield Publishers.

Foreword

Chela Sandoval

This book, *Spoils of War: Women of Color, Cultures, and Revolutions,* enacts the very narrative told in its title: those who were once "spoils of war" become its despoilers, a force that shatters war from within. The studies collected here were produced by feminist scholars, women of color and their allies, twenty-first–century warriors against war. Their research disrupts the meanings by which war is waged; their findings re-place the violence and confusion of war with a new poetics from which love is not absent. Their project is this challenge: to wage revolutionary peace. The weaponry they bring to this project are a hermeneutics, a specialized set of methods, techniques, and technologies, that interrupt the rationality of war.

Around 1969, the advance guard of a developing transnational political class of women of color identified and mobilized itself in relation to women's, decolonial, and ethnic liberation movements. Since that time, the United States has not stopped reverberating from the insertion of a radical form of difference into every cultural arena. When "difference" is defined as the point where sameness is disrupted, its meanings provide a paradigm for war. This paradigm addictively chains whatever is dominant to its potential disruption in a circumscribed marriage of meanings. The result are binary oppositions such as white/black, male/female, mind/body, same/different, high/low—those antagonistic couples that guide dominant rules of perception and social meaning. Third-world liberationists from Derrida to Anzaldúa have argued that the in-between can have no presence in this two-term system of difference that makes the war machine rumble.

Instead of the dominant or its binary partner, a third force, a radical form of difference, has swept Western cultural terrains. *"La conciencia de la mestiza,"* "womanism," "strategic essentialism," "differential conscious-ness," and the technologies of "U.S. third-world feminism" insist upon a strategic form of being that goes beyond any previous understanding of "difference:" it is from within this realm, argues one school of feminist scholars of color, that peace becomes possible. During 1970s social move-ments, feminists of color including Barbara Noda, Audre Lorde, Gloria Anzaldúa, and Paula Gunn-Allen identified this third space that is different from difference as an alternative technology: an "erotics" of power. This erotics moves between, through, and with meaning and brings about alter-native identities, citizen/subject positions, and possibilities for action. Lorde's rallying call for "Sister Outsiders" to recognize this erotics *as* "power," Anzaldúa's *"la conciencia de la mestiza,"* Spivak's "strategic essentialism," Noda's "lowriding through the movement," Gunn-Allen's "Dykes are like Indians," all represent varying descriptions of a similar methodology for peace that has been developed in relation to this in-between place, this borderlands of being. Early 1970s feminist intra-movement conflict was often caused when white feminists misheard the continual demand by feminists of color for this strange "difference" as a presumptive and destructive intervention in movement politics. Whether welcomed or dismissed, however, this particular form of U.S. third-world feminism eventually became the historical basis from which new approaches, methods, knowledges, aesthetics, and alliances have become available, not only within feminist thought, but also within cultural studies across disciplines. *Spoils of War: Women of Color, Cultures, and Revo-lutions* is a book that advances this late twentieth-century transdisciplin-arity and the forms of knowledge it produces. If the thesis of this book is that women of color and children are under siege and in rebellion, then this book seeks to identify the specifics of this war and resistance, while calling upon those allies who can help develop the tactics and strategies necessary for waging peace.

Upon what principles do twenty-first–century warriors against war wage revolutionary peace? Today, the zones are clear. Postmodernism is a neo-colonizing force. Yet oppositional alliance forces are mobilizing under equally mobile, eclectic, and presentist banners. These oppositional equiv-alencies, however, escape neocolonial, dehumanizing effects when the substance, values, and degrees of force of rebellion alliances are guided by the methodology of the oppressed. Alliance warriors who are guided by the

methodology of the oppressed are interventionists, assimilationists, nego-
tiators, radical transformers, and separatists who, as distinct cadres, become unified under the banner of a specific social movement theory. The
principles of the methodology of the oppressed are these:

1. To develop sign reading skills, reading power everywhere and always.
2. To engage in interventionary tactics designed to shift the powers
   of war that operate inside any sign system. The choices on the
   level of the sign are to deconstruct, or metaideologize.
3. To self-consciously inhabit and deploy differential consciousness,
   the identity that shifts to permit practitioners the ability to enact
   these principles.
4. To evaluate and guide each exchange wherein the self has a role
   with the aim of equalizing power among interlocutors. This eth-
   ical principle directs the previous three principles toward the goal
   of egalitarian redistributions of sexual, gendered, raced, physio-
   logical, social, cultural and/or economic powers.

Each of these principles can be operated independently. But when
utilized as a single apparatus they become an interrelated hermeneutics
of peace, a methodology of the oppressed. Commitment to this methodology has permitted feminists of color to ally across cultural geographies.
Moreover, this shared methodology generates other kinds of cross-national
coalitions. Its guerrilla operations call new peoples into being: country-
women, -men, and -children of the same psychic terrain. Their aim? To
carry on irresistible revolutions, to wage love across the postmodern world.

Preface

T. Denean Sharpley-Whiting and Renée T. White

History of the Project

Spoils of War: Women of Color, Cultures, and Revolutions evolved out of a discussion by the women's studies faculty and program affiliates at Purdue University on women in the war-torn Bosnia, Herzegovina specifically, and our responsibility and commitment as feminist activists and academics. A petition of sorts was discussed, and then the idea for an anthology emerged. However, following the women's studies retreat in the fall of 1994, the breadth and scope of the project changed considerably.

On 11 February 1995, the Women's Studies Program cosponsored the Spoils of War: Women, Cultures, and Revolutions conference with the Department of Foreign Languages and Literatures and with the support of the African American Studies Research Center, the Department of Sociology and Anthropology, and the Office of the Dean for the School of Liberal Arts. As the participants were heavily concentrated in the field of literature, we selected for this study only two papers from the conference. We envisioned a collection of essays that cut across not only disciplines but also cultural divides. And thus, in our attempt to open up the anthology to scholars in various fields, we broadened our conception of war and our geographic parameters and simultaneously refocused whose experiences of war the volume would articulate.

In his seminal study *On War*, Karl Von Clausewitz writes, "War is an act of force . . . which theoretically can have no limits." Clausewitz's discussion of war's theoretical limitlessness as an act of force refers explicitly to the escalation of physical force and the lack of restraint in the use of weaponry between opposed forces, resulting in indiscriminate killing and inconceivable brutality toward a state of "absolute" war. Using Clausewitz as a point of departure, our interpretation of war's theoretical limitlessness is subtended by its manifestations and, as Michael Walzer argues in *Just and UnJust Wars: A Moral Argument with Historical Illustrations*, its context:

> War is not usefully described as an act of force without some specification of the context in which the act takes place and from which it derives its meaning . . . it's not what people do, the physical motions they go through, that is crucial, but the institutions, practices, conventions that they make. Hence, the social and historical conditions that "modify" war are not to be considered as accidental or external to war itself, for war is a social creation.[1]

Within *Spoils of War: Women of Color, Cultures, and Revolutions*, the theoretical limitlessness of war is discussed as a struggle or conflict— cultural, economic, sexual, or racial—contextualized historically or presently, nationally or internationally, collectively or individually (in the DuBoisian sense of "warring souls"/ "double consciousness" or identities trapped within one body) as incited by patriarchy, and meted out through its social institutions, structures, mores, conventions, and racist-sexist practices. Social science conflict-theorists recognize that social inequality, which is mediated through race/ethnicity, gender, and social class, results in conflicts and competition for power. According to Marxian theory, war can be perceived as the efforts of the ruling class to maintain control over the proletariat. Economic exploitation and control over labor capital are ways to maintain social control over working people. Within an international context, women of color remain arguably the most economically, politically, and socially exploited "caste." Racism and sexism provide ideological justifications for their continued exploitation and oppression. These ideologies and their manifestations in social institutions can be thought of as acts of aggression and war against women of color.

A sexist and/or racist patriarchal culture and order posits and attempts to maintain, through violent acts of force if necessary, the subjugation and inferiority of women of color. As Joy James notes, "its explicit, general premise constructs a conceptual framework of male [and/or white] as normative in order to enforce a political [racial, economic, cultural, sexual] and intellectual mandate of male [and/or white] as superior." The warfront has always been a "feminized" and "colored" space for women of color. Their experiences in and perceptions of war, conflict, resistance, and struggle emerge from their specific racial-ethnic and gendered locations. *"Inter arma silent leges*: in time of war the law is silent," Walzer notes.[2] Thus, this volume operates from the premise that war has been and is presently in our midst.

"[Women] have a right to become free by their own efforts," John Stuart Mill argues. Yet, women's resistance sets in motion the Clausewitzian theory on escalation. When women resist, be it via organized, mass protests, solitary defiant stances, or merely driving as Shahrzad Mojab's essay reveals, "modifying" principles are introduced into warfare through a myriad of racist-sexist patriarchal stratagems.

Women of color exist within social realities shaped by both race/ethnicity and gender. The very fact that their struggles are often different from those faced by white women makes the use of traditional feminist investigations of women and warfare problematic. The public and private lives of women of color, as well as the struggles ensued therein, have often been interpreted and defined within schema that do not account for the intersection of ethnicity and gender. The ways in which war(s), as interpreted in this anthology, both constrains and constructs the existence of women of color has been largely erased from contemporary discourses on war. Such erasure occurs when attention is paid uniquely to race or gender. The multiplicity of identities embraced, rejected, and negotiated by women of color is delimited within theoretical investigations of struggle, resistance, and survival. Living as bodies imbued with racial and gendered meanings, women of color regularly face and challenge war(s) and struggle against becoming the spoils of war.

Living under colonial and neocolonial political leadership, participating in the economic growth of developing nations, raising families, defending one's territory (whether political, economic, geographic, or individual/ personal), battling physical and emotional assaults/invasions are all themes related both literally and metaphorically to warfare and struggle. As the works of Angela Davis, Toni Cade Bambara, Deborah King, bell hooks, and other activist-scholars recognize, the specific sociopolitical realities of women of color are continuously problematized, minimized, and rendered invisible by larger social institutions and structures. Thus, the warfront, "that masculine space," is necessarily feminized as long as economic systems, social constructions, and structures exist that adversely impact the lives of women of color. It is merely a question of naming the war and identifying the "hows" and "whys."

Unlike the preponderance of anthologies that address women of color and war in an essentially Third World context, the uniqueness of this volume lies in its transdisciplinary nature, its interdisciplinary approaches, and its national and international multi-ethnic/racial gendered experiences and metaphoric and symbolic representations of war(s). That is, we traverse the world cartography. As the Fourth Annual United Nations World Conference on Women held in Beijing highlighted, the violation of women and girls' human rights is a global issue, that inter/intraracial gender-specific wars, such as higher incidences of sexual abuse, rates of poverty, and educational inequalities, are as prevalent for U.S. women of color (those who openly identify and who are inescapably identified as such), whose social ills are exacerbated by their racialization, as for women of color in the Third World.

The Work

Spoils of War is divided into four thematic sections. Part one, "Working Women, Activist Academics, and the Politics of Academe," sets the tone and begins chronologically with Joy James's "Ella Baker, 'Black Women's Work,' and Activist Intellectuals," a discussion of activist and public intellectual Ella Baker's organizing of black women domestic workers in the 1930s. James analyzes excerpts from Ella Baker and Marvel Cooke's study, "The Bronx Slave Marts," of the economic exploitation, powerlessness, and sexual abuse experienced by black women workers at the slave marts in New York. She equally discusses the federal and state-sanctioned economic wars waged against black communities that forced black women into the occupation known as black women's work, literally out onto street corners, "auction blocks" to sell their labor and bodies. James powerfully contrasts the economic and sexual exploitation of the 1930s variety with that experienced by black slave women in the antebellum South. Lewis R. Gordon's essay picks up James's analysis in his "Struggling along the Race-Gender Academic Divide," an examination of how black women's historic relationship to work and in the workforce as loci of labor and production has determined their positionality in the academy as simultaneously "public property" and invisible, and the tensions that coexist for these women, ensconced primarily in African American Studies, with women's studies over the politics of representation, affirmative action, and liberation discourses.

Part two of this volume, "Spoils of War: Women, Sexual Identity, and Violence," tackles questions of sexual identity and sexual violence. Renée T. White's essay, "In the Name of Love and Survival: Interpretations of Sexual Violence among Young Black American Women," provides an ethnography of young black women and their experiences and interpretations of sexual and domestic abuse. White's data demonstrates the ways black women normalize and rationalize the existence of violence in their lives along sociopolitical contexts. The young women struggle to mesh ideas of romantic love and femininity with their assertions of strength, inde-pendence, and individual control—thus resulting in paradoxical perceptions of black femininity, womanhood, and the role of violence. T. Denean Sharpley-Whiting's "When a Black Woman Cries Rape: Discourses of Unrapeability, Intraracial Sexual Violence, and *the State of Indiana v. Michael Gerard Tyson*" continues with the themes of sexual violence, black women, black sexual politics, and "unrapeability." Sharpley-Whiting specifically analyzes the *State of Indiana v. Tyson* rape case to reveal how "race" functions in black sexual politics and in the dominant culture to elide violence visited upon black female bodies. As White's essay reveals the ways black women normalize and rationalize violence, Sharpley-Whiting equally addresses the cultural and legal normalizing of violence against black females from within and without black communities.

Both Shahrzad Mojab's and Janet Afary's essays in part three, "Middle Eastern Women, Feminism, and Resistance in the Postcolonial Era," discuss Middle Eastern women, patriarchy, feminism, and feminist resistance. Mojab's "Women and the Gulf War: A Critique of Feminist Responses" uses the Gulf War of 1991 as a point of departure to reveal the ways the war reinforced the subjugation of women in the region. Mojab also issues a critique of feminist responses to the war and the failure of the international women's movement to play a prominent role in prompting peace and the liberation of women. In "Feminism and the Challenge of Muslim Fundamentalism," Afary provides a comparative and cross-cultural critique of theoretical perspectives on feminism and gender in Islamic ideology. The basis and attraction of fundamentalism, maintains Afary, is its holding out of the "illusion that a return to traditional/patriarchal relations is the answer to the many social and economic problems that Third World countries face in the era of late capitalism." Hence, a battle is waged against a liberatory praxis rooted in gender equality or feminism as well as against those women who subscribe to it. In the main, Afary examines the various manifestations of the gender ideology in Islamic tradition in countries such as Pakistan, Sudan, and Algeria.

Alienation, exile, feminist consciousness, and collectivities figure prominently in part four, "Literary and Autobiographical Portraitures and Landscapes of Identity, Exile, and Gender." Valerie Orlando's "Women, War, Autobiography, and the Historiographic Metafictional Text: Unveiling the Veiled in Assia Djebar's *L'amour, la fantasia*" positions Algerian woman writer Assia Djebar's *L'amour, la fantasia* as a collective autobiography that interweaves Djebar's own story with the long, bloody history of French colonial occupation in Algeria. By creating a historiographic metafictional text, Orlando suggests that Djebar lends voice, identity, and subjectivity to "the feminine collective" hitherto silenced and erased.

"Contested Crossings: Identities, Gender, and Exile in *Le baobab fou*" by Marjorie Salvodon elaborates on Martinez's dilemma (of chapter 9) in a postcolonial African context. "Contested Crossings" investigates the complex relationship between exile and cultural identity in Senegalese woman writer Ken Bugul's autobiographical *Le baobab fou*. By situating *Le baobab fou* within the specific historical context of "post"-colonial crossings to the métropole in the twentieth century, Salvodon's essay defines the parameters of the warring relationship between two languages, two cultures, and two distinct locations. Geographic boundaries as well as linguistic, cultural, and social affiliations are destabilized and rendered obsolete by the black female protagonist's adjustment to the "new world."

Jacqueline Martinez evokes autobiography, biography, and colonial history to discuss the sociocultural and geographic tensions and identity politics around the Chicana lesbian body in "Radical Ambiguities and the Chicana Lesbian: Body Topographies on Contested Lands." Martinez examines the situation of war for the contemporary Chicana lesbian in light of the land and history of the southwestern United States. As Martinez notes, the Chicana lesbian, by virtue of her sexual orientation (perceived as Western), yet her politicization or nationalist identity (contained in the very name Chicana), occupies a place of radical ambiguity, whicha when read through a history of the land, problematizes the "assimilationist versus nationalist" and "complicitous-traitor versus loyal culturalist" binarisms. Meshing autobiography, the biographical-scholarly writings of activist academic lesbian Cherríe Moraga, and the colonial history of "ancestor mothers" to demonstrate her thesis around the rigid binarisms of cooptation and nationalism and Chicana lesbian subjectivity, Martinez suggests how the emergence of the Chicana lesbian as a site of "warring" demands reconsideration. Her reading creates different possibilities for understanding and achieving radical transformation for both the person and the social world.

Our title, *Spoils of War*, suggests that women are the booty, or victims of patriarchy. We, the editors, concede that women are oppressed and repressed culturally, socially, politically, and economically by a racist and/or sexist male hegemony, that women in patriarchal cultures exist as booty to be consumed, used, and traded off, that war(s) are indeed waged against women of color, but as the essays in this volume reveal, counterwars, resistances, and discourses are importantly waged by women of color.

Notes

1. Michael Walzer, *Just and UnJust Wars: A Moral Argument with Historical Illustrations* (New York: Basic Books, 1977), 24.
2. Walzer, *Just and UnJust Wars*, 3.

Part I

Working Women, Activist Academics, and the Politics of Academe

1

Ella Baker, "Black Women's Work," and Activist Intellectuals

Joy James

> In my organization work I have never thought in terms of "making a contribution." I just thought of myself as functioning where there was a need. And if I have made a contribution I think it may be that I had some influence on a large number of people.
>
> —Ella Baker

Intellectuals and Political Choice

A brilliant strategist in the civil rights movements, Ella Josephine Baker (1903–1986) was field organizer for the National Association for the Advancement of Colored People (NAACP) in the 1930s and 1940s, the first director of the Southern Christian Leadership Conference (SCLC) in the 1950s, and convener of the student conference in 1960 that led to the formation of the Student Non-Violent Coordinating Committee (SNCC), for which she served as advisor. Baker's "organizational work" expanded U.S. democracy and helped to redefine and radicalize intellectuals and activists in the civil rights era. Her radicalism transformed criticisms of racism into critiques of both capitalism and liberal acquiescence to oppressive state practices. Baker also channeled her critiques into confrontation with oppressive state practices as well as political opposition to exploitation through civil disobedience and grassroots organizing for a democratic society. Merging rhetoric about black liberation with activism, she embodied both political worker and intellectual.

Ella Baker's influence on a large number of people extends to generations who, knowing very little about or having never heard of Miss Baker,[1] were shaped by her political legacy. Baker's obscurity is as instructive as

3

her political thought and action. Charles Payne observes, "That Ella Baker could have lived the life she did and remain so little known even among the politically knowledgeable is important in itself. It reminds us once more of how much our collective past has been distorted—and distorted in disempowering ways."[2] Part of the distortion stems from which actors are privileged in political memory and knowledge. Reflecting the conservative/liberal bias that privileges men, whites, and the affluent, male civil rights leaders, contemporary civil rights historians minimized the role of African American women activists in this movement.[3] For most, leadership and agency have been distorted as primarily the attributes of male political and intellectual elites. It is not surprising that the contributions of radicals, particularly black women such as Ella Baker, who spoke and organized not only against racism but also capitalism and imperialism, go unrecognized.

Even the "knowledgeable" who remember Ella Baker's political contributions may do so in disempowering ways, this is, in ways that deradicalize her political commitments. For some, Ella Baker may represent the "organic intellectual" described in Antonio Gramsci's *Prison Notebooks* as the strategist whose theorizing to end oppression forms the "ribs corseting the masses." The organic intellectual as activist works with a theoretical and experiential political base, which is precisely how Ella Baker positioned herself. However, Miss Baker would likely reject as elitist any Gramscian characterization of her as a member of a political vanguard. One of her often-cited comments is that "a strong people don't need strong leaders." As an activist-intellectual with democratic vision, Ella Baker's thought reveals a strong sense of social change determined by "ordinary" people who wage political movements. Her relationships to impoverished and militant workers forged political perspectives that identified African American laborers and workers as political leaders. Such views on mass leadership shaped her facilitation of grassroots activism for the NAACP, SCLC, and SNCC. It also led to her resignations from NAACP and SCLC because their bureaucratic leadership, in her estimation, refused to commit to mass political activism. A study of her political life reveals the class, gender, and ideological differences simmering and erupting within the civil rights movement. A review of some of her earliest writings, published over half a century ago, reveals how her critique of violence incorporated an analysis of economic, sexual, and racial exploitation.

With political instincts grounded in lessons accumulated through organizing in New York City during the Great Depression, Ella Baker preferred to take her political directives from poor or working-class African Americans, rather than civil rights elites. This preference led some to marginalize her. Labor activism in Harlem planted the roots of her praxis in the political-economic conditions and collective leadership of black workers, youth, and women. With these roots, as a young, black woman worker during this era, Baker used her caste position to explore the relevancy and efficacy of various political views on black liberation.

Black Workers and Labor Activists

During Ella Baker's lifetime, "black women's work" generally meant field or domestic labor for whites (in the North it expanded to include factory work). For a more privileged minority of African American women, it also included teaching, which brought both status and a reprieve from the dehumanizing physical labor characterizing black women's work.[4] A graduate from Shaw University, the young Baker recognized the limitations of pursuing antiracist radicalism within a conservative, or racist profession. Refusing to acquiesce to white-controlled school boards, she rejected a career teaching school. In 1927, joining hundreds of thousands of black women migrating north in search of work and relief from Jim Crow, Ella Baker left a somewhat protected, privileged place in her hometown of Littleton, South Carolina, for New York City. Once there, she secured employment in the menial and racially-sexually exploited labor reserves, considered traditional "black women's work."[5] Refusing to accept exploitation, Baker began organizing with other African American workers for collective economic goals.

Racist and sexist hiring policies—the few African American businesses tended to hire men for clerical workers with the bias that men were, and should be, the primary "breadwinners"—meant that for several years Ella Baker's first and only paying job was as a restaurant waitress. Later obtaining factory work, and eventually employment as a journalist and paid political organizer, Ella Baker gained a wide range of work and social experiences.[6] These traditional and "nontraditional" jobs, along with organizing with Harlem trade unionists during the depression, deepened her understanding of economic exploitation in racism.

At the height of the depression, national production decreased by half; thousands were left homeless due to bank foreclosures; and millions were left jobless without compensation. By 1933, an estimated 66 percent of the "potential labor force of Harlem was unemployed."[7] In 1935, over two million African Americans were on relief. Concentrated in northern cities—eleven had African American populations of over 100,000 by the end of 1935—African Americans used their votes to increase the numbers of black city officials; yet the majority were impoverished.[8] In response to their conditions, largely unmitigated by electoral politics, African Americans formed Unemployed Councils, which supported multiracial organizing and organized nationwide "hunger marches" to agitate for immediate emergency relief and unemployment compensation legislation.[9]

Ella Baker describes New York City in the 1930s, with its "race" men and women, socialists, communists, and union activists, as a stimulating "hotbed of radical thinking." During the depression, Baker herself began to consider the structural nature of black exploitation and the need for organized responses to it:

> I began to see that there were certain social forces over which the individual had very little control. It wasn't an easy lesson for me to learn but I was able to learn it. It was out of that context that I began to explore more in the area of ideology and the theory of social change. So during the Depression years, I began to identify to some extent with the unemployed, the organization of the unemployed.[10]

Faced with increasing economic hardship, racist riots, hatred strikes, exclusion from better paying jobs and unions by northern white workers, and the racism of the federal government, African Americans increased their labor agitation, strengthening ties to socialist and communist organizations.[11] Although the majority of Harlem blacks did not join radical parties, many organized to create alternative economic relations in their personal survival and that of their families during the depression. The Young Negroes Cooperative League, which Ella Baker joined in 1932, was one attempt at community organizing for black economic self-sufficiency. Eventually working as coordinator of the league, Miss Baker administered its offices in Chelsea, organizing with others to establish stores and buying clubs throughout the country. Ella Baker worked in the league with George Shuyler, whom she called the originator of the "buy black" campaigns.[12] These campaigns attempted to discourage consumers from patronizing businesses with racist hiring practices. "Buy black" campaigns focused on black customers patronizing black businesses, yet intended more than "black capitalism" in that the campaigns critiqued structural unemployment and used economic boycotts as a labor strategy against racist businesses. The Harlem Labor Union picketed for jobs on 125th Street with "don't buy where you can't work" as its slogan, foreshadowing the picket lines and boycotts of the civil rights movement in the South.[13] Devastated by the depression, many blacks became (ideologically) receptive to cooperative, noncapitalist economic and social relations. In the league, people collectively banked funds, purchased goods, and donated services and resources to the cooperative. The leagues also offered a set of social relations similar to the extended, southern families familiar to Harlem residents. By 1930, nearly half of Manhattan's African American population had been born in the South.[14] African Americans also gathered in cooperative classes in settlement houses and Negro women's clubs.[15]

According to Ella Baker, young African Americans joined the Young Negroes Cooperative League during the depression because they "were feeling the pinch, so when people feel the pinch they do certain things that they wouldn't do otherwise." The Young Negroes Cooperative League offered an alternative to Darwinian production and consumption during the depression. Necessity made it popular among young African Americans. After the depression, the league's structures for communal/socialist economic interdependence and black independence from white society dissipated. Organizing with the league had provided Ella Baker with many opportunities as a strategist in confronting the poverty of black workers. However, it was probably not until she worked with New York City's AfraAmerican domestics, that Ella Baker analyzed how state exploitation of black workers was exacerbated by gender and sex.

On the Auction Block: Sex, Race, and Class Exploitation

In 1932, Ella Baker began freelancing for the NAACP's publication, *The Crisis,* which as its editor, W. E. B. Du Bois had developed into a major intellectual vehicle for civil rights politics. In 1929, prior to working for the *Crisis,* she had joined the editorial staff of the *American West Indian News* and later served as office manager and editorial assistant for the *Negro National News.* Work as an investigative journalist, translating ideas gathered from political activism and research into written analyses, was instrumental in clarifying Baker's politico-economic critiques.

In 1935, as an experienced labor organizer, Ella Baker cowrote "The Bronx Slave Market" with Marvel Cooke for the November issue of *The Crisis.*[16] "The Bronx Slave Market" describes sexual and racial exploitation unique to African American women, particularly black domestic workers. As her most detailed, analytical piece, "The Bronx Slave Market" appears to be Baker's only published essay focusing on the exploitation of African American women laborers/workers. Although less well known than her 1960 article "More than a Hamburger," which dealt with the desegregation of southern lunch counters by student activists, this article, like the 1960 piece, maintained economic justice for poor and working-class African Americans as the primary objective for black political struggles.

To research their essay Baker and Cooke posed as domestic workers seeking employment in the "slave marts."[17] Institutional sexism and racism in employment segregation rendered black female employment synonymous with menial labor, even for college-educated black women such as Baker and Cooke who, struck with the dilemma that white society largely defined black women's work as domestic service for whites, easily assumed their role-play as "servants." Although a few African American men stood in line waiting to be chosen for day labor, the slave markets of domestic work were overwhelmingly reserved for African American women. The auction blocks were located at 167th Street and Jerome Avenue and at Simpson and Westchester Avenues in the Bronx (now the "South Bronx"). Black women exercised the least control over their labor and bodies at the Simpson slave market, the most dehumanizing of the two auction sites, according to Baker and Cooke. For paltry wages, workers negotiated salaries with employers who paid anything or, after the work was com-pleted, nothing to women with few political or legal rights. The treatment of African American women domestics as "disposable" was a feature of the markets.

An overwhelming number of AfraAmericans in the 1930s was trapped in domestic work. The depression forced middle-class African American women who had previously earned factory wages, or whose husbands' or fathers' salaries enabled them not to work outside of the home, back into domestic "slavery." Later, the opening up of factory jobs first to white and then black women during World War II created another AfraAmerican exodus from domestic service for whites. The depression, with fifteen million Americans without jobs and savings, intensified the economic conditions tying African Americans to domestic and food service. According to Baker and Cooke, while it eviscerated conditions of middle-class and working-class black women, it also elevated the social status of working-class white women, increasing their access to AfraAmerican servants: "Paradoxically, the crash of 1929 brought to the domestic labor market a new employer class. The lower middle-class housewife, who, having dreamed of the luxury of a maid, found opportunity staring her in the face in the form of the Negro pressed to the wall by poverty, starvation and discrimination."[18] Baker and Cooke's criticisms of white working-class women as employers included those who set their clocks back an hour or two to cheat black women domestics of their wages. Ironically, even the wives of union activists engaged in these practices.

Grappling with economic deprivation and exploitation, AfraAmericans turned to the federal government for assistance. Government emergency relief provided a desperately needed cushion for those African Americans able to obtain it. Yet, it was riddled with inequities: Franklin Delano Roosevelt's policies excluded blacks from most of the Department of Labor's Federal Emergency Relief Administration assistance (e.g., the Wagner-Lewis Social Security Bill failed to cover farm and domestic work where the majority of African Americans were employed); blacks received less relief assistance than whites; and the Federal Housing Administration denied mortgage financing to blacks seeking to buy homes in white neighborhoods.[19]

Baker and Cooke found that subsistence levels of relief, paradoxically, forced women into the slave markets and, by providing a meager "safety net," allowed them to negotiate for better wages: "As inadequate as emergency relief has been, it has proved somewhat of a boon to many of these women, for with its advent, actual starvation is no longer their ever-present slave driver and they have been able to demand twenty-five and even thiry cents an hour as against the old fifteen and twenty cent rate."[20] Yet, the government neither regulated for decent wages to enable worker independence from relief nor provided adequate assistance to free workers from the need to "sell" themselves. Despite crucial federal aid, African American women were dehumanized in seeking government assistance and further debased in the free enterprise zones of the slave marts.

Black women (domestic) workers had to contend not only with the government's indifference to their economic exploitation but also with the duplicity of employment agencies, which ostensibly were their vehicle for gainful employment. Although Baker and Cooke cite the positive role of some employment agencies' organizing in curtailing the activities of illegal agencies and establishing minimum and maximum wages for workers, they also critique agencies for neglecting workers' needs. Agencies tended to blame women workers in the slave markets for driving down wages, and consequently the reduction in agencies' fees. Employment agencies' economic self-interest, as well as class bias, fueled antiworker sentiments; Baker and Cooke summarize one agency's contempt for women in the slave marts: "Deserving domestics are finding it increasingly difficult due to the menace and obstacles presented by the slavish performances of the lower types of domestics themselves, who unlike the original slaves who recoiled from meeting their masters, rush to meet their mistresses."[21]

Countering these stereotypes, Baker and Cooke suggest economic devastation, rather than slavish opportunism, as the primary motivation forcing women to auction themselves in the marts: "Who are these women? What brings them here? Why do they stay? . . . whatever their standing prior to the Depression, none sought employment where they now seek it. They come to the Bronx, not because of what it promises, but largely in desperation."[22] Baker and Cooke also note that AfraAmericans seeking wages in the marts faced not only the derision of "respectable" wage earners but also exploitation from ineffective or fraudulent employment agencies: "Hours of futile waiting in employment agencies, the fee that must be paid despite the lack of income, fraudulent agencies that sprung up during the Depression, all forced the day worker to fend for herself or try the dubious and circuitous road to public relief."[23]

Pointing out how government and employment agencies invest in workers' exploitation, the writers also addressed the public's general indifference toward AfraAmerican domestics, suggesting this public aloofness stemmed from its perception that desperate poverty was peculiar to "lower-class" domestics. Ella Baker and Marvel Cooke instead judged the workers' plight as an indictment of the economic system and systemic racism, arguing, "The real significance of the Bronx Slave Market is that the mart is but a miniature of our economic battle front."[24]

Part of the social censorship and moral condemnation directed against the workers came from the fact that in the markets women also sold sex in order to feed themselves and their families. Sexual exploitation and violence are, in general, an occupational hazard for domestics. Control over women's bodies is the dangerously contested terrain mapping out Black women's work.[25] Rather than investigate the sexual harassment or assaults of domestic workers, Baker and Cooke focus on women who "voluntarily" engaged in prostitution in the markets. Without moralism, their descriptions of sexual trafficking within household wage labor emphasize economic constraints: "Not only is human labor bartered and sold for slave wage, but human love also is a marketable commodity . . . whether it is labor or love that is sold, economic necessity compels the sale."[26] Forced by poverty into the marts to sell themselves to "mistresses" and "masters" who bought by the hour, day, or week, African American women grappled with dual commodification on the block as both domestic and sexual worker[27]:

> Rain or shine, cold or hot, you will find them there—Negro women, old and young—sometimes bedraggled, sometimes neatly dressed—but with the invariable paper bundle, waiting expectantly for Bronx housewives to buy their strength and energy for an hour, two hours, or even a day at the munificent rate of fifteen, twenty, twenty-five, or, if luck be with them, thirty cents an hour. If not the wives themselves, maybe their husbands, their sons, or their brothers, under the subterfuge of work, offer worldly-wise girls higher bids for their time.[28]

Euphemistically labeled, the "human love" purchased from "worldly-wise" women mirrored the southern sex trade, which many AfraAmericans had migrated north to escape. On the northern battle front in the economic war, they found the same struggles and countered with the same tactic: selling, at subsistence wages, their bodies for survival.

As evident in its inadequate provisions for relief, the government shared some of the public's deep indifference toward black women trapped in domestic/sexual labor. Baker and Cooke recount their own experiences with a white male plainclothes detective who attempted to entrap and arrest them for prostitution while they were posing as domestics. Their story intimates the hypocrisy within punitive and protective aspects of the "law." Police entrapped or demanded bribes from black women domestics while ignoring white johns, pimps, and employers who sexually/physically abused or robbed the women workers; police punishment was as selective and discriminatory as police protection.

Despite the obstacles posed by state agencies, economic institutions, and debilitating labor, African American women organized an "embryonic labor union" at the slave marts. According to "The Bronx Slave Marts," domestic workers forced black women who bargained for wages less than thirty cents an hour to leave the market; they also organized workers to collectively demand thirty-five cents an hour on Jewish holidays. However, Baker and Cooke write that neither their conditions nor their nascent labor activism led these women workers to critically examine the political-economic structures that created the slave marts and drove Black women to them. Baker and Cooke surmise, "Largely unaware of their organized power, yet ready to band together for some immediate and personal gain either consciously or unconsciously, they still cling to the American illusion that any one who is determined and persistent can get ahead."[29] According to the activists, such beliefs in the limitless opportunities of free enterprise and the "American illusion" hindered the development of a broad-based radical consciousness among black women.

Forgoing "American illusion" for labor militancy, Baker and Cooke maintained that the abolition of the slave market required eradicating its causes:

> The roots . . . of the Bronx Slave Market spring from: (1) the general ignorance of and apathy towards organized labor action; (2) the artificial barriers that separate the interest of the relief administrators and investigators from that of their "case loads," the White collar and professional worker from the laborer and domestic; and (3) organized labor's limited concept of exploitation, which permits it to fight vigorously to secure itself against evil, yet passively or actively aids and abets the ruthless destruction of Negroes.[30]

The oppressive conditions that Baker and Cooke point out, and their remedies based on labor activism as well as alliances between "welfare" agencies, social workers, middle-class workers, and manual laborers are important reminders of the centrality of economic struggles and the repositioning of class alliances for the civil and human rights of African Americans in general, and black women workers in particular.

Gender, Race, Class, and Work

Ella Baker's historical and political significance is usually remembered through her contributions to SCLC and SNCC. Yet, decades before helping to develop these organizations, her labor activism placed "work" central to critiques of racism, classism, and sexism as well as made the struggles against racism and sexism indispensable to dismantling economic oppression.[31] Theorizing on women's "multiple" oppressions, "The Bronx Slave Market" anticipated analyses of the intersections of race and class, and their relevance to progressive struggles, fifty years before Black women's studies, women's studies, and cultural studies embarked on their current endeavors.[32] Despite its limitations, the article's insights remain salient.

For example, although the conditions surrounding contemporary black women's work differ, patterns of job segregation, economic exploitation and sexual violence persist, reflecting the sexism and racism in labor practices of previous generations.[33] Today black women workers are hindered by racist/sexist wage differentials in the formal economy and by gross exploitation in the underground economy of the labor of undocumented workers in present-day "slave marts"—homes, fields, sweatshops, the sex industries, as well as prisons, another site for the exploitation of workers denied civil and human rights.

Social inequities still make domestic labor an economic mainstay for black women. In 1980, more African American women were employed as domestics than professionals.[34] Angela Davis notes the constraints shared by historical and modern domestic workers:

> The enervating domestic obligations of women in general provide flagrant evidence of the power of sexism. Because of the added intrusion of racism, vast numbers of Black women have had to do their own housekeeping and other women's home chores as well. And frequently, the demands of the job in a White woman's home have forced the domestic worker to neglect her own home and even her own children. As paid housekeepers, they have been called upon to be surrogate wives and mothers in millions of White homes.[35]

The roles of African Americans in (mis)using black women's labor also determine the constraints surrounding domestic work. Affluent black women and men employ and exploit African American domestic laborers, while poor, working-class, and elite African American men may all benefit from exploiting black women's work in their own households. African American women work more hours outside the home than do European American women, and receive less pay given employment segregation, and wage and educational hierarchies. They also labor, without pay, more hours inside the home than black men. For many, black women's work means double or triple shifts in unpaid domestic work and inadequate compensation for wage labor.[36]

Black women's work includes not only employment in domestic, field and factory work, but also unpaid labor within African American families and communities. Women's indispensable unpaid reproductive or domestic labor, as "free" labor, maintains the family and reproduces the workforce.[37] Naturalized, African American women's exploitation in black households escapes consideration,[38] while racist and state violence and exploitation as "public," overshadow the "private" violence and exploitation within black families.[39]

Focusing on racism and sexism in the economic market, society, and government, "The Bronx Slave Market" makes no reference to sexual violence, domestic abuse/exploitation in black women's personal lives; however, it still provides a window for responding to the multiplicity of black women workers' struggles. Part of that response details deconstructing (neo)colonial sites,[40] which devalue African American women's labor in (1) childbearing or biological reproduction; (2) raising children or social reproduction and household management; (3) wage labor; (4) sexual commodification; (5) volunteerism in church/civic/community activism (i.e., disproportionately African American women serve on and lead PTAs, religious charitable work, community development, and environmental activism in black communities; Cheryl Gilkes refers to this as the "occupationalization" of black liberation). Every form of black women's work has its own occupational hazards: depression, domestic violence, ill health, labor exploitation, lack of job safety, and community organizing "burn out."

Conclusion: Role Models and Activist Intellectuals

For nearly half a century, Ella Baker organized a praxis for black liberation movements, establishing models for radical intellectualism, activism, and black women's work. That she worked as a "facilitator" rather than a spokesperson, had little time to write, and did not seek to establish herself as a "public intellectual" outside of a community of radical activists reveals another feature of black women's work—its community focus can lead to anonymity in the larger society. That her life's work (mirrored in her few, obscured essays) touched so many people—and that activists, political students, writers, film markers, and artists keep her memory alive—speaks to the incredible power of intellectualism rooted in radicalism, communal relationships, and political counsel to younger activists.[41]

Ella Baker's lifelong activism does not in itself qualify her as an intellectual; likewise, her pursuit of a teaching career would not have made her an intellectual either (neither oppressed workers nor celebrated elites are inherently moral, social leaders). Amid conflicting modes for intellectuals, Ella Baker provides an important model of intellectual as progressive activist. Defying the media marketing of black intellectuals, Baker provides a framework for progressive debates about the role of the "public intellectual" in societies crippled by economic and social crises shaped by white supremacy.[42] As an *engagé,* her political speech was concretized in resistance to labor exploitation where race and gender are denigrated for economic advantage. Transforming debates into strategies and theorizing into democratic agency, her autobiographical model suggests that the intellectual as political actor, rather than distant spectator, has the roots to resist deradicalization.

Her standing as activist-intellectual, or Fundi, comes from her ability to analyze the necessary conditions for African American equality in a democratic state, while rejecting the seductive diversions of class pretensions and assimilation. Most important, Ella Baker worked to maintain and expand an existential base upon which people could confront their relationships to their own exploitation and their exploitation of others. In this light, Ella Baker's insights, shared through writing and activism, pass on a political vision which to this day illuminates our own progressive struggles against economic exploitation and violence.

Notes

1. For sources on Ella Baker used in this article see: Joanne Grant, *Fundi: The Story of Ella Baker* (New York: First Run Films, 1981); Ellen Cantarow and Susan O'Malley, *Moving the Mountain: Women Working for Social Change* (Old Westbury, N.Y.: Feminist Press, 1980); Gerda Lerner, ed., *Black Women in White America* (New York: Vintage, 1973); Charles Payne, "Ella Baker and Models of Social Change," in *SIGNS* 14, no. 4 (Summer 1989): 885–899; Carol Mueller, "Ella Baker and the Origins of Participatory Democracy," in Vicki Crawford et al., eds., *Women in the Civil Rights Movement* (Brooklyn, N.Y.: Carlson Publishing, 1990); and John Britton's 19 June 1968 interview with Ella Baker, Civil Rights Oral History Documentation Project, Moorland-Spingarn, Howard University, Washington, D.C.

2. Payne, "Ella Baker," 898–889.

3. Taylor Branch's *Parting the Waters: America in the King Years, 1954–63* (New York: Simon and Schuster, 1988) and David Garrow's *Bearing the Cross: MLK, Jr. and the SCLC* (New York: William Morrow and Company, 1986), for example, are largely silent about the contributions of Ella Baker to the civil rights movement.

4. A few of the better known African American women fired from teaching positions because of their political activism include Ida B. Wells, Septima Clark, and JoAnne Robinson.

5. Even though Ella Baker married former Shaw University classmate T. J. Roberts in the early 1930s, marriage did not alleviate the need to find work (Baker rarely referred to this brief marriage in her later life). Most African American men were also segregated into low-paying subsistence wages in public "domestic work." (Jacqueline Jones, *Labor of Love, Labor of Sorrow: Black Women, Work, and the Family: From Slavery to Present* [New York: Vintage Books, 1985], 161.)

6. In 1930, 5.5 percent of African American women were employed in industry compared to 27.1 percent of foreign-born and 19 percent of U.S.-born white women (Jones, 166).

7. Joanne Grant, ed., *Black Protests: History, Documents and Analyses, 1619 to the Present* (New York: Ballantine Books, 1968), 213.

8. Paula Giddings, *When and Where I Enter: The Impact of Black Women on Race and Sex in America* (New York: William Morrow, 1984), 218.

9. Grant, *Black Protests*, 216. According to Grant, in the 1930s, the expanding Congress of Industrial Organizations challenged the American Federation of Labor's racist and exclusionary practices.

10. Britton, "Interview," 4.

11. See Jones, *Labor of Love* as well as Herbert Shapiro, *White Violence and Black Response: From Reconstruction to Montgomery* (Amherst: University of Massachusetts Press, 1988).

12. Author interview with Dottie Miller, New York City, 1987.

13. Grant, *Black Protests*, 216.

14. U.S. Bureau of the Census, *Fifteenth Census of the United States 1930, Population*, vol. 2, General Report (Washington, D.C.: Government Printing Office, 1933), 216–218, cited in Mark Naison, *Communists in Harlem during the Depression* (Urbana: University of Illinois Press, 1983), 32.

15. Cantarow and O'Malley, *Moving the Mountain*, 64.

16. Ella Baker and Marvel Cooke, "The Bronx Slave Market," *The Crisis: A Record of the Darker Races* 42 (November 1935): 330–340.

17. Fifty years later, African American Judith Rollins also posed as a domestic worker to research her book, *Between Women: Domestics and Their Employers* (Philadelphia: Temple University Press, 1985).

18. Baker and Cooke, "The Bronx," 330.

19. Federal administrators exacerbated racial inequities and fueled the migration of the 1930s, giving local Southern officials overseer powers in the distribution of federal funds.

20. Baker and Cooke, "The Bronx," 330.
21. Baker and Cooke, "The Bronx," 330.
22. Baker and Cooke, "The Bronx," 330.
23. Baker and Cooke, "The Bronx," 330.
24. Baker and Cooke, "The Bronx," 340.
25. African American women generally cautioned their female children since many adolescent girls had to seek work as domestics. Proximity to white families brought dangers of sexual exploitation and violence. This was particularly true during slavery. For Ella Baker these were family stories of how the "demotion" of her grandmother, Betsey Ross, from house to field slave brought an element of safety through greater distance from whites in the plantation house. See Cantarow and O'Malley, *Moving the Mountain*.
26. Baker and Cooke, "The Bronx," 340.
27. Patricia Hill Collins writes that the first appearance of American pornography appeared on the auction block with the selling of African women. Although this is perhaps one of the most graphic illustrations of marketing sexual commodities, pornography of European or Indigenous American women likely preceded and coexisted with the pornographic auctions of black women. Collins notes the consequence of sexual objectification and violence: "Treating African-American women as pornographic objects and portraying them as sexualized animals, as prostitutes, created the controlling image of Jezebel. Rape became the specific act of sexual violence forced on black women, with the myth of the black prostitute as its ideological justification" (Collins, *Black Feminist Thought* [New York: Routledge, 1990], 171).

The historical auction block is supplanted by the largely white-dominated pornography and prostitution industries. However, black porn magazines such as *Players*, which featured a "Daddy's Little Girls" issue in the 1980s, also effectively market sexual violence and incest.
28. Baker and Cooke, "The Bronx," 340.
29. Baker and Cooke, "The Bronx," 340.
30. Baker and Cooke, "The Bronx," 340.
31. The use of these terms as analytical categories rather than descriptive terms as well as their difference and relationships, requires further explorations not possible within the limitations of this essay.
32. Gloria Hull and Barbara Smith maintain that "only a feminist, pro-woman perspective that acknowledges the reality of sexual oppression in the lives of black women as well as the oppression of race and class, will make black women's studies the transformer of consciousness it needs to be." See Gloria Hull, Patricia Bell-Scott, and Barbara Smith, eds., *All the Women Are White, All the Blacks Are Men, But Some of Us Are Brave: Black Women's Studies* (New York: Feminist Press, 1982), xxi. Other black feminist writers on black women studies include Barbara Christian, Deborah King, and bell hooks.
33. Kay Lindsey writes, "Large numbers of black women earn their living, either part- or full-time as prostitutes, the most outrageous and flagrant form of sexual oppression, in which an individual is forced to sell her body on the basis of both sex and color, rather than use her mind to survive. . . .While white

females are sexual objects, black women are sexual laborers." See Lindsey, "The Black Woman As Woman" in Toni Cade, ed., *The Black Woman: An Anthology* (New York: Mentor, 1970), 88.

34. Carole Marks documents that over 50 percent of African American women employed outside the home were domestics in 1920; increasing to 60 percent in 1930, this figure dropped to 33 percent in 1960, and currently remains about 13 percent. "Limits to the Decline of White Supremacy," unpublished paper presented at the University of California-Santa Barbara, April 1990.

35. Davis, *Women, Race, and Class* (New York: Random House, 1983), 238.

36. According to a *New York Times* 29 March 1990 report, the economic gains of the 1980s were tied to property, higher corporate profits, interest, and dividend payments. From 1980–1989, U.S. personal savings rates of the net national income declined (8.9 percent to 3.6 percent), average hourly wages decreased (9.84 percent to 9.66 percent), and the percentage of population working rose (59.6 percent to 63.3 percent). During that decade, U.S. families earned more because they worked more, with women workers outside of the home largely responsible for gains in family income.

37. *Women in the World Atlas* cites that for every 100 hours of household labor that U.S. women perform, U.S. men perform 51, possessing 141 hours of leisure time for every 100 hours of leisure acquired by U.S. women.

38. Mary I. Buckley notes: "Women and the subsistence work of neocolonial peoples are treated as if they were part of nature, like water, air, and land." See "Encounter with Asian Poverty and Women's Invisible Work," RNEW (Religious Network for Equality for Women) *Update*, no. 11 (Winter 1990).

39. Loretta Ross, Alice Walker, bell hooks, et al. Black feminists have written about sexual violence in black women's lives inflicted by black men.

40. Using "colonized" as an analytical category rather than as metaphor, Judith Rollins describes AfraAmerican domestics:

Are the conceptual leaps from the mistress ignoring the presence of her servant to Asians being portrayed as non-humans in films to the colonizer treating the colonized as an animal or object too great? I think not . . . all of these behaviors are manifestations of similar mental processes . . . having been socialized into cultures that define people of color as worth less than whites and having observed material evidence that seems to corroborate this view of them as inferior, white . . . to varying degrees, devalue the personhood of such people. This devaluation can range from the perception of the persons as fully human but inferior, to conceptualizing them as subhuman (Fanon's colonized animal), to the extreme of not seeing a being at all. And though this mechanism is functioning at all times when whites and people of color interact in this society, it takes on an exaggerated form when the person of color also holds a low status occupational and gender position—an unfortunate convergence of statuses for the black female domestic servant (*Between Women*, 212–213).

41. Ella Baker is also memorialized in song: Bernice Johnson Reagon, who worked with Ella Baker in SNCC, quotes Miss Baker in Sweet Honey in the

Rock's "Ella's Song": "Until the killing of black men, black mother's sons is as important as the killing of white men, white mother's sons, we who believe in freedom cannot rest."

42.   Payne writes, "What I know of Ella Baker's thinking does not strike me, and never struck her, as offering any complete set of answers, but I think it does offer a more promising way to begin framing questions about where we are and how we get to the next stage than ideas of many activists who did not become media figures." See Payne, "Ella Baker," 898–899.

2

Struggling along the Race-Gender Academic Divide

Lewis R. Gordon

Recent times have been marked by a high level of sophistication in the continued effort to dismantle the constructions of empowerment that fostered the creation of African American studies and women's studies. These efforts come to the fore in a number of factors both "internal" and "external" to these disciplines. Many of them connect with the identity construction of women with work.

I would like to say straight away that the concept of women in the workforce has never been a mystery to me. My mother worked for most of her life before she gave birth to me at the age of nineteen. From my birth onward, she has been a member of the public work-space, a space in which her humanity was constantly invisible. Since I have known my mother, then, the notion of work as a contingent feature of a woman's identity hasn't been a living reality.[1]

The irony of placing work as a contingent feature of a woman's identity is, of course, displacement of the fact that the quality of life of the families women support is displaced in the global sphere of priorities. It is no secret that there is a direct correlation between the treatment of women in the public labor space and the abysmal levels of global poverty. I do not here intend to deny that the systemic levels of poverty that are functions of a small demand for labor, which is a consequence of the current efforts to make the worker obsolete in contemporary capitalism, especially for women and their families, raises serious questions on the political economy of the structures of what might be called a more just society.

That I have raised the normative question of justice brings us back to the points of intersection between African American studies and women's studies with which I am concerned, for it should be clear right now that the intersection, it would seem, is the convergence of race and gender—

concerns embodied, in virtue of the matrices of American sexism and racism, in "racialized" women. Since in the United States racialization fundamentally means blackness (to the chagrin of many nonblack ethnic groups), this convergence is embodied by black women.

African American studies has gone through an evolution in which its subject matter has become simultaneously more precise and more vague. When "Black Studies" was the name of the discipline, it represented a global concern of people of the same racial background. But with the politics of difference that marked the period of the 1980s and the bewildering 1990s, the construction of racial problems has generated more splintered ethnic and other social formations. At Yale University, for instance, this fragmentation took the form of there being an African American studies program and an African studies program. Since blacks are not necessarily African American, nor are they all African, the conclusion to be borne in mind is that African American studies isn't fundamentally a study of race.[2] Its possibilities are therefore opened in ways that raise different levels of debate among blacks, with the political problematic looming in the distance of struggle over small segments of the academic pie.

I mention this point of struggle because that dimension has been a two-edged sword in the political climate of our time. If blacks can be pitted against each other for academic space, how about a similar tension on the level of gender?

I recently had a conversation with some colleagues on the impact of postmodern forms of praxis in the academy. I pointed out that it is interesting how right-wing devices like "political correctness" and white sites of victimization emerged alongside postmodern turns. I held no punches. In practice, at least, postmodernism has presented cultural progressivism on a par with politico-economic praxes. The problem is that power in the United States is far more sophisticated than that. Celebrations of everyone's "difference" has been subsumed and consumed under the current scheme as "marketable."[3] But marketability has specific manifestations of power. The consequence is that the excluded "other" becomes marketable when her "otherness" has been misappropriated.[4] We live now in an age of exoticized otherness, a situation that obscures the focus of struggles primarily because, in dominant-cultural appropriations of struggle, "struggle" has been rendered meaningless.

Some cases in point. It was a tactic of the Reagan and Bush administrations to pit obvious confusing examples of exoticized otherness to the test of its own logic in the public space. By hiring Clarence Thomas to do a demolition job on the Equal Employment and Opportunity Council (EEOC)—a demolition job he did rather well by failing to process over thirteen thousand discrimination cases, and by blocking the funneling of millions of dollars to historically black colleges—the ball was set in motion for an inevitable collision of intraracial concerns.[5] Thomas's hiring the conservative Anita Hill to accompany him with this task gave momentum to the strategy. In the congressional hullabaloo, the complexity of cultural, racial, sexual, and class concerns was evaded. The illusion was that a black upper-class male (upper-class, that is, by black standards) standing accused by a black upper-class female (both of whom took all hog the American up-from-poverty ideology) stripped the political dimensions down to matters of gender and the failure of race. What a *coup*! The whole logic of difference became suspect by virtue of the underlying query: How could we seriously regard Anita Hill and Clarence Thomas as ideal symbols of liberating praxis?

The ripple effect became fixed, of course, in the class dimension of the professional academic. After all, people who teach women's studies and African American studies are regarded as members of Hill and Thomas's "class." But class is murky business in the United States. As Antonio Gramsci once observed, one's profession doesn't necessarily determine one's organic relation to a group.[6] That there is no black bourgeoisie in the proper sense of the term, which means "ruling class," raises serious questions about the convolution of race, gender, and class categories. It is true that racism divides classes. It is also true that racism divides gender. But isn't it also true that both class and gender divide race? The effect is a complex network of identity crises in these disciplines. And amid this complex network is the continued hegemony of methodological tools that affect the reality of displacement.

What do I mean?

In the effort to forge identities, both women's studies and African American studies have been pitted against each other on the question of hegemonic representation of those identities. As one black faculty member of a women's studies program relates, "My experiences in women's studies suggest that 'race' is the most heated and contested battle around multiculturalism. Perhaps because, unlike 'women' and 'class,' and 'sexuality,' as a category it cannot easily be projected as 'White.'"[7]

Whatever solidarity by way of sisterhood may be expressed here and there, the bottom line on political matters, as a friend in the sociology of education once related to me, is where both the money and the hires go. Although some black women educators like Barbara Smith have "equalized" the matrices of discrimination against black women in terms of racist white women's studies and sexist (male-dominated) black studies, the fact remains that most college students have a greater potential of meeting black female faculty in black studies or African American studies courses than in any other discipline.[8] In many of these institutions, even if black women are joint-appointed faculty with African American studies, the job searches and source of funding for their salaries came from African American studies. Of the black women faculty I knew as an undergraduate at Lehman College of the City University of New York, only one wasn't a member of the black studies department. As a graduate student at Yale, the number of black female faculty who were not joint-appointed with African American Studies was zero. All of these institutions have women's studies programs. As of 1995, Purdue University, whose hiring dynamics I am most familiar with (by having been a faculty member and having worked on numerous job-search committees there), has the distinction of having a women's studies program with no black women faculty members. Although not all of the black female faculty are affiliated with African American studies, black women comprise 50 percent of the African American studies' faculty. Of the teaching assistants, black female graduate students comprised 80 percent in 1995. It should be borne in mind, however, that these figures do not pertain to all academic institutions for the obvious reason that not all academic institutions have women's studies programs nor African American studies programs. The implication from these cases is that we should consider those institutions in which both programs exist. Still, even though African American studies programs generally hire black female scholars, it would be an error to conclude that there are not sexist men in African American studies programs across the country. An obvious site of criticism, for instance, would be the key administrative roles of chairpersons and directors.

In the context of women's studies, it is important to note the extent to which the untranslatability of black women into whites has had an impact on the allocation of important resources on the structural level. Gender solidarity hasn't translated into the distribution of resources, whereas race solidarity seems to have done so with great consistency. In some cases, the women's studies program may regard itself as attempting to maximize the number of women on a college campus by expecting African American studies to hire black women while women's studies hires the rest. The problem, however, is that if both programs hired black women, the number of women, over all, would increase by the same number, whereas the number of *blacks* might increase significantly. The strategy of reserving black hires for African American studies, therefore, has a negative impact on the total number of black hires that could occur. It is racist—at least in its consequence.

Such a consequence is a function of the artificial scarcity that emerges in many institutions. With limited power to hire a limited number of people, cold-blooded hiring practices emerge. In most institutions, women's studies and African American studies are programs, not departments. Their identities are therefore subject to the identities of departments whose attitudes toward the role of programs is generally condescending. In terms of the opening theme of work, this is a serious situation, for these disciplines are intimately linked to a form of self-determination that we may call group-determination. One can, in a university, be a professor of Russian or German who is judged solely according to one's knowledge of Russian or German by colleagues whose sole area of scholarship is Russian or German. Can we say likewise for women's studies and African American studies?

When we speak of struggles in the academy, we invariably encounter the historical conflict of the spirit, which I have elsewhere referred to as the *Geist* War—the struggle for humanity's self-perception.[9] At stake is the role such programs as women's studies and African American studies play in the development of their society's future "image." We need now to start recognizing the complexities of the fact that imaging a new America calls for an America that is not merely an image and a random collage that hides torrential currents beneath a calm surface of phony inclusion.[10] We cannot, and I dare say should not, have individuals "represent" excluded groups. No institution of power in the United States "has" blacks. It is a façade of current identity politics to conclude that Purdue, for example, "has" black professors in virtue of the composition of, say, a panel of black presenters. The presence of blacks, and black women in particular, is a far more complex political phenomenon. We are here when we no longer function as representatives of those who are not.[11]

Notes

1. My experiences of my mother's relation to work is typical of most black people's experience of their mothers. The classic text on the intersection of black women and work is Angela Y. Davis's *Women, Race, and Class* (New York: Random House, 1983). For a fascinating recent discussion, see also Joy James, "Ella Baker, 'Black Women's Work' and Activist Intellectuals" (chapter one of this volume).

2. For the distinction among these various black and Africana identities, see my book *Bad Faith and Antiblack Racism* (Atlantic Highlands, N.J.: Humanities Press, 1995). See also *Existence in Black: An Anthology of Black Existential Philosophy*, ed. by Lewis R. Gordon (New York and London: Routledge, 1996) and *Black Texts and Textuality: Constructing and De-Constructing Blackness*, ed. by Lewis R. Gordon and Renée T. White (Lanham, Md.: Rowman & Littlefield, 1998).

3. For a discussion of this phenomenon, see my essay, "Uses and Abuses of Blackness: Postmodernism, Conservatism, Ideology," in my book, *Her Majes-*

ty's Other Children: Philosophical Sketches from a Neocolonial Age (Lanham, Md.: Rowman & Littlefield, 1997).

4. I place "other" in quotation marks primarily because blacks are not ultimately the Other in Western societies. Blacks are the "not-self-nor-Other." In Hegel's introduction to his *Philosophy of History*, for instance, the black is a point without universality or subjectivity, literally and merely a point in nature as the rest of the purely animal world. The human Other is another human being. Such an egalitarian possibility is denied in antiblack racism. See my discussion of this dimension of antiblack racism in *Her Majesty's Other Children*.

5. For a discussion of the Thomas-Hill situation, see "The Clarence Thomas Confirmation: The Black Community Responds," a special issue of *The Black Scholar: Journal of Black Studies and Research* 22, nos. 1 and 2 (Winter 1991–Spring 1992): 1–156, and Joy Ann James's *Resisting State Violence in U.S. Culture* (Minneapolis: University of Minnesota Press, 1996).

6. See Gramsci's *Selections from the "Prison Notebooks,"* trans. and ed. Quintin Hoare and Geoffrey Nowell Smith (New York: International Publishers, 1971), part I, chap. 1, "The Intellectuals."

7. Joy Ann James, "Paradigms of Exclusion and the 'Integration' of Multiculturalism," *The Black Scholar* 23, nos. 3 and 4 (1993): 64.

8. For Smith's position, which raised the question of a black women's studies program, see Gloria Hull, Patricia Bell-Scott and Barbara Smith, eds., *All the Women Are White, All the Blacks Are Men, But Some of Us Are Brave: Black Women's Studies* (New York: Feminist Press, 1982), especially xxi. Today, there is an Africana women's studies program at Clark-Atlanta University.

9. See my essay on academic activism in *Her Majesty's Other Children*.

10. See, for example, Ruth Farmer's article, "Places But No Importance: The Race for Inclusion in Academe," *Spirit, Space, and Survival: Black Women in (White) Academe*, ed. Joy James and Ruth Farmer (New York: Routledge, 1993), 196–217, and Joy James's discussions of the academy in *Resisting State Violence in U.S. Culture* and *Transcending the Talented Tenth* (New York and London: Routledge, 1996).

11. For a collective discussion of the situation of black academics, see *Spirit, Space, and Survival*.

Part II

Spoils of War: Women, Sexual Identity, and Violence

3

In the Name of Love and Survival: Interpretations of Sexual Violence among Young Black American Women

Renée T. White

Violence against women is far from a new phenomenon. Every few decades it appears as if the social reality of violence is "discovered" within the public consciousness of this country. Given the recent controversy regarding a number of black celebrities and public figures who have been accused of, or formally charged with, some form of violence against their female partners, this issue has taken on a new cast. We now hear debates raging concerning the "cultural" differences in the ways people understand, define, and respond to violence against women. Critics have begun to investigate whether or not race is associated with violence. Given this perspective, one would be left to question whether or not race, often referred to as culture, is somehow associated with the experience or perpetuation of violence.

So, then, to what extent are there cultural (i.e., racial-ethnic) differences in the experience of violent encounters among men and women? For example, if more black women than white women and Latinas report having been victimized at some point during their lifetimes, can this fact be explained in *cultural* terms? If not, what else might explain any real or imaginary racial-ethnic differences in sexual violence? As a starting point, I will consider the ways young women who have experienced sexual violence in their personal relationships understand and explain it. For the sake of this discussion I will consider forms of sexual violence occurring in intimate relationships rather than other forms of family violence, such as incest.

For almost two-and-a-half years in the early 1990s, I was engaged in an extensive field study of forty-one teenagers—mostly black—in a small city in the Northeast. While the primary topics concerned sexuality, AIDS, and the socially determined nature of risk, a powerful and sometimes troublesome subtext emerged, that of sexual violence. What I intend in the following reflections and analyses of my conversations is to highlight how some young black women in my project differentiated between sexual violence and other forms of physical violation. In large part, sexual violence did not exist as a *functional* category for them, though many reported encounters that were clearly instances of rape and other types of sexual abuse. They created boundaries that distinguished violent and nonviolent behavior. These boundaries were developed and maintained in response to the social and environmental realities in which they functioned.

Many of the teenagers embarked on a process of interpretation and reinterpretation of violence. This process was affected by, and maintained within, a sociopolitical context. Sexual victimization in particular was seen as an outgrowth, or a reflection, of the gendered nature of sociocultural barriers to power in U.S. society, namely, that their boyfriends, lovers, and husbands were acting out the frustration they faced as racialized (i.e., black) men in a society that fundamentally rejected and devalued them as men. Consequently, the young women recognized a distinction between the public and private spheres, while at the same time understanding how they and their partners were socially defined in the public realm was directly connected to their identities in the private realm.

Young black women created boundaries concerning the kinds of behavior they would tolerate from their boyfriends and lovers. These boundaries were distinctly different from the ones they maintained in other close relationships. Violent behavior rarely included sexual assault, or other forms of sexual violence.

These perceptual distinctions were not readily apparent in many of the comments made by some of the young women. As Andie explains during a conversation, "I think it is wrong to hit someone, especially when they done nothing wrong." "If a man ever touched me, he'd be gone. Maybe dead if it got really bad," explained another young woman. On the surface, these comments, as well as many others I heard in the course of this field project, imply that the speakers are self-possessed young women who value themselves enough to find any kind of physical abuse unacceptable and intolerable. Unfortunately, this was not always the case. In fact, some of the attitudes expressed during the course of this study made clear the fact that these young black women had internalized very traditional social expectations regarding gender-appropriate roles for men and women. While they expressed a strong sense of self and a commitment to their own socioeconomic independence and identity development, many were concurrently conflicted about the limitations faced by young black men. In a sense, they saw a need to alter how they represented themselves within intimate relationships in order to maintain the perception of their male partners as masculine. As will be seen, this process often required that they look to other male modes of behavior for evidence of their boyfriends' masculinity/masculine identity.

Traditional views of gender expectations greatly affected the boundary-setting process. Though most young women surveyed expressed intolerance for violence, they frequently contradicted themselves when talking about personal experiences with violent behavior. The image of the active, aggressive man and the passive, to-be-controlled woman, time honored archetypes of gender identity, often contradicted the gender reality experienced by these young women. These gender stereotypes were only functional in their intimate sexual relationships.

The Hurting of Young Women

Violence against women is at epidemic proportions. According to a 1990 report released by the U.S. House of Representatives, rates of rape rose four times as fast as the overall crime rate during the course of the 1980s. In 1990, 683,000 adult women were raped—according to a victimization survey conducted by the National Institute on Drug Abuse. About 61 percent were less than eighteen years old. Currently, as indicated by the 1994 Uniform Crime Reports, an estimated 80 out of every 100,000 females are raped each year. Most sexual violence goes unreported, and many surveys might not accurately reflect the experiences of respondents because the findings are influenced by how sexual violence is defined by the researcher and interpreted by the respondent.[1] This is particularly of concern when considering the kinds of violent behavior experienced by young women, who may be least likely to define it as such and to report it.

It is frightening to note that even with these liabilities in reporting and documenting sexual violence, all research indicates that young women are at greatest risk of sexual assault. Those between sixteen and nineteen are the most likely victims of sexual assault—about four of every one thousand. Those between twelve and twenty-four years old report victimization rates that are four times the rate reported by twenty-five to thirty-four-year-old women.[2] Sixty-three percent of rape cases among victims twelve to eighteen years old were acquaintance rapes.[3] Increasing numbers of young women report being the targets of unwanted sexual attention, ranging from touching and fondling to rape.[4]

There is some disagreement about racial differences in victimization rates. Some argue that black women are particularly affected by the specter of sexual violence, that they are at-risk the most.[5] Some claim that few or no racial differences exist.[6] Others, however, observe that:

> [In 1991] white women were 50 percent more likely to be victimized than black women. . . . There is no research to explain this change in the rate of victimization; nevertheless, the white rate has remained relatively constant over time while the black rate has fluctuated dramatically. It appears that the black rate has stabilized for the time being while the white rate has taken one of its periodic increases. The rates of victimization for blacks has been significantly reduced since 1987. It is possible that black women have become more assertive and thereby reduced their chances for victimization.[7]

What are black women experiencing in actuality? And more specifically, what are black teenage females experiencing?

According to the 1994 *Sourcebook of Criminal Justice Statistics*, the rates of victimization because of violent crime are comparable for black and white teenagers ages twelve to nineteen. However, the rate of rape and sexual assault among black teens twelve to fifteen, 7.3/1000 persons, is noticeably higher than the rate for white teens, which is 3.8/1000 persons. Young black teenagers are at greater risk for sexual violence than their Caucasian counterparts. The effects of adolescent abuse continue into adulthood for black women. Black women who are sexually abused as children appear to be at great risk of abuse as adults. According to a 1994 study of community college students by Urguizo and Goodlin-Jones, 61.5 percent of black women abused as children reported repeat abuse as adults, while 18.8 percent of those not abused as children were assaulted as adults.

Criticism of the method and analysis of such data remains great (see note 2).[8] National data are scarce on rates of victimization by race and age among adolescent females.[9] Most studies resort to assuming racial-ethnic differences without actually researching the population in question. Researchers are thus left to two devices: drawing on regional or small-sample data for trends, or using data on adult women as a representation of what might be happening among younger women and girls. The latter option is especially complex given that many studies question whether the nature and catalysts of victimization as adolescents are comparable with those occurring during adulthood.[10] This is especially the case when comparing courtship with marital relationships. Consequently, none of these approaches is sufficiently illuminating or satisfying. Given that so many young women report facing sexual coercion and assault in school, at home, and in intimate relationships, it seems realistic to presume that there is probably much more that we hear little about.

As far as black females are concerned, some research has shown that at any age they are even less likely to report assault or harassment than their white peers. If they underreport to this extent, then how accurate are the data on black women's victimization? And if teenagers are the least likely to recognize and report what they have experienced, then the situation among black teenagers may be troubling indeed.

Although the data remain contradictory, I wish to argue that there might be ways to account for any continuing racial-ethnic differences in both the rates and the perceptions of sexual violence among adolescents in particular. First, the highest incidence of rape occurs among single, low-income, young women of color.[11] Additionally, research has shown that many women are at great risk for sexual and other physical assault during pregnancy.[12] Black teenage females are at greater risk for pregnancy than white teenage females, due to differences in contraceptive usage and black women's disinterest in abortion. Third, these teenagers are often, though not always, involved with men who are substantially older than they are—increasing the possibility of role conflict between the partners.

Further, some research indicates that covictimization, "the witnessing of others being victimized (e.g., sexually abused, murdered)" is extremely high among black teenagers living in urban areas.[13] Since there is a strong association between witnessing violence and experiencing it as a perpetrator or victim, the implications for these black teenagers in urban areas is clear.[14] They could be at great risk of being assaulted or hurt. As Hill et al. observe, violence in urban areas "Is a predictable outgrowth of historical oppression and inequities among an oppressed people. . . . Yet little is known about how the context of violent urban environments impacts effective coping strategies for women."[15] Therefore, I believe that this combination of factors might illuminate what young black women face in their intimate relationships, and how they adapt to the interactions occurring within these intimate experiences.

Having said all of this, I wish to add a few caveats. First of all, this essay is not a treatise on the sociocultural proclivity of young blacks to perpetrate or be victimized by violence. The commonly held attitude that "black culture" is to blame for sexual violence among blacks is at best fallacious and at worst racist.[16] Reducing such a complicated phenomenon to racially determined and socially maintained values, norms, and beliefs is an ineffective and unenlightening mode of analysis. Instead, any presumed racial differences in sexual violence among young women need to be understood in a different context based on a different view of culture.

Our national culture is one filled with overly sexualized imagery of women, and black women in particular.[17] The gendered history of this country, as well as many other countries influenced by European tradition, includes the invocation of "women-as-property": women being victimized in times of war and revolution, women treated as chattel (of the economic and sexual varieties) in their domestic lives, and women being perceived as the catalysts of unbridled sexual passion in men. The fact that marital rape was not recognized legislatively until the latter part of this century, and that women's past sexual history was deemed admissible in rape trials until very recently, are all examples of this complicated gendered environment.

Coexistent with this culture is the continuing reign of patriarchy and traditional views of masculinity.[18] Men are primary breadwinners. Masculinity comes with independence and expressions of power. Social norms dictate that men are to be more successful than women in word and deed. But what if there are a host of other societal barriers preventing men from satisfying these requirements? Functionalists would argue that when faced with restrictions to attaining widely held norms, ones internalized by those facing the barriers, the solution is to use nontraditional means to attain these goals. In the case of some young black men, this might involve relying on the presumption of "women-as-property" and thus engaging in claiming one's territorial domain in intimate relationships through sexual violence. Conversely, this would mean that young black women might be inclined to *explain* instances of sexual/domestic violence using the same lens. Such a restructured cultural analysis explains differences in the perceptions of and formal reporting of sexual violence rather than emphasizing the search for racial-ethnic differences in the rates of sexual violence.

Perceptions of Sex, Rape, and Coercion

"People who have sex might fight sometimes, but it's not about the law or anything," explained Reed during one conversation. "In fact, the only ones who get hit are the stupid ones." Reed's understanding of violence in relationships excluded the possibility of sexual violence. To her, and many others surveyed, being hit, kicked, or punched might be construed as violent behavior, but rape or coercive sex was not. Approximately 30 percent (n = 12) of those surveyed described instances of unwanted physical attention. Yet, if I relied on the survey distributed to participants, the proportion would have dropped to 11 percent (n = 9). Rather than argue that these young women don't know what sexual violence is, I would rather claim that they know what it is, yet opt to avoid applying such definitions and labels to themselves. I say this because in many cases they would clearly and strongly condemn what they observed in their peers' relationships.

For example, the following conversation concerns a rumor that had circulated involving a young woman and her then former boyfriend. Apparently, she had reconciled with him, resumed sexual relations, and was raped by him at a party.

> Angie: I don't know what that fool's problem was. He got her back, so what was he proving by jamming her up like that?[19]

> Chris: Yeah. And like at a party? I guess he figured nobody's going to notice how she was all messed up.

> RTW: What happened? I'm missing something.

> Sherry: Oh, right. You're not going to believe this, but [Kathy] had gotten back with Bill a few days before, and they were fine and all that, and then . . .

> Chris: And then that mf-er took her to a party and fucked her up pretty good. For real. He was drunk, and out of control.

> Sherry: Don't even start with that drunk shit. That man, excuse me, *boy*, tried to play like he only did that 'cause he was drunk. Well he did it to teach her a lesson about messing with other guys. Like now that she's ruined or something no other guy'll want her or something.

> RTW: Would guys look at her as if she were dirty or tainted?

> Angie: If word got out about her.

> RTW: So both guys and girls think like that?

> Chris: I guess. . . . Well, maybe not. I think girls would understand, umm, sympathize and all, but guys wouldn't be that way, unless it was their mama or baby sister. Most girls would be mad. Really pissed about a guy being so foul and evil.

> Angie: That could be anyone. Kathy could be one of us.

During the course of this exchange, Angie, Chris, and Sherry described other instances of sexual violence that happened to other young women. Yet, though one of them in private conversation detailed at least three instances of violent behavior on the part of her boyfriend, she never identified it as such. One lesson to be learned is that often the most vocal critic is the one in the greatest pain. Why, though, did so few view clearly abusive behavior in their own relationships as such?

The concept of "rough sex," popularized by Robert Chambers's defense team during his trial for the murder of Jennifer Levin in New York City, is useful here as well. Behaviors associated with sex and sexual contact were likely to be categorized as a part of sex-play. The sex might be rough, even out of control, but it was always sex, and thus either consensual, or "deserved." Whatever was a by-product or outgrowth of sexual activity was commonly viewed as either wanted or subconsciously elicited. Sexual violence only occurred in other people's lives.

Additionally, these young women's perceptions of socially determined gender categories reflect traditional norms. Male sexuality is associated with the maintenance of male identity and power. Female sexuality exists in relation to, or as an extension of, male sexuality. Therefore, what might be formally recognized as sexual violence becomes translated into a reinforcement of necessary gender categories. Young women cannot be victimized by someone who is merely accessing what is his prerogative/ territory as a man. Thus, sexual violence became categorized in the following ways:

1. Coercion—sometimes included rape and physical violence, always involved some physical contact

2. Sex-play—normally involved what is formally recognized as rape, as well as coercive physical behavior, and verbal pressure to have sex

3. Rape—being sexually assaulted by a stranger

4. Violence—physical contact, as in being beaten, but not rape

Considering the ways young women were categorizing these kinds of behavior, it was not surprising to discover the number of young women in this study who have been coerced into sexual activity and otherwise physically abused. Particularly those who identify their sexual relationships as committed report questionable sexual behavior—what they would normally consider to be excessive pressure to have sex—with their partner or with his friends. Although aware of the implications of their partners' behavior, they justify these actions as expected within the framework of a romantic partnership or as being "natural" behavior among men:

> We were chillin' out for a while, and then started to mess around. I knew he wanted to do it, but I wasn't feeling too good, and just wanted to take it easy. . . . [H]e got pissed, and was going to walk . . . so we end up doing it. He just couldn't wait, you know? Maybe I shoulda been stronger, but he got what he wanted anyway. Got hot pants. Was pushy and all—I shoulda been stronger. They always want it, all the time, so what else is new, right?

This seventeen-year-old young woman had been involved with her partner for two years, and described numerous situations when he would physically force her to engage in some sexual activity with him. She appeared aware that this behavior was unacceptable, but either passed it off as "typical boys stuff," or argued that rape or coercion could not occur in a long-term relationship. Another young woman, this one fifteen, expressed few objections to how her boyfriend treated her. "He always tells me about who he could do if I don't, then I tell him to go ahead, and then I figure he should just stay with me, be my man, so I let it go."

In U.S. culture, both male and female gender identity are defined in terms of what roles they play in public and private spaces. Work, parenting, spousal responsibility, and sexual attractiveness are among many of the qualities held as characteristics associated with masculine and feminine "being." If some of these are not readily attainable in one's life, others will gain importance. Furthermore, in intimate settings, couples are aware of the fine balance to be managed between the private (internal) and public (external) personae, and each partner is aware of his or her role in maintaining the gender identity of the other.

Sexual coercion is effective because both parties *understand* the gender codes and what is at stake. Maleness comes from being able to satisfy a number of expectations, from assuming the role of provider to being sexually capable (attractive to women). Femaleness is associated with being able to attract and hold onto men. Particularly in the case of older boyfriends, many of whom were not able to represent themselves as male-as-breadwinner to their girlfriends, asserting sexuality gains importance. Therefore, the consequences of recognizing and resisting sexual violence are substantial. Gender-role maintenance becomes so important that young women deny or minimize the seriousness of their experiences.[20] As sexuality in our society is connected with heterosexuality and power, it becomes important to assert one's maleness/manhood or one's femaleness/womanhood at any cost. Considering the institutional barriers young men face regarding the assumption of breadwinner status, they may be forced to assume the only other social roles available to them: those associated with sexual aggression and power.

Young women have also internalized these social definitions. Woman-as-self-sufficient entity is not an available option, but woman-as-sexual-object/being is feasible. Given this framework, they will be less likely to recognize or act on sexual aggression, because it either indicates that they aren't sexually available enough or because the backlash will lead to their sexual isolation. Consequently, they may be able to identify and respond to any other instances of sexual violence except ones they experience.

People in Love Don't Hurt Each Other

Justifications or explanations for ignoring sexual violence hinge on the concept of romantic love. This has been especially evident in relationships between younger teenagers and older men (in their twenties), but was also true of older teenagers. What distinguished these two age cohorts was the extent to which each formally recognized how important being loved was to them. Especially for younger teenagers, love could include expressions of violence.

Much of the literature surrounding violence in intimate relationships explains "why women stay" in terms of the Battered Woman Syndrome, cousin to the Stockholm Syndrome, and Post-Traumatic Stress Disorder. Battered Woman Syndrome refers to "a series of characteristics common to women who are abused, psychologically and physically, over a period of time by the dominant male figure in their lives . . . learned helplessness, depression, and incapacitation affect the battered woman; additionally, the woman holds false hope that the batterer will change . . . feelings of ennui, as well as economic, social, and *sex-role stereotypes*, prevent the woman from leaving."[21]

The cycle of dependency between victim and victimizer, social isolation of the woman, and the woman's regular experience of devaluation all help explain why she might redefine abuse in her personal life, and why she may remain in the relationship. Most of the teenagers who described sexual violence in their relationships were not solely reliant on their partners for financial stability, yet they recognized that their partners financial contributions improved their lifestyles. Further, many teenagers, as already stated, were involved with older men who alternately verified their value as women and threatened to devalue them by seeking out other female partners if the teenager resisted or challenged their advances. While many of these characteristics were easily identifiable among the young women in this project, what still remained the predominant influence on their perception of violence, apart from a reification of traditional gender roles, was romanticized love.

Young women who identified a primary relationship, and who believed that these relationships were loving in nature were the most likely to ignore violent partners or to redefine any violent behavior as a manifestation of the partners' love: "Look. He gets pissed off sometimes," one seventeen-year-old states, "but it's nothing. Anyhow, everything else, it's all good. If we fight, then we fuck, and that's that." When asked if these sexual resolutions are always consensual, she said, "he wants it, I give it, and that's all there is." Another young woman, Shirlene, explains her relationship thus: "He's crazy, but he loves only me. When he freaks, it's because of that." Her definition of "freaks" included anything from shouting to hitting and forced sex. Interestingly, for Shirlene, the hitting was violence, but it wasn't abuse or battery, "because there ain't many bruises . . . and I fight him [as well]." Forced sex was also seen as a logical resolution to conflict, but not as a symptom of that conflict.

By defining these teenagers' ideas as romanticized love, I refer to the ways they collapse idealized gender roles into the expectations they have regarding the ways love can be expressed in intimate relationships. In romanticized love relationships, stereotypical gender roles shape how the young women behave, and what they expect from their partners. The young men are viewed as aggressive, independent, and more inclined to show their feelings through either controlling behavior or through sexual intercourse. The young women see themselves as more passive and emotional, and less likely to initiate sexual behavior with their partners. What is essential to note is that while these traditional female gender norms hold true within their relationships with boyfriends and husbands, they do not hold true in other social relationships. In any interactions occurring outside of the romanticized love relationships, those teenagers who reinterpreted sexual violence saw themselves in much more egalitarian and thus non-gender-typed ways. This contradiction can best be understood by considering how they defined and identified the causes of men's behavior.

Explanations for Sexual Violence

Given this previous argument, these young women create explanatory models that reflect traditional expectations about womanhood and they also transform and adapt these expectations within their particular social world. Whether critical of sexual violence or not (in their own lives or in the lives of their peers), their conceptualization of the phenomenon reflects "the cult of true womanhood": a paradigm regarding womanhood/femininity and manhood/masculinity. Men who behave violently do so either because that is simply how they are or because this is how they are forced to behave. In either instance, agency and direct responsibility are somehow nullified, and with it the recognition that they—young women—can potentially be physically or emotionally harmed by violent men.

They Are All Dogs

The most common coercion experienced by these girls consisted of men reminding them that there were few available and acceptable men to date. Consequently, if one woman is unwilling to have sex, there remain many others who will. This strategy has been identified in communities where the young men are at greater risk of incarceration or early death.[22] Sexual manipulation by their partners, as well as the issue of sexual commitment, were factors that were clearly relevant to those young women who described sexual violence in their own lives.

Many of these young women sought to explain such behavior in terms of the "nature" of masculinity: "I know that they all got a burning," said Marta. "So you just know that they gonna go step out on you sometimes." Does this translate into coercion within the relationship? "Well, I know that there are other girls out there, and I know that I gotta keep him happy, so maybe it kinda affects what I do with him." Another young woman, nineteen years old, was dating a man in his late twenties. "We love each other, and all of that, but I also can say that he still is a dog. They all are on some level." While she did not report sexual violence in her own life, she certainly echoes the perspective of a number of the young women in this study.

Being "dogs," or sexually and emotionally unreliable in relationships, was a trait commonly associated with male behavior. Many anticipated that their partners, even those who never behaved inappropriately, might do so one day because of this presumed trait. A feeling of resignation regarding the potential kinds of encounters between woman and man was apparent in some of these teenagers. A subset of those who had experienced violence explained this behavior as merely a manifestation of what men do because that is what is expected of them as men. Aggressive and violent behavior was not explicitly identified as such. It became transformed into a validation of typical male behavior. As such, violent behavior looses its urgency; it simply becomes "what men do." So, for these teenagers, male violence is expected, but not because violence is acceptable nor because they, as women, should be mistreated.

There is a presumption that men are likely to use sex as a form of conflict resolution. In situations where conflict is intense, the form of resolution is expected to be equally as intense. The potential for sexual violence is thus a product of the nature of the relationship itself as well as the nature of the individuals in the relationship. The violence becomes reformulated into what is to be expected because it merely reflects what men are inclined to do anyhow. Given this view, the optimal resistance to the threat or reality of violence was self-defense within the relationship, not ending the relationship altogether.

Black Men Are in Crisis

An alternate explanatory model used by young women also concerned gender identity and gender norms. In this situation, violent behavior was seen as a symptom, or a by-product, of the compromised position faced by black men in our society. As Jo-Ellen Asbury has noted,

> economic difficulty is the factor that most often triggers violent episodes. Focusing on the African-American experience suggests that this factor may be even more problematic for African-American families. . . . [R]acial discrimination has prevented African-American males in many cases from fulfilling the traditional male role of head of household and provider. Thus, to the extent that African-American males internalize mainstream standards for the appropriation of masculine roles (the focus of some debate), they are confronted with the conflict between what they are and what they have been led to believe they should be.[23]

She further observes that,

> This state of anomie[24] among African-American males represents one aspect of the African-American experience that has not been considered in mainstream spouse abuse literature. Such consideration is important not only because it represents a potential causal factor that has yet to be investigated but because it may play a part in the African-American woman's response to being battered.[25]

Since it is apparent that the young women in this project were aware of what was socially expected of them as women, and of their partners as men, and that these social proscriptions are to be maintained by any means, then it follows that they find ways to alter both the means of expressing gender identity, and what these gender identities represent.

This mode of explanation and justification was mostly utilized by teenagers who were involved with older men. In these cases, the relationship appeared more domestic; occasional cohabitation, sharing of social and financial resources, and occasionally caretaking of children were characteristics in some of these intimate relationships. Even when the relationships were not particularly domestic, the age difference, and the likelihood that the male would be either employed full time or looking for work greatly affected the way the teenagers perceived their partners as men.

Many described situations where the boyfriends were made to feel insignificant by "the system." For Andie, her boyfriend's frustration with encountering social institutions that regarded him with suspicion seemed to render him emasculated, or at least unable to maintain control over his life. The public reality of being a black male affected the private reality of being her boyfriend: "It's hard being a black man these days. There's no way for you to turn. These people [security force in a department store] got you guilty before you do anything . . . so how you gonna be a man? You always have to explain yourself."

Apart from the degradation her boyfriend felt from being detained and questioned by this store's security detail, Andie sympathized with the anger and frustration he shared with her regularly. "It's not like we just talk about white folks, and about black folks, but it can wear you down after a while." In some conversations she talked about violent moments between the two of them: "He nearly knocked me down," "we got into it," "he grabbed me—*hard*," were but a few of the passing comments Andie made. Though aware that this behavior was not acceptable, it became transformed through the lens of racial injustice to be but another indication of the ways institutions frustrate black men.

Few participants clearly identified a connection between sexual violence and racial-gender identity. Most made remarks about the nature of life as black men, and a sense of sympathy regarding the struggles men would face in finding alternate masculine identities. Sexual violence in particular was reinterpreted as a way for men to be men. By being complicit, the teenage girls were also ascribing themselves to traditional roles. They too experienced race and gender oppression in "the real world," as one recognized. They are aware, as black women, of the kinds of gender-ego challenges regularly faced when interacting with wider social institutions. It is possible that in response to the challenges faced in the private realm, it becomes important to validate their own roles as women in addition to verifying that their partners can be traditionally masculine. Yet again, the urgency with which gender scripts are kept hypertraditional within relationships becomes the most reasonable means of *innovation*.

But I Take Care of Myself

The common perception of victimization and sexual violence connotes inactivity and nonresistance on the part of the female victims, according to a few young women. For them, violence is a unidirectional occurrence, from victimizer to victim. For this reason, many of them could not understand how sexual violence was possible in a relationship, where one ostensibly has the power to resist her partner's actions. As long as she is willing or able to fight back, sexual violence would not be viewed as a reality in intimate settings. In the case of Lee, arguments with her boyfriend involved frequent shoving, slapping, and other physical contact. On rare occasions, sexual contact would be rough and painful for her. In these moments, Lee would communicate her displeasure to her partner. "I just bit his lip this time. I wasn't in the mood for that kiss-and-make-up action, and he just was not listening to what I was trying to say. He's way too big to be throwing his weight around with me like that." During this scenario, by retaliating against her boyfriend's advances, Lee actually shifted the focus away from the fact that he thought this behavior was appropriate. As long as she successfully avoids harm, whatever happened would not be recognized as violent, coercive, or hurtful. His attention, while unwanted and unacceptable, was not to be understood as potentially violent in nature.

The perception that resistance is the acceptable and preferred way to deal with sexual violence was a pervasive one. It appears as if the conflicting gender identities of these young women is at play here. While in need of affirmation of their value in the eyes of men, they are also trying to assert their own power as independent and self-determining young women. Hence, while sexual violence may not lead to the severing of their relationships, it certainly would result in their actively resisting unwanted advances. A willingness to "fight back" is obviously evidence that many of these young women clearly understand what unwanted sexual attention is and they recognize that they have the power to counter negative attention; at the same time, their willingness to redefine the nature and meaning of this violence in order to remain in these relationships is problematic.

Resisting Sexual Violence: The Transformation of Gender and Sexual Identity

The fact that these are young women is an important one. As they are processing many conflicting messages about manhood and womanhood, it is not surprising that they can be simultaneously very stereotypic in their views about gender and vocally critical about the limitations they personally face. Black teenage females, as with all young women, are experiencing many changes in their lives; they are in a period of transition and growth unlike anything they will experience as adults. Sexual experimentation, friendship development, independence from parents and guardians are all part of this process. They are just beginning to build relationships with men, and are formulating their identities as women. Considering all of this, doesn't it make sense to claim that the causes, meaning, and effects of sexual violence are going to be substantially different for them than for their mothers, aunts, and grandmothers? To what extent, then, does current research recognize this fact?

Information on young black women and sexual violence is virtually nonexistent. This includes both data and theory on the phenomenon. Without these resources it becomes extremely difficult to produce much in the way of useful observations that can lead to challenging preconceived notions about the "nature" of violence in their intimate relationships. Out of this particular project, I see a few important questions that are deserving of further attention.

In reviewing theories concerned with racial differences in sexual violence, many troubling trends became apparent. As previously mentioned, there is a great deal of emphasis on the cultural differences in the perception of violence; black men and women are viewed as living in a social reality where violence is more common, has little negative meaning, and thus is often the "glue" that keeps couples together. The evidence used to make these claims consists of data reported by hospitals, law enforcement, and occasionally the victims and perpetrators themselves. As has already been noted, such sources are only partially useful. Black men and women are generally mistrustful of formal institutions, viewing them with healthy doses of skepticism. Further, since black men are disproportionately more likely to be processed through the criminal justice system for a range of reasons, most statistics are likely to overrepresent the numbers of men accused of sexual violence. Women do not report what they actually experience in their personal lives, and this is particularly true for black women. What all of this means is that those who work in the area of sexual violence will find their efforts severely compromised by the quality and quantity of data made available to them.

Traditionally, theorizing on black couples and sexual violence falls into two camps: cultural adaptation and structural functionalism. According to the first perspective, black-on-black sexual and domestic violence is a manifestation of the way violence is generally valued by blacks. In contrast, structural functionalists claim that social conditions compromise the ability of black men to attain all of the traditional trappings of male success; they subsequently become frustrated and take their frustration out on their partners. As the first perspective has been effectively dismissed, we are left to explain sexual violence among black adolescents by utilizing the second theory. This, of course, is inadequate for many reasons.

Throughout my conversations with these teenagers, I was continually struck by their heightened awareness of the place they have in the world as black women. They all clearly articulate that being a black woman in public (particularly outside of their communities) is very different from being a black woman in private. How does this affect their self-perceptions given that they are in the midst of such turbulent changes common in adolescence? Furthermore, to what extent does this tension between the progressively nontraditional women they wish to be and the stereotypic women they are expected to be (either as a reflection of the European cult of true womanhood, or as the mythic sexually aggressive and angry Sapphire/Jezebel) affect the boundary-setting and gender script-writing processes in their relations with men?

Much more attention should be focused on the nature of sexual violence in the lives of young black women rather than on explanation of the rates of violence. The claim that blacks are more violent in personal relationships has been unconvincing. Most young women, regardless of race, experience unwanted sexual attention, sexual pressure, and other forms of harassment and violence. What is more sociologically interesting, in terms of young black women, is how those who experience sexual violence perceive it, and how they perceive the perpetrators. The women in this project who had been somehow violated were aware of what had happened to them—these same women were critical of similar kinds of behavior in the relationships of their female peers. They believed in resistance and fighting back, and were upset when their friends did not use these measures. Naturally, this indicates that the process of growing up, dealing with gender and power constructs, and emerging whole is a complicated territory that needs to be traversed.

Notes

1. S. Sorenson and J. Siegal, "Gender, Ethnicity, and Sexual Assault: Findings from a Los Angeles Study," *Journal of Social Issues* 48, no. 1 (1992): 93–104.

2. Victimization in this case refers to the percentage of women surveyed who faced some form of assault. A sample of adult women is directly approached and surveyed. In contrast, crime statistics refer to data on sexual assaults reported to the police. In that case, precincts provide information on the number of reports filed within a given year. The obvious difference here is that most women do not report assaults to the police. Thus, victimization surveys are perceived as more accurate representations of the actual proportion of women who have been assaulted.

3. See K. Kulp, "Acquaintance Rape," *WOARpath* 7 (Fall 1981): 2–3.

4. See S. Small and D. Kerns, "Unwanted Sexual Activity among Peers during Early and Middle Adolescence: Incidence and Risk Factors," *Journal of Marriage and the Family* 55 (1993): 941–952.

5. See P. H. Collins, *Black Feminist Thought* (New York: Routledge, 1990); Angela Davis, *Women, Race, and Class* (New York: Random House, 1983); L. George, I. Winfield, and D. Blazer, "Sociocultural Factors in Sexual Assault: Comparisons of 2 Representative Samples of Women," *Journal of Social Issues* 48, no. 1 (1992): 105–125; and G. Wyatt, "The Sociocultural Context of African American and White American Women's Rape," *Journal of Social Issues* 48, no. 1 (1992): 77–91.

6. See K. Pape and I. Arias, "Control, Coping, and Victimization in Dating Relationships," *Violence and Victims* 10, no. 1 (1995): 43–54.

7. See Southerland's essay in *Women, Law, and Social Control*, ed. A. Merlo and J. Pollock (Boston: Allyn and Bacon, 1995), 187.

8. See Carolyn M. Sampselle, ed., *Violence against Women* (New York: Hemisphere Publishing, 1992).

9. See H. Hill, S. Hawkins, M. Raposo, and P. Carr, "Relationship between Multiple Exposures to Violence and Coping Strategies among African-American Mothers," *Violence and Victims* 10, no. 1 (1995): 55–71; J. White and S. Sorenson, "A Sociocultural View of Sexual Assault: From Discrepancy to Diversity," *Journal of Social Issues* 48, no. 1 (1992): 181–195; and Wyatt, "The Sociocultural Context."

10. See A. Demaris, "Male Versus Female Initiation of Agression: The Case of Courtship Violence," in Emilio Viano, ed., *Intimate Violence* (Washington, D.C.: Hemisphere Publishing, 1992); D. Follingstad, L. Rutledge, K. McNeill-Herkins, and D. Polek, "Factors Related to Physical Violence in Dating Relationships," in Emilio Viano, ed., *Intimate Violence* (Washington, D.C.: Hemisphere Publishing, 1992).

11. See Wyatt, "The Sociocultural Context."

12. See Campbell's essay in Sampselle, *Violence against Women;* C. Costello and A. Stone, *The American Woman, 1994–95: Where We Stand* (New York: Norton, 1995).

13. See D. Garret's "Violent Behaviors among African American Adolescents," *Adolescence* 33, no. 117 (1995): 212.

14. See Demaris, "Male Versus Female," and M. Pirog-Good, "Sexual Abuse in Dating Relationships," in Emilio Viano, ed., *Intimate Violence* (Washington, D.C.: Hemisphere Publishing, 1992).

15. Hill, Hawkins, Raposo, and Carr, "Relationships between Multiple Exposures," 57.

16. E. Barbee, "Ethnicity and Woman Abuse in the United States," in Carolyn M. Sampselle, ed., *Violence against Women*; Hawkins's essay in R. Hampton, *Violence in the Black Community.*

17. See Davis, *Women, Race, and Class*; D. Clark-Hine, "Rape and the Inner Lives of Black Women in the Middle West," *Signs* 14, no. 4 (1989): 912–920; and White and Sorenson, "A Sociocultural View."

18. See White and Sorenson, "A Sociocultural View."

19. All names of participants have been changed. In subsequent excerpts, the author is identified as "RTW."

20. Wyatt, "The Sociocultural Context," 86.

21. See Hale and Menitti in A. Merlo and J. Pollock, eds., *Women, Law, and Social Control* (Boston: Allyn and Bacon, 1995), 206. Emphasis added.

22. E. Anderson, *Streetwise: Race, Class, and Change in an Urban City* (Chicago: University of Chicago Press, 1990); D. Feldman, ed., *Culture and AIDS* (New York: Praeger, 1990); D. Garrett, "Violent Behaviors among African-American Adolescents"; and W. J. Wilson, *The Truly Disadvantaged* (Chicago: University of Chicago Press, 1987).

23. Cited in Hampton, *Violence in the Black Community* (Lexington, Mass.: Lexington Books, 1987), 96.

24. Anomie, as defined by Robert Merton (1968), refers to the feelings that result from the realization that traditional, institutional means for attaining socially proscribed goals are not available. Because these social goals are widely valued

and expected of members, this individual has to consider alternate means for attaining these same goals. In the case of black men and women, this might involve seeking out alternate means of expressing one's masculine or feminine identity when traditional avenues remain closed, especially when the barriers are due to institutional and structural racial oppression.

25. Hampton, *Violence*, 98.

4

When a Black Woman Cries Rape: Discourses of Unrapeability, Intraracial Sexual Violence, and *The State of Indiana v. Michael Gerard Tyson*

T. Denean Sharpley-Whiting

Case # 91116345 *State of Indiana versus Michael G. Tyson* both shook the boxing world and captivated the American public during the fall months of 1991 and the early winter of 1992. Basketball was the number one sport in the nation, yet sports editors and broadcasters voted the Tyson rape conviction the Associated Press's top story for 1992.

Indeed, the charge of rape by Desiree Washington was the stuff of America's primal fixations: sex, race, violence, and wealth. Praised by some for her courage in speaking out and seeking justice against the lionized role model, Washington was equally publicly scorned as a "money grubbing gold digger and a liar to boot" by Tyson's famed appellate counsel Alan Dershowitz. Washington's detractors appeared to be nonetheless heavily concentrated in black communities across the nation. The gender-biased political strategy of sacrificing the particular for the interest of the whole community reverberated.

While a guilty verdict was handed down in the trial, a 1993 poll conducted by the Indiana University Opinion Laboratory revealed that 67 percent of blacks believed that Tyson was unfairly convicted. The cry of racism and for race loyalty took a stronghold, obscuring the issue of sexual abuse. As black journalist Joan Morgan bitterly quipped in her interview with Barbara Kopple, the producer of the documentary *Fallen Champ: The Untold Story of Mike Tyson*, "this just shows how expendable we are in our own community."[1] The retrenchment evidenced in the greater Indianapolis black community and the partisan closing of ranks advocated by the black clergy in response to Washington's charge of rape point to the larger issues in American culture and in black sexual politics of victim credibility, sexual racism, sexual violence, and self-effacement for community with which black women have been continually confronted.

Washington's cry of rape put her in the unenviable position of challenging sexually racist mythology—directed against black women as promiscuous, and reinforcing the mythology of black men as "natural" rapists—and simultaneously attempting to claim a space in which Mike Tyson has held a peculiar monopoly—that of victim. Victim of the judicial process, victim of racism, victim of the "unsavory" Don King, victim of society, "the hapless victim of intentional fraud" by ex-wife Robin Givens, Mike Tyson has occupied all of these roles.[2] And thus, on 21 July 1991, when accused of rape, Michael Gerard Tyson, affectionately known as "Iron Mike," was cast in the all too familiar role of victim with an ironic and fateful twist: victimizer.

To the boxing world, Mike Tyson represented a multimillion dollar enterprise. To many in the African American community, he was a role model whose boxing skills had brought him to the pinnacle of athletic success. Sports is a mainstay of American culture, and athletes themselves epitomize American maleness, heroism, and virility: modern-day gladiators competing in twentieth-century Roman coliseums. For many Americans, the sport of boxing serves as the ultimate test of manhood. In his controversial book *Soul on Ice*, Eldridge Cleaver writes,

> The boxing ring is the ultimate focus of masculinity in America, the two-fisted testing ground of manhood. . . . Our mass spectator sports are geared to disguise, while affording expression to, the acting out in elaborate pageantry of the myth of the fittest in the process of surviving . . . boxing, and the heavyweight championship in particular, serves as the ultimate test of masculinity, based on the perfection of the body and its use.[3]

Joyce Carol Oates, author of "Rape and the Boxing Ring," equally observes,

> Yet, even within the very special world of sports, boxing is distinct. Is there any athlete, however, celebrated in his own sport who would not rather reign as the heavyweight champion of the world? . . . Boxing celebrates the individual man in his maleness, not merely in his skill as an athlete—though boxing demands enormous skill, and its training is far more arduous than most men could endure for more than a day or two.[4]

While boxing offers the premiere carrot of American machismo, for a great number of African American youth, the sport represents a meal ticket—one of a very few limited avenues out of urban ghettos. And Tyson's life reads much like a classic success story: young, black male from the impoverished Brownsville ghetto in Brooklyn, New York, in and out of training schools, literally fights his way to the top to become not only the youngest heavyweight champion in history at the tender age of twenty, but one of an elite few to hold all three boxing titles (WBA, WBC, IBF). Tyson was the symbol of exalted manhood, "the people's champion" as Don King once said. Although not the champion of the world at the time of his arraignment on the charge of rape, Tyson, scheduled to fight reigning champion Evander Holyfield for a reported fifteen million dollar purse on 8 November 1991, was nevertheless revered as one of the world's greatest and most bankable boxers.[5]

The woman who accused him of rape, Desiree Lynn Washington, was an eighteen-year-old freshman at Providence College in Providence, Rhode Island. Born and raised in Coventry, Rhode Island, an integrated, working-class community just outside of the state's capital, Washington was an honor student, a Sunday school teacher, a church usher, and a member of a big sister organization. Unlike Tyson, she was not from a "broken home," but similar to Tyson, her homelife was also troubled. In October of 1989, Donald Washington was arrested and charged with assault and battery against Desiree. He had reportedly pushed his daughter under a kitchen sink and repeatedly hit her head against the wall and floor upon discovering she had lost her virginity.[6]

In July of 1991, at the twenty-first annual Black Expo in Indianapolis, Indiana, Washington was a contestant in the Miss Black America beauty pageant. Tyson was invited to the expo by the event's organizers. On 19 July, he was scheduled to rap in a promotional video with the pageant's contestants. The stories of their ill-fated encounter differ enormously. Whether "Iron Mike" boldly told Washington that he wanted to "fuck her," to which she responded, "That's rather bold of you. Okay," or whether he inquired if she was a "Christian girl" and then politely asked for a date, to which she replied, "sure," was contended throughout the trial. But what was evidently and uncontestably clear was that the two went to Mike Tyson's hotel room, suite 606 at the Canterbury Inn at approximately 2:00 A.M. 20 July and on 21 July at 2:52 A.M., Desiree Lynn Washington made a call to 911 alleging rape by a "famous person."

The Grand Jury Deposition

On 13 August 1991, the chief prosecutor for Marion County, Indiana, Jeffrey Modisett, convened a special grand jury of six persons. In a highly unusual legal move, uncontested by the Tyson legal team until after the boxer's conviction, Modisett also selected Judge Patricia Gifford to over-see the proceedings. Gifford was ironically a former sex crimes prosecutor who helped to legislate the rape shield law. Perhaps one of the most pro-gressive acts to pass in a conservative state, Indiana's rape shield law prohibits the introduction of evidence relating to the victim's sexual his-tory.

On 18 August 1991, Tyson presented his version of events: heavy pet-ting, oral sex, consensual intercourse, and an angered Washington by the interlude's end because Tyson would not escort her to his limousine. On 9 September 1991, the grand jury indicted Michael Gerard Tyson on one count of rape, two counts of criminal deviate conduct, and one count of confinement:

The Indictment

THE STATE OF INDIANA, MARION COUNTY, SS:

      In the Marion County Superior Court,
      Criminal Division Four
      Special Grand Jury—August, September, October 1991

THE STATE OF INDIANA
INDICTMENT FOR:
VS.   COUNT I: RAPE IC 35-42-4-1
MICHAEL G. TYSON   CLASS B FELONY
                                     COUNT II: CRIMINAL DEVIATE
                                         CONDUCT IC 35-42-
                                         4-2
                                     COUNT III: CRIMINAL DEVIATE
                                         CONDUCT IC 35-42-
                                         4-2
                                         CLASS B FELONY
                                     COUNT IV: CONFINEMENT
                                         IC 35-42-3-3
                                         CLASS D FELONY

      The Grand Jury for the county of Marion in the State of Indiana, upon their oath presents:
Count I
      Michael G. Tyson, on or about July 19, 1991, at and in the County of Marion in the State of Indiana, did knowingly or intention-ally have sexual intercourse with Desiree L. Washington, a member of the opposite sex, by use of force or imminent threat of force;
Count II
      Michael G. Tyson, on or about July 19, 1991, at and in the County of Marion in the State of Indiana, did knowingly or intention-

ally cause Desiree L. Washington to submit to deviate sexual conduct, by inserting Michael G. Tyson's finger or fingers into the sex organ of Desiree L. Washington, when Desiree L. Washington was compelled by force or imminent threat of force to submit to such deviate conduct;
Count III
Michael G. Tyson, on or about July 19, 1991, at and in the County of Marion in the State of Indiana, did knowingly or intentionally cause Desiree L. Washington to perform or submit to deviate sexual conduct, an act involving a sex organ of one person and the mouth or anus of another person, when Desiree L. Washington was compelled by force or imminent threat of force to submit to such deviate sexual conduct;
Count IV
Michael G. Tyson, on or about July 19, 1991, at and in the County of Marion in the State of Indiana, did knowingly or intentionally confine Desiree L. Washington without her consent by restraining her on a bed in Room 606 of the Canterbury Hotel, 123 South Illinois Street;

all of which is contrary to the statute in such case provided and against the peace and dignity of the State of Indiana.

JEFFREY MODISETT
Prosecuting Attorney
Nineteenth Judicial Court

Reinforcing and Combatting Sexual Racism: The Church and the Mobilization of the African American Community

Like the Clarence Thomas/Anita Hill hearings, white America would again become spectator to the intricacies and intimacies of black sexual politics, filtered through misconduct or criminality, and entangled with the legal tactics of subversion and reinforcement of culturally racist stereotypes of black male and female sexuality. Indeed, beside the charge of rape, two counts of sexual "deviancy" against Tyson hammered home dominant representations of black men. On 27 January 1992, as the State of Indiana, represented by hired gun and lead prosecutor J. Gregory Garrison and cocounsel Barb Trathen, squared off with Team Tyson's five-thousand-dollar-a-day defense attorneys Vincent Fuller, Kathleen Beggs, F. Lane Heard, and Indianapolis counsel James Voyles, half of the prosecution's work—attacking Tyson's moral turpitude—was ironically undertaken by the defense. Tyson was cast as an insatiable, black brute who clearly made his intentions known to Washington by lead defense strategist Vincent Fuller whose list of infamous clients also included John Hinckley, Jr., Michael Milken, and Don King himself. The dating rituals of black Americans were referred to as "different" from whites, playing on a theme that Harvard professor Orlando Patterson had promoted in his writings on Clarence Thomas and Anita Hill. Fuller's description of black male-female relations hinged upon age-old stereotypes of black sexuality as pathological, animalistic, and vulgar. Further, the patrician Fuller continuously presented a picture of a smiling Desiree, clad only in a swimsuit from the pageant photo sessions, as proof of her sexual availability and licentiousness.

The prosecution countered by presenting Desiree Washington as a doe-eyed, eighteen-year-old so in awe of Tyson, who was also her father's hero, that she acted against her better judgment. And while the prosecution's strategy attempted to subvert the deeply entrenched "come and get it" American images of black women, the strategy appeared all too contrived, feigned even. Perhaps this is because one gets the impression, and lead prosecutor Garrison readily admits in his book *Heavy Justice*,[7] that he initially did not believe Washington. Throughout the trial and the book, Garrison subverted dominant stereotypes by describing Washington as "thin," "slight," "wide-eyed," "frightened," "barely developed": "a beautiful child with nothing to hide—one hundred and six pounds, five foot five inches tall—just a little twig, little tiny voice, sweet beautiful eyes." He ritualistically referred to Washington as a teenager, a girl who loves animals and children, a freshman just one month into college in an effort to minimize her threat as the prototypical black woman invested with sexual desires and soliciting gratification. In the end, the prosecution and defense strategies proved effective. The jury, at least, believed both sides: Tyson was a crude, sexual brute and Washington was his childlike victim.[8]

Yet, what Garrison was selling, some in African American communities were not buying. Perhaps America's sexually racist constructions of black female bodies as available and ripe for the taking have too long meandered about, for as Nation of Islam leader minister Louis Farrakhan comfortably articulated to a crowd of listeners, from which a five-minute soundbite would be extracted and televised nationally: "Now ladies, you know when you say no, you don't mean no."[9] A caller to the local Indianapolis radio station, WTLC-FM, said, "She should be the one to be charged because he didn't force her to come to his room. Didn't nobody make her."[10]

Throughout the trial, the crowded lobby of the courthouse overflowed with Tyson supporters and Washington detractors. One supporter from

Little Rock, Arkansas, maintained: "I don't really think he's guilty. I guess the woman figured if she lost the pageant at least this would advance her career." Another Indianapolis man said, "It's all about a buck. . . . When the trial first started, Tyson was sluggish, but now we are bringing his confidence up. When he saw that the people were for him, the women were for him, he started shaking everybody's hands." A sixty-six-year-old Indianapolis woman offered in disgust: "I think its terrible that she calls herself a Sunday school teacher. If that's the case, she has no business prancing around in skimpy clothes in a beauty pageant. If you are in a beauty pageant, there are certain rules to follow. I'm sure that one of the rules are that you don't go to a man's hotel room at 2:30 in the morning." And finally, at a vigil held at the Christ Missionary Baptist Church in Indianapolis where more than two hundred supporters gathered, a black woman, adhering to "the cult of true womanhood" and Christianity, spoke: "Black women, we must remember that our bodies are our temples, and we control them. If we don't respect ourselves, who will?"[11]

With the delivery of a "not guilty" verdict in the 1991 Will Kennedy Smith date rape trial and the 1991 confirmation of Clarence Thomas to the Supreme Court despite charges of sexual harassment by Anita Hill, many believed that Tyson would also be acquitted. All three trials alleged sexual misconduct or abuse. However, only the black males dealt with the burdensome stigma of sexual savagery that racism created and continues to perpetuate. While Tyson, with the help of the prosecution and defense, was depicted as the quintessential sexual brute and Thomas reportedly had a taste for hardcore pornography, Smith, who had been accused by at least three other women of sexual assault, was presented as a clean-cut American boy by the media. Indeed, *Time* deemed Smith "an unlikely candidate for the rapist's role."[12] Having all the ingredients of a sensational trial, the televised Bowman/Smith saga nonetheless lacked that racial flavoring which vulgarizes sex, making it all the more tantalizing to the white American psyche. The name Thomas, rather than Senator Robert Packwood, would become synonymous with sexual impropriety in political culture, and Tyson, not Smith, would come to represent the poster "bad boy" for date rape.

The charge of rape, Tyson's indictment, and his eventual sentencing created fervor and fury in Indianapolis black communities. During the two-week trial, from 27 January 1992 to the pronouncement of "guilty" on 10 February 1992 on one count of rape and two counts of sexual deviant conduct, African Americans, led by religious leaders, mobilized and rallied behind the besieged hero. Much of the rhetoric opposing Tyson's conviction resembled that of Clarence Thomas's. The word "lynching" was liberally tossed about. In comparing Tyson's trial to the historic and heinous lynching of two black men in Marion, Indiana, in 1930 for the alleged killing of a white man, Chuck D of Public Enemy raps, "Never liked what I saw in the law/Indiana trees hangin' us instead of leaves" (*Hazy Shade of Criminal*). The 1992 video to *Hazy Shade of Criminal* nonetheless features Anita Hill as a victim of the Senate Judiciary Committee. Ten thousand supporters signed a petition for leniency; Donald Trump offered to buy out Tyson's rape conviction.[13]

Chief Prosecutor Modisett, who had previously courted black voters, gloated during the sentencing, calling Tyson a "sick man" and stating that "Mike Tyson, the rapist, needs to be off the streets." The Democrat would later face the wrath of many of his black constituents, as he was accused of using Tyson to further his political ambitions. In a rally hosted by Ebenezer Baptist Church, guest speaker Don King urged the crowd of black voters to oust Modisett.[14] Protesters in support of Tyson carried placards that read "Kissing + Teasing leads to Pleasing," "Put the Pressure on your local Politicians in the Name of Mike," "Truth or Justice?," "Desiree Washington Tell the Truth." Across the nation, Tyson supporters wore t-shirts with the logo "I'll Be Back."

The black clergy not only provided space in their religious sanctuaries for Tyson rallies, drives, and vigils, but also were especially active in the leniency and petition drives. A rally in support of Tyson was headed by the Reverend T. J. Jemison, president of the National Baptist Convention, U.S.A., the largest black denomination with 7.9 million members. Jemison would later be investigated by the U.S. Attorney in Indianapolis for offering a bribe of up to one million dollars to Desiree and Donald Washington to drop charges.[15] Reverend Girton of the Christ Missionary Baptist Church held a "Fairness for Tyson" rally on 29 January 1992 with an estimated 350 supporters, including 40 ministers.[16] The Reverend S. R. Shields of the Pilgrim Baptist Church spearheaded a "Mercy for Mike Tyson" petition.

Amid criticisms from black men and women, like William G. Mays, publisher of *The Indianapolis Recorder* and Indianapolis University-Purdue University professor of theology Karen Baker-Fletcher concerning sexism and the church's unwavering support for a convicted rapist, Reverend Shields responded: "I would not want and would not condone any man raping my daughter. But I feel mercy is in order if there are extenuating circumstances. We have never been anti-Desiree."

The male rank and file members of black churches have long been accused of sexism. Even though black women generally make up 80 percent of congregations, they rarely lead the religious flocks. Certainly advocating leniency for Tyson does not necessarily indicate an anti-Washington stance. However, the church leaders were not as steadfast in their efforts to mobilize their congregations around the discussion of sexual abuse in black communities, neither did they rush to provide space for rape crisis centers, educational programs, or shelters within their churches. But what is even more disturbing, underscoring the sexist positions of the clergy and lay people, is that Washington, not Tyson, was an active member of the Baptist Church.

To maintain that one does not condone rape, yet remain silent on the issue of intraracial sexual violence, to be vociferous with regards to the racist injustices of the legal system toward black men, reveals a partisanship that designates black males' sexual violence against black females as secondary or peripheral to violence against black men. As the Reverend Thomas Brown of the Ebenezer Baptist Church stated: "I am more concerned about the many black-on-black killings and police injustices."[17]

But all the communities' protestations, pleas for leniency, and cries of racism were fruitless, for on 26 March 1992, Judge Gifford sentenced Mike Tyson to a six-year jail term, four years probation, and a thirty-thousand dollar fine. "Iron Mike" was to serve out his time at the Indiana Youth Center as prisoner # 922335 with eligibility for parole in 1995.

"A Rage in Harlem": Parades and Parole

After a number of unsuccessful appeals to the Indiana Court of Appeals and the Indiana Supreme Court for a retrial based upon Gifford's exclusion of three defense witnesses before the trial, the charge of discrimination against blacks in the jury selection process, and Washington's contingency fee agreement with attorney Ed Gerstein, Mike Tyson was eventually paroled on 26 March 1995.[18]

A little less than three months after his release, community and religious leaders and elected officials in Harlem planned a redemption parade for Tyson at which he was to present a check for $100,000 to the Children's Foundation. Protests against the celebration abounded. Coalitions formed and debates were borne out in the *New York Times, Amsterdam News, Village Voice*, and on Jesse Jackson's 25 June 1995 CNN-sponsored syndicate, *Both Sides*. As Jill Nelson, a member of the Harlem-based community group African Americans Against Violence, writes: "That Mike Tyson served time entitles him to a second chance, not a heroes welcome. To embrace him as a redeemed man . . . sends a cynical and dangerous message to all people. It says to black women that no one cares about us: not our politicians, pastors, leaders, not our men."[19]

Indeed, the oft-skirted realities of intraracial violence against black women and black women's value in their own communities was at the heart of the standoff in Harlem, and continues to plague black sexual politics. That Tyson could be so easily embraced, and the violence against Washington so quickly forgotten, does not bode well for future rigorous engagements on the issue of intraracial sexual abuse. The "rage in Harlem," headed by African Americans Against Violence (AAAV) and the Committee of Rational African Americans Against the Parade (CRAAAP), nonetheless represented a much-needed rupture with the time-observed codes of racial honor and sexual silence.

Unrapeability: Codes of Racial Honor/ Codes of Sexual Silence

The legacy of black women's unrapeability, in this case, functioned as much as a code of silence, self-erasure, in the name of race solidarity, as it did to unequivocally deny Washington's rape. To some, Washington did the unforgivable. Rather than forsake herself for the sake of communities that "Iron Mike" came to represent, she hobbled an African American role model; but more important, she denied Tyson his freedom. Just as Anita Hill attempted to deny Thomas his freedom, that is, a seat on the U.S. Supreme Court, Washington blocked Tyson's freedom to box the richest fight in history with an estimated gross of over $100 million in revenues, and helped send him to state prison.[20]

The silence demanded of Washington, and her pariah status in many black communities, deflects from the fact that 90 percent of all rapes are intraracial, and black perpetrators of intraracial sexual violence are given lesser sentences than white perpetrators of intraracial forcible rape. Moreover, according to author Earl Ofari Hutchinson, "the Dallas Herald reviewed all felony cases in the country for 1988 and found that when a black male was charged with the rape of a white woman the average sentence was ten years. When a black woman was the victim, the average sentence was two years."[21] The worthless status of black female bodies is reified in U.S. judicial practices. These are issues that black women, in particular, and black communities are struggling to confront. While believability, "mis"understandings concerning black women's sexual availability in U.S. cultural productions, and their inexcusable collusions in the legal system present road blocks, they are not insurmountable.

Black women cannot afford to be silent objectors to intraracial sexual violence, nor complacent puppets whose strings are pulled in the higher service of communities. The Crime Victims Research and Treatment Center estimates that this invasive crime will affect the lives of over twelve million American women by the year 2012.[22] If black women opt to remain silent on the issue of intraracial sexual abuse, they will continue to "not be counted" in mainstream strategies and studies for prevention, intervention, and rigorous prosecution, and "not count" in their own communities.

Notes

1. *Indianapolis Star*, 4 February 1993, B-1 and 2.

2. In his countersuit for divorce from Givens, Tyson contends that she tricked him into marriage with the claim of pregnancy.

3. Eldridge Cleaver, *Soul on Ice*, with preface by Ishmael Reed (New York: Dell, 1992), 87.

4. Joyce Carol Oates, "Rape and the Boxing Ring," *Newsweek,* 24 February 1992, 60–61.

5. Tyson was injured shortly after the arraignment and the fight was tentatively rescheduled for 20 January 1992.

6. See the *New York Post*, March 1993.

7. J. Gregory Garrison, *Heavy Justice: The State of Indiana v. Michael G. Tyson* (Reading, Mass.: Addison-Wesley, 1994).

8. "Jury Believed Both Sides," *Journal and Courier*, 12 February 1992, A-1.

9. Featured in televised documentary by Barbara Kopple, *Fallen Champ: The Untold Story of Mike Tyson*, premiered 12 February 1993.

10. February 1992, WTLC-FM, host Jay Johnson.

11. See "Lobby Crowd Is Mostly in Tyson's Corner," *Indianapolis Star*, 12 February 1992, A-10; *Time,* 24 February 1992, 25–27.

12. Cited from the article "Sisters Act," *Village Voice*, 25 July 1995, 15.

13. *Indianapolis Star*, 19 February 1992, C-1; *Indianapolis Star*, "Trump's Offer," 20 February 1992, C-1

14. See *Indianapolis Star*, "Voters to Oust Modisett," 29 March 1992, A-1. As of August 1995, Modisett is still in office commenting on the O. J. Simpson trial and drawing comparisons to *State of Indiana v. Tyson.*

15. See *Journal and Courier*, 20 February 1992, A-1; See also *Indianapolis Star*, 22 March 1992, A-1.

16. See *Indianapolis Star*, "Black Church Is Torn," 22 February 1992, A-8.

17. *Indianapolis Star*, "Black Church Is Torn," A-1.

18. This was the basis of Dershowitz's attack on Washington as a "money grubber, gold digger, and liar to boot." Dershowitz claimed that Washington had secured Gerstein in order to file a civil suit for damages. Hence, her cry of rape was premeditated and calculated to get Tyson's money.

19. Jill Nelson, "Not Ready for Redemption" *New York Times*, 17 June 1995, 15.

20. See Nell Painter's essay on Clarence Thomas and Anita Hill, "Hill, Thomas, and the Use of Racial Stereotype," in Toni Morrison, ed., *Race-ing Justice, En-gendering Power: Essays on Anita Hill, Clarence Thomas, and the Social Construction of Reality* (New York: Pantheon, 1992).

21. Earl Ofari Hutchinson, *Beyond OJ: Race, Sex, and Class Lessons for America* (Los Angeles, Calif.: Middle Passage Press, 1996), 11–12.

22. Emilie Buchwald, Pamela Fletcher, and Martha Roth, eds., *Transforming a Rape Culture* (Minneapolis, Minn.: Milkweed Editions, 1993), 7–9.

Part III

Middle Eastern Women, Feminism, and Resistance in the Postcolonial Era

5

Women and the Gulf War: A Critique of Feminist Responses

Shahrzad Mojab

In spite of its brief duration, the Persian Gulf War of 1991 (16 January to 27 February) was a major event in the international arena. The war has left its mark on every aspect of life in the region and throughout the world and continues to shape the course of events in the region and among the countries that participated in the conflict. While the military, economic, political, environmental, and mass media dimensions of the war are being intensively studied, the impact of the war on women and the role of the feminist movement has largely been ignored. In this chapter, I deal with the relationship between the Gulf War and women. In spite of its contradictory impact, the war reinforced the subjugation of women in the region. I will discuss the feminist response to the war and demonstrate both the weaknesses of the international women's movement and its potential to play a prominent role in promoting both the cause of peace and the liberation of women. This will be followed by a critique of the theory and practice of the feminist movement in the West.

Women and the Gulf War

The Gulf War was a conflict between two belligerent sides that acted against the interests of the peoples of the Middle East and the peoples of the world. The countries directly affected by the war—Iraq, Saudi Arabia, and Kuwait—are ruled by dictatorial regimes that have used their enormous oil revenues to protect their own rule, which aids and abets the domination of Western powers. They ruthlessly repress the popular demand for democracy, freedom, and independence. In spite of their rivalries, the Western countries that played a leading role in the war, the United States,

Britain, and France, were interested in maintaining their hegemony over the region. While the continuous flow of cheap oil was certainly a main objective of the war, the overall strategy was aimed at protecting the pro-Western regimes of the region, including Israel, Saudi Arabia, United Arab Emirates, and Turkey, and intimidating less-cooperative states like Iran and Syria. Maintaining the status quo is equally important for preventing the upsurge of revolutionary movements in a volatile region where poverty and repression, in the midst of enormous wealth, act as a powder keg always ready to explode.

The states of Saudi Arabia, Kuwait, and Iraq were created by Britain at the end of World War I when England and France defeated the Ottoman Empire and cut it into smaller states ruled by these two powers. The creation of these states was based primarily on colonial interests. The present ruling families of Saudi Arabia and Kuwait were installed by England in order to maintain British interests.[1] Later, after World War II, the United States gradually replaced the declining British and French power in the region. However, in spite of their rivalries, the Western nations continue to dominate the Gulf region, which provides cheap oil and other resources.

The Gulf War was one of the most destructive neocolonial wars of the century. More than one hundred thousand were killed; millions of people were displaced; the lives of tens of millions of people were disrupted; hundreds of billions of dollars of property were destroyed; millions of individuals are suffering from permanent physical and psychological scars; hundreds of thousands of children were orphaned; and the environment was permanently damaged. The United States, the chief architect and leader of the war, committed numerous war crimes against the people of Iraq.[2]

As in other modern wars, the impact of the war on women was contradictory. On the one hand, the war opened new opportunities for women to enter the nontraditional domain of politics and war, and to challenge the patriarchal system. On the other hand, it reinforced their subordination. I will provide evidence of both trends, and discuss their significance for the women's liberation movement.

Women in the Middle East

Opportunities: The Struggle for Women's Rights

It is a well-known fact that during major wars, women are usually recruited to serve the cause of war. Women replace men who are dispatched to the war front and, as a result, they enter male domains in both private and public life. This allows women some leeway to break the ties that traditionally bind them.

The women of Saudi Arabia and Kuwait are among the most subjugated human beings in the world. It is official policy to segregate women and exclude them from participation in politics, the economy, and defense in Saudi Arabia and other sheikhdoms of the Arabian peninsula.[3] A strict gender division of labor is imposed by both religion and the ruling tribal and feudal patriarchy.

Contrary to the widespread image of Middle Eastern women as an ignorant, veiled, subordinate, and inactive mass of humanity, there is a century-long history of feminist struggle in countries like Egypt, Turkey, Iran, Iraq, Lebanon, and Algeria. This feminist movement, like other revolutionary struggles, has been the target of unceasing repression by the pro-Western regimes of the region. Western powers, especially the United States and Britain, have been involved in this repression by providing military, intelligence, and financial support to their client states.[4]

The Gulf War inevitably changed the balance of forces in these countries. The despotic regimes involved in the conflict were threatened and weakened and, as a result, women had a better opportunity to fight for their demands.

Saudi Arabia. During the crisis, the Saudi government organized civil defense training programs for women.[5] Also, King Fahd called on government agencies to accept women volunteers who were willing to serve in medical and social services. The royal edict was apparently motivated by the requirements of the war at a time when about a million foreigners were being expelled and Saudi men had to be freed up for military service. Some female members of the Saudi elite responded to the king's call positively, hoping it would open up more opportunities for women.[6]

Two months later, on 6 November 1990, some fifty women met in the parking lot of a supermarket in the capital city of Riyadh. The women dismissed their drivers and drove their cars through the streets. This was a dramatic defiance of a strictly observed ban on women's driving. The government and religious authorities quickly suppressed the movement.

Kuwait. After the war, Kuwaiti women stepped up their struggle for equal rights, including suffrage rights. During the October 1992 parliamentary elections, however, women were excluded. The right to vote was reserved for 81,400 males, about 14 percent of all Kuwaiti citizens. During the election campaign, many opposition candidates advocated the extension of the franchise to women and foreign nationals with long-standing residency. On election day, a group of about one hundred women staged peaceful demonstrations at polling stations to protest the denial of voting rights to Kuwaiti women.[7]

Suffering of Women

The gains of women during the rather short war were dwarfed by the enormous suffering caused by killings, destruction, and economic, social, and psychological hardships. The following is a brief account of the women's side of this major human disaster.

Kuwait. After the Iraqi invasion, women suffered as a result of the hardships of the occupation, the military action, and the destruction of the environment and the infrastructure. According to a Kuwait University psychologist, about five thousand women were raped by Iraqi soldiers. By November 1991, some one thousand women were expected to give birth to children who would be rejected by society and whose existence would shatter the lives of their mothers.[8] Some of the women abandoned their children before hospitals and mosques while some expectant mothers committed suicide. Under Islamic law, abortion is prohibited unless the mother's health is at risk.[9]

Since the discovery and extraction of oil several decades ago, Kuwait has relied on foreign workers. By 1990, foreign workers and their families (from neighboring countries and south Asia) made up 62 percent of the country's population. Iraqi occupation led to a massive dislocation of these workers. After the war, according to a study of the situation of Asian maids in Kuwait, the government declared the non-Kuwaitis "a threat to national security."[10] By 1992, there were approximately 75,000 to 100,000 Asian maids, roughly one for every seven Kuwaitis. Interviews conducted with Asian women who had worked in Kuwait before and after the Iraqi invasion revealed "a marked deterioration in their treatment after the war's end." One-third of the cases investigated involved rape or sexual assault, and more than two-thirds involved physical assault.[11] Complaining about abuse, more than 1,400 Filipino women, about 16 percent of the Filipino maid population, fled from their employers between April 1991 and April 1992. Instead of investigating and prosecuting the abusers, the government has often refused exit visas to these women, or simply returned them to their workplaces. In fact, Kuwait's labor laws do not protect the maids against abuse. Women who sought shelter in their embassies were deported.[12]

Iraq. After the secular Ba'th regime came to power in a coup d'etat in 1968, it introduced measures that changed family laws, facilitated women's access to education, the workforce, and the civil and military bureaucracy.[13] The only organization that was allowed to exist was the Ba'th

Party's General Federation for Iraqi Women, which had 18 branches, one in each province, 265 subsections in major towns, 755 centers in larger villages and city quarters, and 1,612 liaison committees that extended to all villages and quarters.[14] However, the thrust of this policy was to bring women under the full control of the Ba'th Party. No one, male or female, was allowed to organize and act independently. Thus, under conditions of extreme repression, women's struggle was clandestine and primarily directed against the regime.

Before the U.S.-led Gulf War, Iraqi people generally, and women particularly, had suffered because of the destructive war between Iran and Iraq that lasted from 1980 to 1988.[15] According to conservative estimates, the number of dead Iraqis was between 1 percent and 1.5 percent of the population (between 160,000 and 240,000), with Iranian losses two to three times that figure.[16] In Kurdistan, hundreds of thousands of women suffered from the destruction of thousands of villages, forced migration to the south, gas bombing, rape, forced prostitution, and execution.[17] In order to finance the war, the Iraqi regime went so far as to rob women of their jewelry. Uniformed soldiers went from door to door bullying women into "donating" their gold. Receipts for donations of gold were required in order to have other official documents processed.[18] Throughout these years, Western powers, especially the United States, supported Saddam's regime until the second Gulf War.

In the summer of 1991, a survey based on interviews with eighty Iraqi women revealed that the war and attendant sanctions had devastated the life of women.[19] The study concluded that, on the one hand, women have been forced to adopt roles and responsibilities traditionally assigned to men, and, on the other hand, they find it more difficult to fulfill their own roles. Hunger and the inability to feed their families is a main burden especially among low-income groups. Females are increasingly vulnerable to losing jobs in the wake of competition from males; and impoverishment has led households to sell their assets and, in the worst cases, women have been driven into begging and prostitution. Women's physical well-being has been greatly reduced; they suffer from psychological and emotional stress, including the trauma of bombings and internal disturbances, the loss of loved ones, and the constant anxiety about the well-being of their families. Social life is disrupted and there is fear of sexual harassment and theft. Marital problems have increased. Widows and divorced and deserted women suffer the most since the pensions widows receive from the state have lost their value due to price increases.

Soon after the war, the people in the south and north, Shi'ite Arabs and Kurds, revolted against the Ba'thist regime. The Iraqi army ruthlessly suppressed both revolts, which resulted in the displacement of millions of people in a short period of days. Tens of thousands perished under the mortars and bullets as well as from hunger and cold in the snowy mountains of Kurdistan. Women and children bore the burden of this tragedy.

Saudi Arabia. When Saudi women drivers moved to assert their right to drive, the government responded to the challenge by brutally punishing them. The Ministry of Interior banned all political activity by women; those who were teachers were fired from their jobs. The interior minister, Prince Abdulaziz, disclosed at a press conference that the women's protest was a "stupid act," especially since it was made during the gulf crisis. The prince remarked, "We are going through a time when other matters for discussion should be left for another occasion."[20] The female staff at the women's campus of King Saud University was fired for participating in the right-to-drive demonstration. Leaflets and petitions were circulated, one of which, entitled "Know Your Enemy," provided detailed information about forty-seven women, their husbands, and their husbands' occupations. The women were described as "whores," and many of the husbands as "criminal communists." The leaflet urged the readers to do as they deemed necessary. This thinly veiled incitement to violence was anonymous, but the detailed information suggests that the writer had access to official sources in this secretive kingdom. There were many calls for the women to be punished and some even wanted them killed.[21] The government ordered the women not to meet Western reporters or to discuss their situation with outsiders.[22]

The repression of women was not limited to Saudi citizens. Women reporters from other countries who covered the war also were harassed. Women reporters had to comply with Muslim laws that hindered their ability to report the news and compete with their male counterparts. The religious police, the *mutawwa*, who can arrest Saudi women for any reason, harassed Western women for exposing their arms, legs, or hair in public or for driving a car or eating alone in a restaurant.[23] The U.S. military chose not to interfere with the official policy on women. Few soldiers were allowed to visit Saudi cities.[24]

Egypt. Egypt was not part of the theater of operations. Assessing the impact of the war on women in this poverty-stricken country, Nawal el-Saadawi, an Egyptian feminist activist, noted that "after the Gulf War things are becoming worse. The gap between classes increases, the gap between sexes increases, the gap between us so-called Third World and so-called First World increases." The war, according to el-Saadawi, reinforced religious fundamentalism in Arab countries. She argues that, "whenever you have fundamentalist movements, women are the first targets. They veil women, they oppress women."[25] As a result of the war, "women's liberation has retreated into the background . . . the patriarchal class system has become more vicious and tyrannical."[26]

Israel. Israel was the target of Saddam's missiles during the war. Under the threat of chemical bombing by Iraq, the Israeli government distributed gas masks only to the Jewish population. Palestinians and foreign nationals were not protected.[27] The Palestinians suffered from the prolonged curfew imposed by Israel while Israelis had to shut themselves up in their homes. In hospitals, patients and mothers delivering babies had to wear the "monstrous rubber-and-glass device," the gas mask.[28] According to one report dated August 1991, since the end of the war, more than a dozen Israeli women were killed by their husbands. Many more were hurt in acts of spontaneous violence. Although some Israelis believed that the war merely brought into the open widespread violence against women, others related the outbreak of violence to the stress triggered by the war.[29]

According to the evidence presented so far, it seems clear that, politically, the main impact of the war on gender relations in the Middle East has been the reinforcement of the patriarchal system and the unleashing of increasing violence against women. Women were under enormous pressure to perform their traditional roles of child-raising and husband-raising, and to do household chores under extraordinary conditions. Tens of thousands of men were killed and many women were left without a source of income. In Middle Eastern economies where women are generally excluded from the job market, widowed mothers find it difficult to support their families. Since women are not recognized as "heads of the family," they find it difficult to have access to financial institutions. In fact, they cannot have access to their husbands' bank accounts or even request loans. Under the circumstances, women and orphaned children are threatened with prostitution, and suffer from hunger and disease.

Women in the West

Although women have always participated in wars in various noncombat capacities, the Gulf War was the first major conflict in which several Western governments allowed women to serve as soldiers. Some thirty-five thousand American women, making up 6 percent of the U.S. military forces, participated in Operation Desert Storm.[30] The British army's female detachment was less numerous, roughly three hundred. Australia sent seven female sailors to a potential war zone for the first time.[31] In Canada, the ban on women's participation in combat was dropped two years before the Gulf War. Among the Canadian forces stationed in Qatar, there were forty women, approximately one for every twenty males.[32]

The rather extensive participation of American women in the war provided a fresh opportunity for the popularization of the debate on women's "right to fight." The issue was debated in the U.S. Senate, in homes, churches, mass media, and the military establishment.[33] Commentator opinion ranged from total opposition to women's combat role to "support for full rights" for women in the military.[34]

American women served in the war in different capacities, including working in supply units, crewing Hawk and Patriot missile units, flying support aircraft, serving aboard Navy tenders, working as mechanics, and standing guard as military police.[35] While these responsibilities did not have high combat probability, some women flew helicopters on air assaults into enemy territory for the first time.[36]

Public opinion favored women's combat roles. According to a poll conducted by *McCall's* during the Gulf War, 84 percent of the people questioned believed that women should serve in combat positions. The war strengthened the opinion that women should fight. In a similar poll conducted a year earlier, 79 percent had approved the idea. Of those questioned who had a daughter, 66 percent said that they would not oppose her combat position, a 6 percent increase over the previous year.[37]

By the time a cease-fire was announced, American female casualties had reached eleven. Five women had been killed "due to hostile action," six were killed due to accidents or natural causes, and two were taken as prisoners of war.[38] Although women's role in military duties had expanded from such traditional positions as nursing and administration to teaching jet fighter pilots, servicewomen were excluded from combat, faced sexual harassment and job discrimination, and did not easily get promoted to higher ranks.[39] Lesbians were a target of official discrimination. When Army Specialist Donna L. Jackson revealed that she was a lesbian, she was told that she would be discharged after the war was over. When she went public with her criticism of the discriminatory policy, the army gave her an immediate honorable discharge.[40] Racism was another problem. An estimated 40 percent of the thirty-five thousand servicewomen were Afro-American. Three lost their lives and many who survived expressed deep frustration over racism.[41]

The Feminist Movement and the War

The feminist movement's response showed both its weakness and enormous potential to affect the course of the war. I will now provide a snapshot of feminist action in North America, Japan, and the Middle East.

The Middle East

In early December 1990, two hundred women and fifteen children from different countries boarded the ship *Ibn Khaldun* in Algiers and sailed toward the port of Basra, Iraq (three-quarters of the women were from Arab countries, the rest came from Sweden, Japan, Britain, Italy, Spain, and the United States). Organized by the Union of Arab Women, the trip was declared to be "purely humanitarian. It is a call for peace and love, a rejection of war, and an appeal for international solidarity and dialogue." Its purpose was "to achieve a global and lasting solution to the Middle East conflict and the crisis in the Gulf by peaceful means; the women seek to preserve world peace and security."[42] Carrying gifts of food and medicine to Iraq, the "Ship of Peace" theme of the voyage was "Food and Medicine—a Human Right for All."

The "messengers of peace" planned to stop at ports in six countries, taking on more people and gifts, and send the message worldwide. They faced political harassment at several ports and were attacked by U.S. Marines in the Persian Gulf. Upon entering the Suez Canal, the ship was searched by the Egyptian police, who delayed its release apparently to prevent contact with Egyptian women who supported the mission.[43] The day after Christmas, when the ship had entered the gulf, contingents of U.S. Marines stormed aboard and fired over the heads of the women who had been awakened by the noise. According to one of the women, "The Marines rushed about the ship kicking and beating the women with their rifle butts, all the while screaming obscenities. They fired electrical stun guns pressed against the women's bodies and fired tear gas at us. They also sought out the journalists and smashed much of their video and other recording equipment, and confiscated the rest."[44]

The ship was held at anchor for eleven days. Finally on 13 January, the ship was allowed to sail for Basra without the gift food. On 14 January, they reached their destination. The 15 January deadline was approaching and, although some of the women doctors and nurses told the Iraqi authorities that they were willing to stay in case war broke out, the Iraqis refused the offer due to the danger involved.[45]

Egypt

In Egypt, where women have a long history of struggle, radical and secular women opposed the war. The Egyptian government, a client regime of the United States, joined the war and suppressed the antiwar opposition. In September 1990, participants in a seminar on women's publishing issued a statement demanding the withdrawal of all foreign forces from the gulf, of Iraqi troops from Kuwait, and of Israeli troops from the occupied territories. They also demanded the use of oil revenues for the benefit of the majority of the common people.[46] In November, the Egyptian Association for Arab Women's Solidarity was ordered by the government not to discuss politics or religion. The association, a pan-Arab international association that has status with the United Nations, was closed down in June 1991.[47]

The government decreed that the association's funds and assets should be given to a fundamentalist group called Women of Islam.[48]

Japan

In Japan, where the constitution does not allow the participation of the military, called Self-Defense Forces, in external wars, the ruling conservative party introduced a bill to the parliament (euphemistically called United Nations Peace Cooperation Law) that would allow Japanese participation in the military buildup. Women united and successfully blocked the bill.[49] While the success of women's opposition was probably due to the reluctance of Japan to join the war, the peace campaign played a significant role in limiting the role of Japan in the war.

Canada

The federal conservative government, closely allied to Ronald Reagan, George Bush, and Margaret Thatcher, joined the war effort in spite of widespread protest. Since the last engagement of Canada in the neocolonial Korean War, Canadian forces have built an image of peacekeepers in the Middle East. In opposing the war, peace activists relied on this peacekeeping image. According to a Toronto newspaper, 18 January was a "loud and noisy national day of protest intended to show 'the human face of war.'"[50] Organized by the National Action Committee on the Status of Women, some one hundred women and children converged on immigration minister Barbara McDougall's office in Toronto. Judy Rebick, president of NACSW, said, "We want to tell Barbara McDougall that your role in cabinet is to represent the views of Canadian women—and 65 per cent of Canadian women don't want this war. We, and our children, are going to bear the consequences." McDougall's staff locked the door and closed the office for that day. Women occupied an adjacent hallway, sang antiwar songs, pinned up children's antiwar art work, and so on.[51]

Women and children conducted similar protests outside government and ministers' offices throughout the country.[52] In Calgary, some fifty women and children occupied the office of a member of the parliament and demanded that Canada should be "peacemaker, not aggressor, in the Gulf."[53]

The United States

The United States organized and led the war and deployed the largest military force in the region. The participation of women in the U.S. military has increased significantly since the Vietnam War. Women make up

11 percent of the all volunteer armed forces compared to 1.5 percent during the Vietnam War. This is the highest percentage of women on active duty of any army in the world.[54] The leading role of the United States in this war and the extensive participation of women in it posed a special challenge to the feminist movement in this country.

Although the feminist movement has fought for women's equal access to the military establishment, many feminist organizations opposed the war. The mainstream National Organization for Women expressed "strong and vocal opposition" to the war without changing its "support for full rights for the women who serve in the military."[55] Other less-known groups like the Revolutionary Sisters of Color, a "socialist feminist autonomous" organization, noted that women of color made up 50 percent of the U.S. female troops in the gulf. The group strongly condemned the "genocidal war, caused by capitalism/imperialism" and said that the best support of the troops was to "bring them home right now."[56]

Opposition to the war included women and men of different political, ideological, and religious persuasions. Activities organized by women were quite diverse, including sit-ins, marches, and conferences. Effort was made to internationalize the antiwar movement. When the Egyptian government closed down the Arab Women's Solidarity Association during the war crisis, NOW organized a demonstration in front of the Egyptian embassy in Washington in October 1990.[57] Between 25 February and 14 March, twenty-three women (from Egypt, England, France, Iraq, Israel, Jordan, the Occupied West Bank Territories, Puerto Rico, and Turkey), traveled throughout the United States and Canada to call for an end to the killing. The mission, called "International Chorus of Women's Voices for Peace," was supported by Church Women United, the Funding Exchange, the Ms. Foundation for Women, and the North Star Fund.[58]

Opposition to the war emerged also within the military. Several women in the reserves challenged Pentagon policy in the Gulf. Two reservists, Pfc. Farcia De Toles and Sp. Azania Howse, applied for conscientious objector status, arguing that since enlisting they had come to the belief that war was immoral.[59] Army Reserve Captain Yolanda Huet-Vaughn, a family-practice physician from Kansas City, invoked the Nuremberg war-crime principles, and refused to go to war. She was confined for her four-week absence and court-martialed. The prosecuting officer declared in his summation that her crime was not deserting but "repeatedly saying that she was opposed to the war and would take no part in it." While her unit was shipping out to the gulf, she "was parading around this country holding press conferences and appearing on TV, denouncing the war. . . . Her calling the war illegal, immoral and unjust was a direct attack on those soldiers who obeyed their orders."[60] The prosecutor asked for a harsh thirty-six month sentence and admitted that the army was pursuing harsher penalties for conscientious objectors than for apolitical deserters. Dr. Huet-Vaughn also faced extralegal punishment for her antiwar stance. The Kansas State Board of Healing Arts voted twelve to two in October 1992 to consider revoking her license to practice medicine on the grounds that she was a convicted felon.[61]

In spite of the initial strength of the opposition, the U.S. government, helped by mainstream media and business, effectively silenced the antiwar movement. "In a mere five days after the launch of the air war . . . American women's opposition to their Government's resort to force contracted from 40 percent to a little over 20 percent."[62]

The Feminist Response: A Critique

Based on the practice of the feminist movement (in North America) briefly documented above, it would be fair to claim that opposition to the war was spontaneous, largely local in scope, isolated, and ineffective. These weaknesses are in sharp contrast with the potential power of the movement.

Like most wars conducted by the great powers, the Gulf War was carefully planned, organized, and carried out. The scope of organization can be gauged by the U.S. military's successful manipulation of language in order to control the minds of the American people.[63] There was, however, no comparable level of organization in the antiwar movement generally or the feminist movement in particular. There was no noticeable coordination within numerous feminist groups, and much less between them and other antiwar groups such as the peace movement, the environmentalist movement, churches, students, alternative media, and antiwar veterans.

The war was international in scope, involving more than thirty countries. Although the global nature of the antiwar struggle was recognized by many feminists, the effort to internationalize it was extremely limited. No doubt, one can hardly expect international coordination when feminist groups themselves fail to unite on the local or national levels.

Organizational problems are related to ideological and political orientation. The feminist movement is inevitably heterogeneous in both ideology and politics because women themselves do not form a homogenous entity and are divided according to class, race, national origin, ethnic, linguistic, religious, and cultural factors. It is only natural that feminist groups will split into prowar and antiwar factions as the experience of the movement throughout this century has indicated.[64] Still, the antiwar component seems to be potentially broader and more powerful than the prowar contingent. Why was there weakness in the midst of strength? I will focus on two issues in order to pose and address this question.

The Question of Internationalism

The Global Nature of Patriarchy and Feminism. The need to forge international solidarity is not simply raised by the international nature of the war. Equally important is the global nature of patriarchy and thus of feminism as a global movement. The movement for liberation has an international character because women throughout the world face a patriarchal system of domination and oppression—a system that operates in all social and economic formations, in precapitalist, capitalist, and socialist societies. Although patriarchy has many faces and forms, it exists as a universal force of oppression that targets women everywhere. The feminist movement is also international in the geographical sense—there is a women's movement in almost every country of the world.

While women have been oppressed throughout the centuries, it was in the capitalist society that they first developed the consciousness, ideology, and political organization capable of engaging in the struggle for liberation. In precapitalist societies, women were simply not able to undertake this historical task. As a result of ideological and political struggles, women in the West won many victories. By the end of the nineteenth century, these achievements left their mark on the women of Asia, Africa, and Latin America. Inspired by their sisters in the West, women in other parts of the world raised their demands for equality. Some concrete demands included suffrage rights, the right of education, the right to divorce, and the right to own property. The international nature of the movement was formalized in 1910 when a socialist congress announced the adoption of 8 March as "the International Women's Day." Soon after that, 8 March was celebrated among socialists, communists, and radical and workers movements throughout the world, including the Middle East.

Thus, one may speak of an international feminist movement, which exists intellectually, ideologically, and politically. Lacking coordination, interaction between various components of this powerful movement has been spontaneous, indirect, and accidental. In spite of its longer history, the feminist movement does not enjoy the level of international trajectory or coordination that has been achieved by the much younger environmentalist movement. Moreover, the feminist movement in the West is not well informed about the problems and potentials of the movement in the developing world, especially in the Middle East. In spite of these limitations, the feminist movement in the West enjoys much respect in the Middle East and inspires other women in their struggle.[65] The potential of the international feminist movement for helping women throughout the world is virtually unlimited.

The Global Nature of Antifeminism. Effective solidarity between the feminist movements of the West and the Middle East is all the more necessary because Western governments, especially in Washington and London, have been directly involved in building and maintaining the dictatorships in the region. The American and British states have also been involved in suppressing women's movements in these countries. For example, the U.S.-led coup d'etat of 1953, which brought Mohammad Reza Shah back to power in Iran, targeted all opposition groups including women's organizations, which were entirely wiped out.

To give another example, American, British, and French propaganda claims that the oppression of women in Muslim societies is part and parcel of their culture, and that everyone, including women themselves, support their subjugation. This big lie has been exposed many times in events such as the Saudi women's attempt to drive their cars and Kuwaiti women's struggle for suffrage rights. Women in Islamic countries not only want freedom but also often take up arms for the cause of equality and social justice.[66] Not surprisingly, the despotic regimes of the Middle East conduct a vast propaganda against the feminists generally and Western feminists in particular. The main purpose of this propaganda campaign is to vilify Western feminism by declaring it an enemy of the family and family life with tendencies favoring streetwalking and encouraging prostitution. Although Western governments and their clients may not coordinate their opposition to women's rights in the Middle East, their policies pursue similar objectives.

It must be noted that Western states have a powerful ally in their opposition to the feminist movement. The mainstream mass media have shown well-documented biases against the feminist movement in the West and in other parts of the world. In dealing with the Middle East, these biases are magnified by outright ignorance, racism, and neocolonialist attitudes. The women of the Middle East are portrayed as ignorant and subhuman entities.

The movie *Not Without My Daughter*, for example, provides a conservative and antifeminist picture of the life of Iranian women. This movie, based on the experience of an American woman married to a Muslim Iranian doctor in the United States, dramatizes the oppression she was subjected to when she returned to Iran with her husband and young daughter. Like other women of her husband's family, she was veiled and segregated. When she decided to return to the United States with her daughter, she was locked up, beaten, and put under surveillance. The movie contrasts this enslavement with the freedom enjoyed by American women.

While the oppression of many Iranian women is as brutal as depicted in the movie, two points must be emphasized: First, Iranian women boast a century-long history of struggle against this brutality; second, various U.S.

governments were involved in the suppression of the feminist movement in Iran during the period between the Second World War and the 1979 revolution.[67] The movie also provides a distorted view of the life of American women who, in spite of a brilliant struggle for equality, suffer from exploitation and violence, including battering and murder, and are raped in their homes, offices, schools, churches, and on streets and college campuses. The movie is widely used in Europe to promote hatred toward Turkish and other Middle Eastern immigrants.[68]

Forging International Solidarity. Facing an international system of oppression, the Western feminist movement should consciously strive to globalize its agenda. First and foremost in such an agenda should be active opposition to the participation of Western governments in the suppression of Third World people's struggle for democracy, freedom, and independence. The women's movement is an integral part of this struggle. The other component of this internationalism is active support—material, political, organizational—to the feminist movement in the Middle East and other parts of the world.

The Western feminist movement has justifiably been criticized for its narrow Eurocentrist and racist outlook, agenda, and activism.[69] While this Eurocentrism has multiple origins (class, ideology, politics, culture), I will focus on its ideological and theoretical dimensions as well as localism and segregationism.

Gender Determinism and Fragmentation of the Movement

The absence of a conscious feminist internationalism is closely related to the tendency of feminist movements in each country to draw an iron curtain around themselves, and to segregate the struggle for justice and equality along gender lines. This tendency is rooted in a worldview, ideology, or theory that assigns gender an overdetermining power. Women are considered to be totally different, usually superior, human beings. Every phenomenon in society, even in nature, is explained in terms of gender. In connection with war and peace, women are said to be, by their very nature, peace loving and men are considered to be inescapably warmongering.[70]

Gender determinism is theoretically untenable and politically destructive. Like all biological explanations of human behavior, gender essentialism fails to understand the social nature of human beings, their thought, forms of social organization, conflicts, and relationships. It cannot see how gender relations themselves are shaped by the unequal distribution of social, cultural, economic, and political power. This biologist perspective has yet to answer why politicians such as Margaret Thatcher, Tansu Giller, Golda Meir, or Jeanne Kirkpatrick are no less warmongering and repressive than any Saddam Hussein or Pinochet.

A major component of gender determinism is its denial of the significance of social class, economic exploitation, race, colonialism, and imperialism.[71] Failing to grasp the multidimensional nature of inequality, it isolates the oppression of women from other forms of oppression.

The Politics of Segregation. Reducing oppression to gender is not a simple theoretical flaw. Much more than that, it serves the agenda of a feminism that perpetuates or at best advocates the fragmentation of women's movement along racial, class, and ethnic lines. It reduces a potentially powerful force into a clearly ineffective entity. Equally harmful, it does not allow cooperation between women's organizations with gender-mixed movements of the environmentalists, peace advocates, Native and Black peoples, and others. An example from the Gulf War would be relevant here.

Everywhere in the antiwar front, the old problem of male exclusion of women surfaced again. In the United States, both the male-dominated mainstream media and the few progressive magazines such as *The Nation* and *The Progressive* chose to silence women in the debate over the war.[72] To give another example from England, according to one report, over one hundred and fifty women in England parted company with one antiwar planning group in October 1990, and set up their own conference on 19–20 January.[73] At the early fall meetings, discussion had been "dominated by the sectarian left; as with early vintage anti-Vietnam war organizing, the tone . . . was set by men shouting at each other."[74]

The London women's approach, quite typical, is an easy "solution" to a difficult problem; it is always easier to retire to a cozy corner with one's sisters, especially if they are from the same racial, educational, ethnic, and linguistic background; it is more difficult to fight on two fronts at the same time—against the Gulf War and against the male chauvinism of antiwar activists. However, the question remains: Which one is more productive? The oppression of women, inequality, and other ills related to male domination may end, if ever, only when the entire system of power relations change; men are part of this system and it is impossible to eliminate oppression without changing men, which can happen in the course of common struggles. It is also important to remember that, in spite of the achievements of the feminist movement, the great majority of women who personally suffer from male violence and other forms of oppression is not involved in the struggle against patriarchy. The revolutionary insights of feminism have yet to be popularized among women and translated into action.

While essentialist feminism draws an oversimplified picture of oppression as a monocausal phenomenon (oppression is determined by gender), the world in general and gender relations in particular are becoming more complex. Patriarchy and capitalism are closely intertwined. Information provided by UN agencies and development organizations indicate that the gulf between the rich and the poor has been widening throughout the world. Far from being a time of peace and prosperity, the early 1990s has seen constant war, mass starvation, displacement of millions of people, and unprecedented violence against women. In Western countries as well, prison riots, tax riots, food riots, and other forms of social upheaval, like the Los Angeles uprising of 1992, are present. In the wars of Bosnia, thousands of women of all ages have been brutally raped and killed. Rape and prostitution have been institutionalized as part of modern wars.[75] Attacks on women and their minor gains are rampant. On 6 December 1990, a male student massacred fourteen female students at a Montreal polytechnical university. The murderer blamed his problems on "feminists." Other, more moderate, attacks are too numerous to count. It would not be unrealistic to claim that, in the foreseeable future, there will be more conflict, more suffering, and more difficult tasks ahead.

While the economic and political situation is getting worse, it is important to note that the feminist movement and other social movements in the West face not only the organized powers of the state and the market but also the mainstream media. The media have regularly supported the capitalist state and economy when they report on labor, women, the elderly, and other disadvantaged groups, and on the peace and environmentalist movements.[76] The media dimension is important because, as Chomsky and others have demonstrated, thought control is—under normal conditions—the dominant system of rule in Western democracies.[77] There is little hope that the mainstream media will be "fair" or "neutral" when they cover the feminist movement or other social movements.[78]

Faced with a powerful array of adversaries, the feminist movement will fail to achieve the objective of equality if it continues to be isolationist. While the adversary seems to be powerful and organized, it can be challenged by the combined forces of people who demand a just and democratic social, economic, and political system, including gender equality. Women hold up half the sky and they have the power to turn the sky upside down if they are ready to face the challenge ideologically, politically, and organizationally. However, as long as feminists insist on separating patriarchy and capitalism, war and economy, and gender, class, race, and sexuality, there will be little hope for the potential power of the movement to actualize. Socialist feminists, with their theoretical insight, can make significant contributions in this struggle, although they are not the only ones capable of or interested in such transformation.[79]

Notes

1. For an account of revolution and counterrevolution in the region see, among others, Fred Halliday's *Arabia without Sultans* (Middlesex, U.K.: Penguin, 1974); Peter Sluglett's *Britain in Iraq 1914–1932* (London: Ithaca Press, 1976) and M. Farouk-Sluglett and P. Sluglett's *Iraq Since 1958: From Revolution to Dictatorship* (London: I. B. Tauris and Co. Ltd., 1990).

2. For a discussion of U.S. war crimes in Iraq, see *War Crimes: A Report on United States War Crimes against Iraq,* ed. Ramsey Clark et al. (Washington D.C.: Maisonneuve Press, 1992).

3. See J. Miller, "Saudi Arabia: The Struggle Within," *New York Times Magazine*, 10 March 1991, 39.

4. A typical example of the repression of the struggle of Omani women is discussed in the Gulf Committee, *Women and Revolution in Oman* (London: The Gulf Committee and Leeds, 1975) and Halliday, *Arabia Without Sultans.*

5. See Cynthia Enloe, "Does Khaki Become You? Are Women Pawns or Players in the War Game?," *New Internationalist*, July 1991, 19.

6. E. Doumato, "Women and the Stability of Saudi Arabia," *Middle East Report* 171 (July-August 1991) 35.

7. *Facts on File*, 8 October 1992, 757.

8. "Raped by Iraqi Soldiers, Shattered Kuwaitis Give Birth," *Globe and Mail* [Toronto], 7 November 1991, A13.

9. "Raped by Iraqi Soldiers," A13.

10. According to a fact-finding mission organized by Middle East Watch 1992, quoted in *Human Rights Tribune* [Ottawa], Fall 1992, 15.

11. Middle East Watch 1992, quoted in *Human Rights Tribune* [Ottawa], Fall 1992, 15.

12. Middle East Watch 1992, quoted in *Human Rights Tribune* [Ottawa], Fall 1992, 15.

13. For a more detailed account of these measures see Samir al-Khalil's *Republic of Fear: The Inside Story of Saddam's Iraq* (New York: Pantheon Books, 1990), 88–93.

14. Samir al-Khalil, *Republic of Fear*, 89.

15. For more information, see Deborah Cobbett, "Women in Iraq," in The Committee against Repression and for Democratic Rights in Iraq, ed., *Saddam's Iraq: Revolution or Reaction?* (London: Zed Books, 1986), 135.

16. See Middle East Watch, *Human Rights in Iraq* (New Haven: Yale University Press, 1990), 5.

17. See Kanan Makiya's article in *Harper's Magazine* entitled "The Anfal: Uncovering an Iraqi Campaign to Exterminate the Kurds," May 1992, 53–61.

18. D. Cobbett, "Women in Iraq," 135.

19. Most of the women were from middle- or low-income families who lived in the north, center, and south of the country. About half of the interviewees were illiterate and around half had at least five children. For more information, see Bela Bhatia et al., *Unheard Voices: Iraqi Women on War and Sanctions* (London: Change, 1992).

20. See "Saudi Authorities Ban Dissent," *Globe and Mail* [Toronto], 17 November 1990.

21. "Saudi Authorities Ban Dissent."

22. See Judith Miller's article in *New York Times Magazine*, "Saudi Arabia: The Struggle Within," 10 March 1991, 39.

23. See Charla Krupp and Maurice Weissinger's article "Newswomen at War," *Glamour* 89, May 1991, 172.

24. See Geraldine Brooks's "Please Do Not Offend the Saudis," *Esquire*, April 1991, 94–96.

25. Nawal el-Saadawi, "Speaking At Point Zero: *Oob* Talks with Nawal El-Saadawi," *Off Our Backs*, March 1992, 1.

26. Nawal el-Saadawi, "Patriarchs and Petroculture," *New Internationalist*, October 1992, 9.

27. "Gulf Dispatches," *Ms.*, March/April 1991, 12–18. Includes reports by women in the Middle East.

28. Galia Peled, "Birth and the Gulf War," *Mothering* 63, Spring 1992, 93.

29. Susan Greenberg, "The War on Women," *Montreal Gazette*, 19 August, B3.

30. David H. Hackworth, "War and the Second Sex," *Newsweek*, 5 August 1991, 24–29.

31. Cynthia Enloe, "Does Khaki Become You?" 19.

32. Harvey Shepherd, "Women and War the Issue for Moral Thinker," *Montreal Gazette*, 2 March 1991, K8.

33. See for example, cover stories of *Newsweek*, 5 August 1991; *National Review*, 18 November 1991; *People Weekly* 35, Special Issue (Spring/Summer 1991).

34. Elaine Donnelly, "What Did You Do in the Gulf, Mommy? (Debate on Women in Combat)," *National Review* 43, 18 November 1991, 41–44.

35. Hackworth, "War and the Second Sex," and Andrea Gross, "Women Under Fire," *Ladies' Home Journal* 107, December 1991, 93.

36. "Women in the War Zone: A Look Back," *Glamour* 89, May 1991, 105–106.

37. Roxane Farmanfarmaian, "Should Women Fight? Even as the Gulf War Raged, You Said Yes," *McCall's* 118, May 1991, 50.

38. Hackworth, "War and the Second Sex," 93.

39. Andrea Gross, "Women Under Fire," *Ladies' Home Journal* 107, December 1990, 93.

40. Rhona Mahony, "Voices of Dissent: Taking on the Pentagon," *Ms.*, March/April 1991, 86.

41. Laura B. Randolph, "The Untold Story of Black Women in the Gulf War," *Ebony* 46, September 1991, 100–102.

42. E. Faye Williams, "The Attack on the Women's Peace Ship," in *War Crimes: A Report on United States War Crimes Against Iraq*, eds. Ramsey Clark et al. (Washington, D.C.: Maisonneuve Press, 1992), 158–63.

43. Williams, "The Attack on Women's," 159.

44. Williams, "The Attack on Women's," 160.

45. Williams, "The Attack on Women's," 163.

46. See el-Saadawi, "Patriarchs and Petroculture," 9.

47. See el-Saadawi, "Speaking at Point Zero," 1.

48. el-Saadawi, "Speaking at Point Zero," 1.

49. Yukiko Tsunoda, "Women Fighting for Peace," *Vancouver Sun*, 2 February 1991, B7.

50. Susan Pigg, "Women, Children Protest for Peace," *Toronto Star*, 19 January 1991, A14.

51. Pigg, "Women, Children," A14.

52. Pigg, "Women, Children," A14.

53. Ron Collins, "Women Want Canada To Be the Peacemaker," *Calgary Herald*, 19 January 1991, B5.

54. Pam Hughes and Nancy Buermeyer, "Women in the Military," *National NOW Times*, March/April 1991, 6–7.

55. Hughes and Buermeyer, "Women in the Military," 6–7.

56. RSC (Revolutionary Sisters of Color), "Women of Color Speak Out Against the War in the Persian Gulf," *Off Our Backs*, April 1991, 11.

57. Nawal el-Saadawi, "Speaking at Point Zero," 1.

58. National NOW Times, March/April 1991, 17.

59. Mahony, "Voices of Dissent," 86.

60. Bruce Shapiro, "The High Price of Conscience," *The Nation*, 20 January 1992, 51.

61. Shapiro, "The High Price," 51.

62. Enloe, "Does Khaki," 19.

63. See Matthew Fisher, "Bandits and Furballs Parts of Military Jargon," *Globe and Mail*, 25 January 1991, A10; George Lakoff, "Metaphors of War," *Propaganda Review*, 8, Fall 1991, 18–21, 54–57; Clarence Page, "Gulf War Blitzkrieg Pulverizes Language," *Toronto Star*, 11 February 1991, A15.

64. Jean Elshtain, *Women and War* (Brighton, U.K.: Harvester Press, 1987).

65. Let me provide just one example of the impact of the American feminist movement on Egyptian and Arab women. We are all familiar with the landmark work of the Boston Women's Health Book Collective, which produced the book *Our Bodies, Ourselves* in 1976. This book created wide repercussions and charted a way for women all over the world to gain personal control over their own bodies, health, and lives. Some Egyptian women, inspired by the book, decided in 1985 to spread the message to Egyptian and Arab women. They formed a collective and after six years of struggle they published an Arabic version in 1991. The book has been received enthusiastically and members of the collective are constantly invited to speak and discuss the book. In one of the meetings, an illiterate Palestinian woman asked a member of the collective to put the information in the book on tape so that she could learn from it (N. Farah, "The Egyptian Women's Health Book Collective," *Middle East Report* 173 (November-December 1991). This is an example of uncoordinated or unorganized solidarity between the feminist movements of the West and the Middle East.

66. See for example, "Mountain Life Prepares Female Kurd Guerrillas," *Middle East Times*, 10, no. 17, April 1992, 16; S. Mojab, "Women in Politics and War: The Case of Kurdistan," Women in International Development, working paper 145, Michigan State University (1987).

67. The feminist movement of Iran has fought both patriarchy and the Pahlavi and Islamic regimes. The CIA-staged coup d'etat of August 1953 overthrew the democratically elected government of Mossadeq and restored the rule of the shah. Once the shah was put back on his throne, women's organizations were eliminated and women activists were punished or exiled.

68. One may imagine feminist filmmakers produce documentaries and a great feature film depicting, for example, the struggle of women in the Middle East or the armed rebellion of peasant women against the feudal overlords in the Telangana uprising of 1948–51 in India (S. S. Sanghatana, *'We Were Making History. . .': Life Stories of Women in the Telengana People's Struggle* [London: Zed Books, 1989]; K. Wilson, "'We Were Making History . . .' by Stree Shakti Sanghatana, Zed Books." *Off Our Backs*, January 1991).

69. Angela Gilliam, "Women's Equality and National Liberation," in *Third World Women and the Politics of Feminism*, ed. Chandra Mohanty et al. (Bloomington: Indiana University Press, 1991), 215–236.

70. For a critique of this position see, among others, K. Pollitt, "Are Women Morally Superior to Men?" *The Nation*, 28 December 1992, 799–807.

71. See for example, Pollitt, "Are Women Morally Superior," 806; Gilliam, "Women's Equality"; on the relationship between class and patriarchy, L. Sargent, *The Unhappy Marriage of Marxism and Feminism* (London: Pluto Press, 1986); A. Kuhn and A. Wolpe, eds., *Feminism and Materialism* (London: Routledge and Kegan Paul, 1986).

72. Colleen Roach, "Feminist Peace Researchers, Culture and Communication," *Media Development* [London] 38, 2 (1991): 5.

73. "Not in Our Names: London Women's Conference on the Gulf Crisis," *Off Our Backs*, March 1991, 4, 9.

74. "Not in Our Names."

75. Rape and War: Enforcing Power," *The ACTivist: Ontario's Peace Newspaper*, 9, no. 1, January 1993, 4.

76. On media and the peace movement see R. Hackett, *News and Dissent: The Press and the Politics of Peace in Canada* (Norwood, N.J.: Ablex, 1991); and S. MacBride, *Many Voices, One World* (London: Kogan Page, 1980). According to Hackett, the mainstream media "have been transmission belts for Cold War ideology and bulwarks against the peace movement" (27). There are numerous studies of media coverage of the Gulf War; see especially *Propaganda Review* 8 (Fall 1991); "Reporting the Gulf War," special issue of *Media Development*, October 1991; and "The Gulf War in the Media," special issue of *The Nordicom Review of Nordic Mass Communication Research*. On women and the media, see "Women's Perspectives on Communication," a special issue of *Media Development* 38, 2 (1992); MacBride, *Many Voices*, 190.

77. Although Western states rule primarily by controlling public opinion, largely through the media, Chomsky warns that "It is important to be

aware of the profound commitment of Western opinion to the re-pression of freedom and democracy, by violence if necessary" ("Force and Opinion," *Z Magazine*, July/August 1991, 19). See also Chomsky, *Necessary Illusions: Thought Control in Democractic Societies* (Toronto: CBC Enterprises, 1989).

78.   According to E. Herman, the mainstream media are not democratic. "A democratic media is a primary condition of popular rule, hence of a genuine political democracy. . . . The media will, of structural necessity, select news and organize debate supportive of agendas and programs of the privileged" ("Democratic Media, *2 Papers*, January/March 1992, 23.

79.   During the Gulf War, individual feminists and some organizations emphasized the link between war and the economic system. The Revolutionary Sisters of Color, for example, wrote in "Women of Color Speak Out against the War in the Persian Gulf":

> We believe that to end this war we must build an anti-war movement that is anti-capitalist, feminist, anti-racist, open and democratic. We encourage the anti-war movement to allow equal input from all political perspectives opposed to the war. . . . We need to bring home to all oppressed peoples that this genocidal war, caused by capitalism/imperialism and provoked by the economic crisis, is directed against us as well as against people in the Middle East. This war is a symptom of a dying economic system based on profit (RSC).

For other, similar analyses see, among others, "Women of Color Speak out against the War in the Persian Gulf," *Off Our Backs*, April 1991, 11).

6

Feminism and the Challenge of Muslim Fundamentalism

Janet Afary

In recent years some postmodern feminists have warned us about the perils of generalizations to feminist theory that transcend the boundaries of culture and region.[1] Feminist critics of postmodernism have argued conversely that abandoning cross-cultural and comparative theoretical perspectives may lead to relativism and eventual political paralysis.[2] The growth of Islamist political movements in North Africa, the Middle East, and Southeast Asia has become an arena where the continued relevance of comparative theoretical perspectives can be ascertained, especially with regard to gender issues, while also some postmodernist concerns related to the meaning and dynamics of power relations are taken into account.

In examining the gender ideologies of several Islamist movements we shall see that despite regional and cultural variations, there is a significant degree of similarity among these movements. Gender relations are not a marginal aspect of Islamist ideologies. Rather, an important strength of fundamentalist movements lies in the creation of an illusion that a return to traditional/patriarchal relations is the answer to the many social and economic problems that Third World countries face in the era of late capitalism. A number of feminist thinkers have tried to explain the appeal of fundamentalism among the middle class and lower middle classes in the predominantly Muslim societies of the Middle East, North Africa, and Southeast Asia. Despite some significant regional variations, these studies can be divided into three groups. One group of writers has stressed the economic and political issues that have contributed to the rise of Islamist movements; a second group has explored the disruptive impact of modernization on the family; while a third group has argued that joining the growing Islamist movements and organizations may indeed empower students and professional women in certain ways, though restricting their lives in others. By critically examining these three approaches we can develop a more integrated and dialectical explanation of fundamentalism, and understand why men *and* women are becoming attracted to such authoritarian ideologies in the late twentieth century.

A Battle over Terminologies or a Battle over Women's Bodies?

Scholars of the Middle East and of religious issues continue to debate the relevance of two terms, *Islamism* and *fundamentalism*, to refer to a growing number of cultural and political movements that have made substantial inroads in the Middle East, North Africa, and parts of Southeast Asia. Some, such as Martin E. Marty and R. Scott Appleby, have argued for the relevance of fundamentalism, not just in the context of the Middle East, but for similar ideological currents around the world that in the last fifteen years have sought political power in the name of religion, be that Islam, Christianity, Judaism, Hinduism, Buddhism, or Confucianism.

Fundamentalism in this view is a late twentieth-century phenomenon and a response to the loss of identity in a modern secular world. Fundamentalism is a militant movement that accepts and even embraces technological innovations of the West, but shuns many social and cultural aspects of a modern society, particularly in the realm of the family. They fight for a world-view based on an ideal and imagined past, yet this past is a carefully selected one that is then elevated to the level of a fetish. Fundamentalists believe they are carrying out the will of God, yet are often intolerant of dissent both within and without the community of believers.[3] Others such as John Esposito and Edward Said have rejected use of the term fundamentalism. In Said's view, by condemning the extremism of "terrorism" and "fundamentalism," the West has claimed for itself "moderation, rationality" and a specific Western ethos.[4] Both groups of writers, however, would agree that despite regional and political differences among these movements, which are significant, such Islamist groups have called for a return to more traditional roles for women, emphasizing women's responsibility for procreation, the adoption of "proper hijab" (Islamic dress code), and submission to patriarchal values. A few examples should suffice to establish this point.

The first dramatic case of retrogression in women's rights took place in Iran after the Iranian Revolution of 1979. To this day, the government of the Islamic Republican Party (IRP) continues to jail and torment thousands of women who refuse to comply with the segregationist rules of the IRP. Strict government enforcement of the hijab and periodic rounding up, fines, and imprisonment of women on charges of "improper hijab" continue in Iran. Despite some recent compromises by the government in the areas of education, divorce and marriage law, and employment, women remain segregated in schools, on buses, and on beaches and are restricted in their choice of career, employment, and education. Prohibitions against dating and casual friendship between unrelated men and women remain strong, while polygamy, encouraged by the government, has increased among the urban middle classes.[5]

A few predominantly Muslim countries have followed in the footsteps of Iran. In Sudan and Afghanistan, fundamentalist groups have assumed control of the government and therefore have significant authority in imposing their views, while in Egypt, Algeria, Jordan, and Lebanon, Islamist movements remain in opposition to the government. These and other religious revivalist movements do not operate in isolation from one another. Indeed, the 1994 UN Population Conference in Cairo became the scene of a new type of alliance between the Roman Catholic Church and a host of Muslim fundamentalist groups. Both groups opposed any reference to abortion rights in the UN documents. Since Muslim jurisprudence has historically been tolerant of birth control methods, one wonders whether Islamist movements are learning new arguments from the Catholic Church or from Christian fundamentalist groups in the United States in their efforts to limit women's reproductive rights.[6]

There have been frequent reports of human rights violations against Sudanese women since the National Islamic Front (NIF) assumed power in a 1989 coup d'etat. The process of Islamization and Arabization of Sudan, where the dissenting southern region of the country is Muslim, Christian, and followers of indigenous religions, is rigidly pursued. The new government has enforced the wearing of the hijab and segregated women in educational institutions.[7] In Afghanistan, the Taliban group that assumed power in 1996 has banned women in the areas under its control from working outside the home. Women are subject to very strict rules of conduct. They may not leave their homes unless they are accompanied by a male relative and then only with completely covered bodies and faces.[8]

In Algeria, the Islamic Salvation Front (FIS) placed first in the 1991 elections but was then banned by the government in January 1992 and prevented from taking power. The FIS has unleashed a campaign of terror against foreigners, all those who have been educated in French schools, as well as feminists. The FIS has vowed that if it comes to power, it will stop women's employment, make sexual relations outside marriage punishable by death, and enforce the hijab.[9] In March 1994, FIS issued a statement in which women who walked the streets without covering their hair were threatened with assassination. Since January 1992, hundreds of women have been assassinated by the fundamentalists for not wearing a head scarf, for wearing Western clothing (such as blue jeans), for working alongside men, or for living without a male guardian in their own apartments. Many more have been stabbed or raped for the same "violations." A large number of women have received threatening letters, and live under death threats for presumably "unclean" activities such as teaching boys in school, running a hair salon, or even visiting one. Algerian feminists have strongly and consistently protested these and other violations of their rights, beginning with the 1984 Family Code, which conformed to traditional Islamic laws that allow a man the right to divorce his wife for any reason and to practice polygamy.[10]

In Malaysia the more liberal customary Malay laws dealing with marriage, divorce, and child custody have been pushed aside by the Islamic Shafi'i laws that oppose family planning policies, and call for punishment in cases of "willful disobedience by a woman of any order lawfully given by her husband." The religious laws have once again sanctioned the marriage of a virgin girl without her consent, and accepted repudiation by husbands.[11]

In Bangladesh, a state that was originally dedicated to the ideals of secularism and socialism during the period after its independence from Pakistan in 1971, Islam was declared the state religion in 1988. Fundamentalist clerics have issued a fatwa (religious decree) calling for the death of the feminist Muslim writer and poet Taslima Nasrin. Nasrin is the author of a popular novel *Shame* (1993) in which she recounts the killing of a group of Hindus by Muslim fundamentalists.[12]

Even in regions where feminists have made some inroads, the struggle to maintain these gains continues. At the plenary session of the 1993 annual conference of the Middle East Studies Association in North Carolina, Egyptian feminist writer and physician Nawal el-Saadawi announced that fundamentalists in both Egypt and Algeria have threatened to kill her. Saadawi's organization, the Arab Women's Solidarity Association, was banned by the government of Egypt in 1991, as a move to appease the fundamentalists, and some of her books remain banned there today.

In Pakistan the respected poet and social campaigner Akhtar Hamid Khan, known for his lifelong support of family planning, education, and employment for impoverished women, has been threatened with execution by both the government and the ulama (clerics). The 1979 Hudud Ordinance practically eliminated the distinction between rape and sex between unmarried consenting adults, calling both adultery, and also sanctioned the flogging of the accused woman. This law was put in place during the government of General Zia' al-Haq and was selectively carried out during that of Ghulam Ishaq. Despite her promises, Benazir Bhutto did not change this situation during her first term, nor has she taken any major steps to revise laws that deny women's rights since her reelection as premier in 1993.[13]

In recent years, Turkish women have campaigned around the issues of domestic violence and helped to create shelters for battered women. They have formed consciousness-raising groups, and have discussed the limitations of legal reforms such as those introduced by Ataturk in the 1920s. They have also become active in environmental issues and demonstrated in the streets against sexual harassment of women. Feminists have set up women's coffee houses (traditionally segregated institutions in the Middle East), thus creating a public space for women's forums, and they have organized art exhibits. The Women's Library and Information Center, the first such center devoted to feminist scholarship and political activity on behalf of women's issues, was opened in Istanbul in April 1990. Recently, Turkish feminists have had to compete with the fundamentalist Islamic Welfare Party (RIFAH) which now heads a coalition government. Followers of the Welfare Party claim to represent women's rights and direct their attacks at the objectification of women under capitalism. The fundamentalists' criticisms of pornography and prostitution, and the many social services they provide for the community free of charge, have helped to legitimate their claim that they represent issues of concern to women. Their outspoken challenge to industrial pollution has also gained them converts. A return to religious values, they insist, would solve the myriad social and economic problems of Turkish society.[14]

Palestinian women in the occupied territories became instrumental in forming decentralized popular committees once the Intifada movement was initiated in December 1987. They also began to address specifically women's issues. Debates on divorce, women's income, and greater respect for women continued to be aired. Many young women activists broke with earlier traditions of arranged and semiarranged marriages and pursued marriage based on individual choice. Others tried to remain politically involved even after marriage. This was a new phenomenon in a movement that had historically insisted that married women must leave the political organizations and instead give "sons to the resistance," and where the birth of boys was glorified under various names such as the "Palestinian womb, " the "factory of men," or the "women's jihad."[15] The Palestinian community took pride in the impressive role of Hanan Mikhail Ashrawi, a feminist and professor of English at Bir Zeit University, who emerged as the official spokesperson for the Palestinian delegation to the 1993 Middle East peace talks.

The Palestinian leadership is divided, however, in its attitude toward women's rights and on women's place in the nationalist struggle. With the ascendancy of the religious right in Israel and the unraveling of the Oslo agreements, a possible political compromise between the Palestine Liberation Organization and the fundamentalist group Hamas in the newly formed autonomous government of Palestine would surely mean greater limits on women. Hamas openly opposes the women's organizing, and projects a theocratic and sex-segregated state as its ideal vision of a Palestinian society, one that undermines the basic civil rights of not only women, but also of Christian Palestinians who have long been active in the resistance movement.[16] The above list could continue since a number of other nations, such as Morocco, Lebanon, and Nigeria, have also made compromises with Muslim fundamentalists.[17]

Feminist Writings on the Roots of Fundamentalism

As the political discourse of the Middle East, North Africa, and Southeast Asia became increasingly dominated by conservative Islamist arguments, a number of feminist thinkers and writers have tried to probe the contradictions of their societies in an attempt to understand the underlying reasons for the growth of Muslim fundamentalism. As mentioned earlier, these studies can be divided into three categories. One group has stressed the economic and political factors that have led to the rise of fundamentalist movements in the late twentieth century. A second group has probed the substantial cultural transformation that has taken place in the realm of the family as a result of modernity, changes that have encouraged women to search for more stable (i.e., protected) relations. A third group has stressed the changing dynamics of power in contemporary Middle Eastern societies and has argued that adherence to the hijab, despite all its limitations, may provide a new public space for young women in the highly patriarchal cultures of the region.[18]

The Political/Economic Explanation

Several sociologists and political scientists have discussed the rapid economic changes that have characterized the region in the post–World War II period, changes that took place under secular and highly authoritarian governments.[19] Iranian sociologist Valentine Moghadam points out that in the 1960s and 1970s, improvements in health and hygiene resulted in drastic demographic changes in the Middle East and North Africa, namely the growth of a youthful population. At the same time, the fall in oil prices in the 1970s and the accompanying unemployment, increased the gap between the upper classes and the middle and lower-middle classes. A crisis of political legitimacy ensued in which the secular and highly authoritarian governments of the region were attacked for corruption, the continued subservience to Western powers, and especially the propagation of supposedly immoral and unethical modernist values and institutions. This last point of contention was fueled by the growth of women's education and employment. The fierce competition for the university entrance exams, and for government civil service jobs, especially affected the lower-middle classes who were the first generation of their families to attend colleges and universities. To pacify this angry and youthful population, and also to undermine the leftist and Marxist groups, the secular governments of the region, whether Anwar al-Sadat in Egypt, or Muhammad Reza Shah Pahlavi in Iran, allowed or sometimes encouraged the activities of Islamist groups.[20]

Fatima Mernissi, who has given us an intimate understanding of Moroccan women's lives through several sociological studies and oral histories, has also focused on the economic and political problems that contributed to the growth of fundamentalism in North Africa.[21] Her point is that the spread of fundamentalism in the last two decades has stemmed from the political and social failures of the secular and authoritarian states of the postcolonial period, states that operate within the rules of the International Monetary Fund (IMF) and the interests of the imperialist powers.[22]

In a 1986 introduction to her classic study *Beyond the Veil*, and in her more recent work *Islam and Democracy*, Mernissi further analyzes some of the sociological reasons for the growth of religious fundamentalism in Egypt. She traces the development of Muslim fundamentalism among the urban lower-middle classes and university students, who make up the great majority of the movements' adherents, to several factors such as rapid urbanization and mass education. The sharp increase in the number of educated and employed women, the fact that most women now delay marriage until their twenties, the greater authority women experience as a result of the earnings they bring home, the greater control they have gained over unwanted pregnancies, and the higher divorce rate, have all helped produce important changes in the relation between the sexes.[23] Given the limited opportunities for advanced education in most Third World countries, there is great competition between men and women for university placement and professional positions, adding fuel to an already explosive situation in predominantly Muslim countries. High unemployment rates in Middle Eastern and North African countries (in Algeria the rate is close to 40 percent) have only increased the tension. Many men, who have been stripped of their old identities as heads of the households and patriarches, find the message of the fundamentalist Muslim clerics and politicians quite appealing. As Mernissi argues:

> The hijab is manna from heaven for politicians facing crises. It is not just a scrap of cloth; it is a division of labor. It sends women back to the kitchen. *Any Muslim state can reduce its level of unemployment by half just by appealing to the* shari'a, *in its meaning as despotic caliphal traditions.* This is why it is important to avoid reducing fundamentalism to a handful of agitators who stage demonstrations in the streets. It must be situated within its regional and world economic context by linking it to the question of oil wealth and the New World Order that the Westerners propose to us [emphasis in original].[24]

In her study of the National Islamic Front (NIF) in Sudan, Sondra Hale presents a similar analysis. She argues that a variety of economic and political factors, such as the emergence of multinational corporations, the uneven nature of economic development, and emigration as a result of high unemployment, have contributed to the "socio-political/economic crises which in turn have had a profound impact on gender arrangements." The process of "romanticizing" women's role in reproduction and the insistence of the NIF that women return to the home and take care of children and husbands is an attempt to force women out of the labor process and to create jobs for the lower- and middle-class urban males, as employees, civil servants, and college instructors, areas in which women have made significant inroads.[25]

Several writers have also pointed to the economic opportunities that fundamentalist institutions provide for believers, among them inexpensive care at hospitals, health clinics, and schools, all of which attract low-income women and their families. Naila Kabeer writes that in Bangladesh the fundamentalist organizations with funding from Saudi Arabia have established a large network of Islamic Non-Governmental Organizations (NGOs) that provide students with a wide variety of educational assistance, from scholarship and vocational training to dormitories, jobs, and medical clinics. The same organizations train Muslim clerics to not only attend to the spiritual needs of the community but also to run the village administration, and to provide basic health care including pre- and postnatal care. These services are dispensed alongside a religious and ideological message that seeks to counter Western and modernist views. For example, the feminist literature in the West that emphasizes women's contribution to the household as a form of unpaid labor is adopted, but then a different conclusion is derived from this literature, that women therefore need not work outside the home.[26] Andrea Rugh points out that in Egypt the services that the private mosques provide for the community not only are more reliable than government services but also contribute to the community's sense of dignity:

> Services may include the provision of subsidized clothing and food, health care, regular educational programs (usually at the pre-primary or primary level), after-school tutoring for children, religious instruction, subsidies for students, evening courses, social group activities, Qur'an reading sessions, and special programs for religious holidays. In poor areas, mosque representatives hand out free food, clothing, and money in exchange, as one poor woman put it, "for our wearing proper Islamic dress." Money can also be borrowed through Islamic banks in the approved "profit sharing" way where a fixed interest is not required.[27]

While these services bring new adherents to the movement, the truth remains that none of the Islamist movements have been able to offer a viable solution to the overall economic problems of their respected societies. Decades ago, Maxime Rodinson had shown in his *Islam and Capitalism* that Islamist economic policies are in no way a genuine alternative to capitalist development.[28] Valentine Moghadam has argued more recently that since Islamist governments in Sudan, Iran, and Pakistan were unable to prevent escalating and structural unemployment, to carry out a program of wealth distribution, or even to reduce government corruption, they have instead focused on issues of family, culture, and law as the root causes of all social and economic problems.[29]

The Cultural Explanation: Modernization and the Family

A second argument that appears in writings on fundamentalism, including those who write on the American Protestant fundamentalist movement, is that women should not be viewed as passive and submissive objects who are coerced or simply duped into such movements. Fundamentalism is not simply "constructed by men and imposed on women," notes Julie Ingersoll.[30] Women are drawn to these movements because of their emphasis on family, and because fundamentalist organizations demand that both women and men place a higher priority on raising children and family relations in general. We are living in a world in which the requirements of capitalist development have placed an enormous strain on married life. Husbands and wives often both work full time; there is appallingly inadequate child care; there are frequent job losses and job relocations; and to make ends meet, couples often work much beyond the eight-hour day. The fundamentalist message, which appeals to a much "higher" authority than corporate owners and manufacturers, falls, therefore, on receptive ears. Women who generally hold low-status jobs in the capitalist market, and are overburdened with responsibility for children as well as for the elderly, may in fact, writes Helen Hardacre, make a "conscious decision to use the fundamentalist message to secure the husband's loyalty and support of them and their children."[31]

Sociologist Deniz Kandiyoti, ethnologist Aihwa Ong, and political scientist Cynthia Enloe have all emphasized the disruptive consequences of shifting gender roles in developing societies, especially changes in the family in the Middle East and Southeast Asia. They suggest that we may be witnessing a growing interest in a return to more traditional and seemingly secure patriarchal cultures of the past by both women and men.

Kandiyoti, a Turkish feminist, suggests that in Asian, including Middle Eastern, societies a tacit intergenerational agreement, a "patriarchal bargain," historically helped to maintain the social structure. A young bride, who was deprived of inheritance rights in her father's house, acquiesced to her subservient position at the residence of her in-laws. She accepted her role and internalized the patriarchal values because she anticipated a day when she herself would become the beneficiary of these traditions and could rule over her daughters-in-law. In the late twentieth century, however, the process of modernization rapidly deprived this social bargain of its necessary economic foundation.[32] Once the built-in insecurities of the capitalist structure and the nuclear family became more obvious (unemployment, lack of child care, or care for the elderly), both younger and older women grew more receptive toward an ideology that called for a return to the old patriarchal bargain in exchange for greater security.

Aihwa Ong probes into why many lower-middle-class women have been attracted by the Islamist revivalist movement in Malaysia. She argues that the process of modernization has had a mixed impact insofar as women are concerned. It has given women greater economic and personal freedom, with paid employment, spending money, and the power accompanying them, but it has also resulted in men abandoning their customary obligations to the family. Given the inherent instability of the capitalist economy and continued exploitation by the West as well as the economic recessions of the last two decades, which have hit many Third World countries especially hard, the newly employed woman often finds herself out of a job, and without the traditional support of the extended family or the community. Ong writes, "Land scarcity, widespread female wage labor, and secularization in many cases reduced men's customary obligations to be the sole supporter of their families."[33]

As Cynthia Enloe argues in her *Making Feminist Sense of Internat-*

ional Politics, "it isn't always obvious that surrendering the role of cultural transmitter or rejecting male protection will enhance a woman's daily security, reduce her burdens."[34] The return to traditional and religious values may thus be intriguing to the overworked housewife, worker, and mother who hopes that her husband and community assume a greater share of her burden. She is also more likely to turn to the religious foundations and their networks of social support. These associations have assumed the customary role as head of the patriarchal clan. They also act as family counselors and help to end conflicts by advising women to be more subservient to their husbands, but also asking men to uphold their traditional obligations to the family.

The Veiling as Empowerment Explanation

A third group of feminist scholars has argued that women who join Islamist organizations do so not only because of the economic support they gain, or the profamily message they cherish, but also because of the alternative social and political power and autonomy they gain in the movements. By donning the veil, young lower-middle-class women may lose many individual freedoms, but they gain access to public spaces, and to employment, and they can become valued and powerful members of political organizations that propagate the Islamist ideology. On the one hand, when a young girl adopts the hijab she becomes physically restrained in certain ways. She may not be able to climb a tree or ride a bicycle so easily (in Iran she is prohibited from biking). On the other hand, she may face a lesser degree of sexual harassment, and she may gain the right from her traditional family to finish high school and even attend the university, to seek outside professional employment, to socialize with her peers in mass organizations that promote the Islamist ideology, and even to choose her own husband in these gatherings rather than submit to an arranged marriage. Those who become active members of militant Islamist groups also gain power over other more secular women. They become the guardians of morality on the streets and public spaces. In countries such as Iran and Sudan where Islamists control the government, activist women of these movements act as police on the streets. They abuse and arrest more upper-class secular women on charges of improper hijab and are tremendously feared in the community.

The Jordanian feminist Lama Abu Odeh writes of the problem of sexual harassment and the dilemma Middle Eastern women have faced ever since they unveiled in the early twentieth century. Negotiating the streets, using public transportation, and working side by side with the men in offices and factories became ordeals for unveiled women. They found that their bodies were constantly under the intrusive gaze of men. In societies where sexual harassment and molestation of women, touching, fondling, stalking, and derogatory comments are rampant on the streets, in buses, and in workplaces, unveiled women often have no recourse to law or higher authorities. Even worse, they themselves are held responsible for the harassment they endure.[35] Under such circumstances, the veil can offer women a certain degree of physical protection. A veiled woman is seldom harassed in public and if she is, she can loudly appeal to the chivalry and religiosity of the men around her who would almost certainly come to her help.

The Syrian feminist Bouthaina Shaaban, who has studied the personal lives of Syrian, Lebanese, Palestinian, and Algerian women, is particularly effective in showing the appeal of Muslim fundamentalism to lower-class single women. Shaaban shows how adherence to the Islamist dress code provides a new public space for young women in traditionally segregated societies. In one case study, a single woman named Zainab, who has a university education and comes from a working class district, has joined the Shi'ite fundamentalist organization Amal in southern Lebanon. She explains how her activity with Amal, and her wearing of the prescribed Islamic outfit, *al-Shari,* have given her both protection and increased freedom of action. She feels safe from harassment, and considers herself a productive member of society, helping to feed and shelter the poor. Above all she has gained greater respect, power, and authority. "My father, who used to be the only supreme authority in the house, never makes any decisions now concerning the family without consulting me first."[36] Zainab can stay out until eleven o'clock at night doing organizational work without her parents questioning her. She has this liberty in a society where even grandmothers cannot stay out late for fear of what the neighbors might say.

There is considerable disagreement among feminist writers on the actual liberating potentialities that the donning of the veil may provide. Leila Ahmed, for example, draws on a study of four hundred veiled and unveiled women at Cairo University that shows that there is a direct correlation between the hijab and the educational level of the female students. The lower the class of the parents, the more chances of the student adopting the veil. She thus concludes that the veil is not a social innovation but a sign of conformity to the social class from which these upwardly mobile young women have emerged. The veil both saves the young student and professional from the expenses of acquiring multiple fashionable outfits and "is a coping mechanism." Joining the Islamist groups carries "the comfort of bringing the values of home and childhood to the city and its foreign and morally overwhelming ways."[37]

While Ahmed recognizes the severe limitations that have been imposed on women in countries where Islamists have entered the government or gained substantial power, she nevertheless believes that the new practice of veiling serves as a transition process for lower-middle-class women. In Ahmed's view, some of the goals of secular and upper-class Egyptian feminists, who were the first generation to demand women's entry into the universities and professional employment, are now pursued in somewhat different ways by the middle- and lower-middle-class women. The new hijab, therefore, in her view, marks a "broad demographic change—a change that has democratized mainstream culture."[38]

Anthropologist Lila Abu-Lughod takes issue with Leila Ahmed on this point. She argues that since Islamist movements are unwilling or incapable of carrying out a serious program of distribution of wealth, they have instead attempted to construct an illusion of equality through the imposition of the veil. She asks why "a political discourse in which morality displaces class as the central social problem is so appealing?"[39]

Arlene MacLeod points to the alienating nature of the labor most women perform. Using Antonio Gramsci's concept of hegemony, she argues that where Islamist movements are in opposition to the state, the wearing of the veil is neither a sign of victimization and subordination, nor an expression of "false consciousness." Rather, it is a measure of women's alienation from modernization and its false promises. The subordinated lower classes are neither forced nor completely duped into accepting regulations and restrictions. Through a series of ethnographic studies, MacLeod describes the enormously difficult lives of women who both take care of the family and work for a living. She shows how alienated and demoralized these women become when they realize that the jobs they fought for at home are so repetitive and uncreative. Most middle-class and lower-middle-class women who have entered civil service jobs find their work to be "boring and unchallenging," as well as "useless."[40] Ambitious lower-middle-class women have few options but to work for the public sector, which provides them with jobs but allows them no true initiative or creativity. Thus, women suffer from a gender division of labor that assigns them to low-status jobs, a class division that limits them to repetitive and boring work, an economic straight-jacket that obligates them to work outside the home in a culture which sees women's primary role to be in the home and blames women who hold outside employment. Women who lack viable and tangible alternatives in life, who have come to view Western women as sex objects through popular culture and television, have therefore turned to traditional alternatives to gain some measure of control over their lives.[41]

MacLeod speaks of the veil as a conscious symbol of resistance in an

Arab society where women work outside the home. But choice involves having access to information and real options. MacLeod says nothing about the fundamentalist message that male sexuality is uncontrollable, and that women induce inappropriate male sexual behavior. Likewise she glosses over the vast unemployment, the pressure on women to return to homes so that more jobs are opened for men. The questions remain: to what extent does the wearing of the hijab empower young students and professional women? What does it mean if you choose your own husband but are then denied the right to divorce, to child custody, or to a fair share of the property you and your husband have acquired during the marriage? How free is a woman who goes to the university and seeks employment but is then deprived, by her husband, of a choice of a career? How much autonomy does a veiled woman have when the very acceptance of the veil means approval of gender segregation, and the admission that a woman is first and foremost a sexual object? What does it mean when the burden of avoiding sexual harassment is placed on women, while men are seen as impulsive creatures with little or no control over their sexual desires? These and other questions indicate that while young unmarried women may gain some control over their lives through wearing of the hijab, or find temporary solutions to the problem of sexual harassment and other issues women face in modern society, donning the hijab is by no means a serious step toward resolution of these contradictions. Emancipation for women means the free exercise of body and mind. That cannot happen when women are deemed inferior and different beings by virtue of their biology.

The emergence of Muslim fundamentalism is a complicated phenomenon stemming in part from the crisis of capitalist development and modernization in the Third World. Muslim fundamentalism has been difficult to confront. This is because in the seminaries and in the mosques it has an organization with ample financial backing and at times state support, and also because the fundamentalists speak to many urgent economic, social, and cultural needs of the community.

Fundamentalism is in part a reaction to rampant problems of migration, unemployment, alienated labor, destruction of the extended family, high divorce rates, single motherhood, and lack of medical care and economic support for families. It fills a void created by the collapse of the secular leftist and nationalist movements, movements that it lumps together with pro-Western politics as essentially foreign and un-Islamic. It claims to bring back the traditional social relationships, the collective and personal loyalties and obligations that maintained the cohesiveness of the community, in place of the alienated social relations that have their roots in capitalist relations of production. The strength of fundamentalism lies in the creation of an illusion that a return to the familiar, the traditional, and the non-threatening, in this case religion, is the answer.

Notes

1. See Linda J. Nicholson, ed., *Feminism/Postmodernism* (New York: Routledge, 1990), 1–16; Judith Butler and Joan W. Scott, eds., *Feminists Theorize the Political* (New York: Routledge, 1992).

2. Nancy C. M. Hartsock, "Foucault on Power: A Theory for Women?" in *Feminism/Postmodernism,* 157–175; Caroline Ramazanoglu, ed., *Up against Foucault: Explorations of Some Tensions Between Foucault and Feminism* (New York: Routledge, 1993).

3. See Martin E. Marty and R. Scott Appleby, eds., *The Fundamentalism Project: Fundamentalisms Observed,* 1 (Chicago: University of Chicago Press, 1991), ix–x. In his "Comparing Fundamentalism," *Contention* 4, no. 2 (Winter 1995): 36, Marty points out that such movements generally share four characteristics: (1) they are literalists (relying on a literal interpretation of religious texts); (2) they adopt a Manichaean worldview; (3) they are zealots in their convictions; and (4) they are highly patriarchal, that is, they uphold "an exaggerated male authority." Bernard Lewis prefers the term *fundamentalism* because in his view use of the terms *Islamic* or *Islamist* to identify such movements implies that "this is what the Islamic religion and civilization is about." See "Un entretien avec Bernard Lewis," *Le Monde*, 16 November 1993; See also Henry Munson, Jr., *Islam and Revolution in the Middle East* (New Haven: Yale University Press, 1988), 3–4.

4. See Saïd, *Culture and Imperialism* (New York: Alfred A. Knopf, 1993), 310. John Esposito, a specialist in Islamic theology, has argued that the term *fundamentalist* has been used and abused by secular scholars to refer to a broad and diverse number of organizations, political leaders, and societies in the Muslim world. See his "Secular Bias and Islamic Revivalism," *Chronicle of Higher Education,* 26 May 1993, A-44. There are, however, many members of Muslim communities who have no affinity for the extremist political movements that operate in the name of Islam, and have objected to characterization of these antimodernist and often antidemocratic versions of Islam as *Islamic* movements. In this chapter, I have used both the terms *fundamentalism* and *Islamism* for such movements, though not the term *Islamic.* Use of the term *fundamentalism* leaves space for other more democratic interpretations of Islam such as those of the contemporary Syrian writer Muhammad Shahrur. His writings call for a reform of Islamic laws along more contemporary lines and he has been greeted enthusiastically by many secular Arab intellectuals. See Dale F. Eickelman, "Islamic Liberalism Strikes Back," *Middle East Studies Association Bulletin* 27, no. 2 (December 1993): 163–167.

5. For a summary of these policies see, Nayereh Tohidi, "Gender and Islamic Fundamentalism: Feminist Politics in Iran," in *Third World Women and the Politics of Feminism*, eds. Chandra Mohanty, Ann Russo, and Lourdes Torres (Bloomington: Indiana University Press, 1991); for discussion of the more recent reforms in family law, see Shahla Haeri, "Obedience Versus Autonomy: Women and Fundamentalism in Iran and Pakistan," *The Fundamentalist Project: Fundamentalisms and Society,* vol. 2, ed. Martin E. Marty and R. Scott Appleby

(Chicago: University of Chicago Press, 1993), 181–213. See also Nesta Ramazani, "Women in Iran: The Revolutionary Ebb and Flow," *U.S.-Iran Review: Forum on American-Iranian Relations* 1, no. 7, (October 1993): 8–9. Ramazani, however, gives much of the credit for these changes to the government.

6. On the availability of contraceptive methods in premodern Arab societies, see B. F. Musallam, *Sex and Society in Islam* (Cambridge: Cambridge University Press, 1989). On the debates at the Cairo conference, see "Vatican Seeks Islamic Allies In U.N. Population Dispute," *New York Times*, 18 August 1994, 1.

7. See Ali Abdalla Abbas, "The National Islamic Front and the Politics of Education," *MERIP* (September-October 1991): 23–25; and *Newsletter of Women Living under Muslim Laws*, 6 July 1992.

8. See John Burns, "With Kabul Largely in Ruins, Afghans Get Respite from War," *New York Times*, 20 February 1995, 1.

9. See "Algeria Again at the Crossroads," *Middle East International*, 24 January 1992, 3; *Le nouvel observateur*, 15 January 1992.

10. See Karima Bennoune, "Algerian Women Confront Fundamentalism," *Monthly Review* 46, no. 4 (November 1994): 26–39.

11. Maznah Mohamad, "Islam, the Secular State, and Muslim Women in Malaysia," in *Newsletter of Women Living under Muslim Laws*, (1989), 13–19.

12. See "Man sukut nakhavaham kard," [I Will Not Be Silenced] in *Keyhan* (London), 6 January 1993. See also Naila Kabeer, "The Quest for National Identity: Women, Islam, and the State of Bangladesh," in *Women, Islam and the State*, ed. Deniz Kandiyoti (Philadelphia: Temple University Press, 1991), 115–243.

13. See *Newsletter of Women Living under Muslim Laws*, 27 October 1992 and "Pakistani Crusader vs. the Mullahs," *New York Times,* 10 August 1992. See also Paula R. Newberg, "The Two Benazir Bhuttos," *New York Times*, 11 February 1995, 50.

14. See Nukhet Sirman, "Feminism in Turkey: A Short History," in *New Perspectives on Turkey* 3, no. 1 (Fall 1989): 1–34. But Sirman also writes that the Turkish feminists' critiques of pornography "at times exhibit considerable affinity with right-wing discourses in Britain and the U.S. on sex and morality couched in terms of extremism and corruption" (25–26). See also Alan Cowell, "Muslim Parties Growth Posing Challenge to Turkey's Secular Heritage," *New York Times*, 30 November 1994, 1.

15. See Rosemary Sayigh, "Palestinian Women: Triple Burden, Single Struggle," *Palestine: Profile of an Occupation* (London: Zed Books Ltd., 1989); Islah Jad, "From the Salons to the Popular Committees, Palestinian Women, 1919–1989," *Intifada: Palestine at the Crossroads*, ed. Jamal R. Nassar and Roger Heacock (New York: Praeger, 1990); Rita Giacaman and Penny Johnson, "Palestinian Women: Building Barricades and Breaking Barriers," in *Intifada: The Palestinian Uprising against Israeli Occupation*, ed. Zachary Lochman and Joel Beinin (Boston: South End Press, 1989), 155–169.

16. This point was eloquently discussed by a longtime Palestinian activist Rabab Abdulhadi at the 1993 meeting of the Association for Middle East Women's Studies at Triangle Park, North Carolina.

17. For example, see "For Another Kind of Morocco: An Interview with Abraham Serfaty," *MERIP* (November-December 1992): 24–27.

18. I would like to stress that these three categories are not mutually exclusive and some authors have used more than one approach.

19. Valentine M. Moghadam, *Modernizing Women: Gender and Social Change in the Middle East* (Boulder: Lynne Rienner Publishers, 1993); Saad Eddin Ibrahim, "Anatomy of Egypt's Militant Islamic Groups," *International Journal of Middle East Studies* 12, no. 4 (1980): 423–453.

20. See Moghadam, *Modernizing Women*, 137.

21. Fatima Mernissi, *Beyond the Veil: Male-Female Dynamics in Modern Muslim Society*, 2d ed. (Bloomington: Indiana University Press, 1987).

22. Fatima Mernissi, *Doing Daily Battle: Interviews with Moroccan Women* (New Brunswick, N.J.: Rutgers University Press, 1989), 3–4.

23. Mernissi, "Muslim Women and Fundamentalism: Introduction to the Revised Edition" in *Beyond the Veil,* vii–xv.

24. *Islam and Democracy: Fear of the Modern World* (Reading, Mass.: Addison-Wesley Publishing Co., 1992), 165.

25. Sondra Hale, "Gender, Religious Identity, and Political Mobilization in Sudan," in *Identity Politics and Women: Cultural Reassertions and Feminisms in International Perspective,* ed. Valentine M. Moghadam (Boulder: Westview Press, 1994), 145–166.

26. Kabeer, "The Quest for National Identity," 134–35. Judith Miller writes that during the 1992 earthquake in Egypt, the government remained ineffectual while Islamist groups provided "temporary housing, emergency feeding centers, and psychological counselors for the bulk of the victims." See *New York Times,* 27 December 1992.

27. Andrea B. Rugh, "Reshaping Personal Relations in Egypt," in *Fundamentalism and Society,* 164.

28. Maxime Rodinson, *Islam and Capitalism* (Austin: University of Texas Press, 1978; orig. pub. 1966).

29. Moghadam, *Modernizing Women,* 167.

30. See Julie J. Ingersoll, "Which Tradition, Which Values? 'Traditional Family Values' in American Protestant Fundamentalism," *Contention* 4, no. 2 (Winter 1995): 93. See also Helen Hardacre, "The Impact of Fundamentalisms on Women, the Family, and Interpersonal Relations," in *The Fundamentalist Project: Fundamentalism and Society,* 129–150.

31. Hardacre, "The Impact of Fundamentalisms on Women," 142.

32. Deniz Kandiyoti, "Bargaining with Patriarchy," *Gender and Society* 2, no. 3 (1988): 274–290.

33. Aihwa Ong, "State Versus Islam: Malay Families, Women's Bodies, and the Body Politic in Malaysia," *American Ethnologist* 17, no. 2 (May 1990): 269.

34. Cynthia Enloe, *Making Feminist Sense of International Politics: Bananas, Beaches, and Bases* (Berkeley: University of California Press, 1989), 55.

35. See Lama Abu Odeh, "Post-Colonial Feminism and the Veil: Thinking the Difference," *Feminist Review* 43 (Spring 1993): 26–37. In his "Women

Regain a Kind of Security in Islam's Embrace," *New York Times*, 27 December 1992, Fouad Ajami writes that the "Islamic dress is a marking out of the physical and moral borders. It sets frontiers beyond which sexually active men may not go."

36.   Bouthaina Shaaban, *Both Right and Left Handed: Arab Women Talk about Their Lives* (Bloomington: Indiana University Press, 1991), 85.

37.   Leila Ahmed, *Women and Gender in Islam: Historical Roots of a Modern Debate* (New Haven: Yale University Press, 1992), 222–223.

38.   Ahmed, *Women and Gender*, 225.

39.   Lila Abu-Lughod, "Movie Stars and Islamic Moralism in Egypt," *Social Text* 42 (Spring 1995): 1.

40.   See Arlene Elowe MacLeod, "Hegemonic Relations and Gender Resistance: The New Veiling as Accommodating Protest in Cairo," *Signs* 17, no. 3 (Spring 1992): 546.

41.   Arlene Elowe MacLeod, "Hegemonic Relations."

Part IV

Literary and Autobiographical Portraitures and Landscapes of Identity, Exile, and Gender

7

Women, War, Autobiography, and the Historiographic Metafictional Text: Unveiling the Veiled in Assia Djebar's *L'amour, la fantasia*

Valérie Orlando

In his documentary novel, *La gangrène et l'oubli* (*The Gangrene and the Forgotten*] author and historian, Benjamin Stora writes, "It is time to put to work a new history . . . of the Algerian war, one which traces the war's colonial beginnings to its survival in the memories of the present."[1] New works in Francophone literature of the Maghreb, such as Assia Djebar's novel, *L'amour, la fantasia*, echo Stora's words. Through a hybrid of culture, language, and historicity, Djebar reconsiders and narrates the legacy of French colonialism that has influenced the identity of Algeria. As a social commentary, *L'amour, la fantasia* confronts difference and marginalization, and champions the important roles of voice, ethnicity, and diversity in forming an historical narrative. Djebar employs a multivalent perspective in order to reinscribe the multiple stories of the Other's[2] past and present. She seeks not to wipe the historic slate clean of former colonial presence, but to refocus the reader's gaze on overlooked and misinterpreted events of France's archival documentation on Algerian history. Layers of history are incorporated into her narrative, creating a palimpsest text, or a text through which multiple views, identities, and subjectivities—French and Algerian—may be read.[3]

Recognizing that both Algerian identity and history, particularly those of women, have been manipulated by colonial European discourse, Djebar seeks to rectify these wrongs through the reconstituted stories that comprise the body of her text. She notes that either misrepresentation, or worse still, no representation at all, has characterized the West's depiction of the colonized Other in the archives of Western history. These misrepresentations have rooted themselves in Western culture, promoting Oriental stereotypes that remain prevalent even in our postcolonial era.[4] According to

Edward Saïd, these modern-day universals are based on mythic ideals stemming from nineteenth-century European colonialist images of sexual pleasure, native exploitation, and rich monetary returns: "The Orient was Orientalized not only because it was discovered to be 'Oriental' in all those ways considered commonplace by an average nineteenth-century European, but also because it *could be*—that is, submitted to being—*made* Oriental . . . . Orientalism [however] is nothing more than a structure of lies or myths which, were the truth about them to be told, would simply blow away."[5]

Orientalizing stereotypes have been doubly detrimental to women of formerly colonized countries. Just as Europeans fostered convenient stereotypes of Maghrebian lands in general, so, too, did they create narrow, self-serving visions of Maghrebian women. Through the colonizing process, the identity of North African women was appropriated into the ready-made sexual diva or dancing girl images depicted in nineteenth-century paintings by such artists as Delacroix and Ingres. These Western stereotypes stifled Maghrebian feminine voice, presence, and individuality.

Assia Djebar's new version of Algerian history reconstitutes the lost identity of the colonized woman as well as the forgotten events affecting all Algerians during the years of French occupation. In her book *A Poetics of Postmodernism*, Linda Hutcheon defines such a reconstituted, historical narrative as "historiographic metafiction," or a narrative that reflects an effort to reinstate history from a different view. Historically reconstituted discourses support the power of difference while forcing the rethinking of "the relation between the past and our writing of it."[6] The manifestation and subsequent creation of difference through historiographic metafiction fosters new expansions toward the realm of the ex-centric, decentered, or fragmented spheres of history, realms that have always bordered on and been subordinate to the Single-Subject-White-European-Colonial-Discourse of the Western World. Assia Djebar exploits this fragmented, ex-centric sphere of history in order to question and promote new codes of identity, culture, past, present, and subjectivity for Algeria.

Djebar incorporates three different, but central, textualities to create her narrative: the autobiographical, the linguistic, and the paradoxical. These textualities are woven within her rendition of Algerian history, which is recounted not in a linear sequence of events, but in a multiplicity of interconnected a-linear experiences.[7] This interconnectedness results in a certain social recontextualization of Algerian history, which equally reflects the collective conscience of a panoply of events, people, and experiences—all of which played essential roles in its construction. This collective conscience challenges and even eclipses the hegemony of the dogmatic European-Single-Subject that has preempted other literatures of the world throughout modern history. Assia Djebar's historiographic metafiction juxtaposes past and future time spectrums with the present, thereby favoring many different sociocultural, linguistic, and ethnic parameters formerly not found in Western-centered historical accounts concerning Algeria.

The Feminine Autobiography: A Painful Testimony

Assia Djebar's novel is a collective autobiography that interweaves her own story with the autobiographies and stories of many women, and the long, bloody history of French colonial occupation of Algeria. This interweaving renders as present three different pasts: the initial invasion of Algeria in 1830, the 1954 war of liberation, and Djebar's own childhood memories.[8] Djebar's collective autobiography demonstrates what Roland Barthes aptly describes as a process "linking form, which is both normal and unique to [her] discourse, to the vast history of others," which in turn demonstrates that "writing is an act of historic solidarity."[9]

Djebar formulates her autobiography on two levels: a personal level, where childhood and family experiences allow her to explore her feelings of dual identity and the difficulties that arise from living a liminal existence between French and Arab worlds and a collective level where the author exposes the need for women to learn to write and thereby empower their own discourse, freed of male and colonial domination.

The author's autobiography is the painful testimony of a young girl growing up between two languages, two cultures, and two traditions. Djebar opens her novel with what is portrayed as a scene from her first day at a French school. Her father, a teacher, walks her to the door of the school—defying village morals by parading his daughter openly and exposing her to Western education and the language of the colonizer:

> Arab girl, going for the first time to school, an autumn morning, hand in hand with her father. He, wearing a fez, his shadow tall and straight in his European suit, holding a book bag, he is a teacher at the French school. Arab girl in a village in the Algerian Sahel. . . . From the first day when a little girl "goes out" to learn the alphabet, the neighbors appropriate the sly glances of those who take pity, ten or fifteen years in advance: on the audacious father, on the reckless brother. Bad luck will inevitably fall upon them.[10]

Ordinary events in Djebar's autobiography become transformed into social commentaries, as she uses her diary to describe the position of women in Algerian society. In another seemingly banal scene, her father sends a postcard written in French to her mother. Djebar tells her readers that the autobiographical incident unveils larger sociocultural issues involving severe ramifications for women. Not only did her father write in French, the language of the colonizer, but he also made public a declaration of love for all the surrounding community to see:

> The revolution had begun: my father, in his own hand-writing, and on a post card which was going to travel from town to town, passing under so many male eyes, even ending up under those of our village's postman, a devout Moslem; my father had dared to write the name of his wife which he had written in western style: "Ms. so and so" whereas all [other] inhabitants rich or poor only evoke wife and children by the vague term "home of."[11]

In presenting this interaction between her mother and father, Djebar alludes to the public pressures on individuals, particularly women, involved in romantic relationships within the Algerian culture. The author informs her readers that such public, amorous demonstrations are not favorably looked upon in a society whose Muslim traditions have divided men and women according to strict domestic codes.

By contrast, in a subsequent chapter, Djebar recedes from her own autobiography to pick up another story from the past. Halting time for a brief instant in 1956, she retells the story of a young French soldier, Bernard, who enters an isolated farm seeking a lovely young girl to whom he feels it is his right to make love. Djebar's reevaluation of this obscure incident mixes both a biography and an appropriated autobiography. She is responsible for telling Bernard's story who, at the same time, tells his own. Djebar is both inside the Frenchman's text as a colonizing soldier, and outside it as an Algerian woman narrating the biography of one of her "sexploited" foremothers. She also appropriates the presence of the other fearful women who are caught in the room when the soldier enters the house:

> He enters without knocking. It must be 1:30 in the morning. He hesitates in the darkness, then lights a match: before him, a group of women, curled up in a circle, watching him; almost all of them are old or seem to be. They are packed against each other; their eyes gleaming with fright and surprise. . . . The Frenchman takes from his pockets supplemental provisions which he distributes hastily. He paces back and forth, relights a cigarette; his searching eyes finally fall upon the "lovely Fatma" who had smiled. He grasps her by the hand, pulls her back. . . . Blackness

has come again. The couple moves to the back of the huge room, there where the shadow is darkest. The circle of old women hasn't moved, hunched up companions, sisters of silence, obscured pupils fixing the preserved present: Does the lake of happiness exist? . . . The Frenchman undressed himself. "I would have thought myself at home," he will admit. He draws the young girl to him, who trembles, who embraces and begins to caress him. . . . "And if one of those old women gets up and stabs me in the back" he thinks to himself. . . ." She kissed me with full lips, like a little girl. Imagine that! Do you realize? . . . Kissed me! . . . Bernard returns to camp around three o'clock in the morning.[12]

In exposing this male autobiography, Djebar conveys a more significant, global message concerning the sexual manipulation of Algerian women at the hands of the French throughout the duration of colonialism. This brief scene stands as a testament, inscribed in the present, to all female identity. It is a eulogy for all women forgotten, maimed, beaten, raped, and mutilated by war; a reminder to women that they must take charge of their own discourse, never forgetting their sisters, mothers, and grandmothers who crouched, silenced by fear, in an obscure corner. Assia Djebar does not forget, and she reminds her audience that the scene is, and will be, repeated, until women find the strength to emerge from silence: "Twenty years later, I am reporting the scene to you, to you widows so that at your turn you look, so that at your turn you silence yourselves. And the old, immobilized women listen to the unknown village girl who offers herself."[13]

The links that women share represent a central theme of *L'amour, la fantasia*. In writing a collective feminine biography, Djebar seeks to illustrate women's struggles to find and establish presence through the strength of their connections with each other. According to Shoshana Felman in her book-length essay, *What Does a Woman Want?*, the need to establish presence and subjectivity is a phenomenon shared by all women. Felman argues that throughout history, women have been the incarnate identity of man's desire, the objects that succumb to his overall picture of "what they ought to be."[14] Under masculine domination, women are socialized to write about themselves through male eyes, thus denying their own identity. Moreover, Felman insists, the only male encounter with femininity has been femininity as an object of desire, or as the mirror-image of himself. A woman orbits around his world, devoid of any independent subjectivity.[15] In order to counter the male mirror image and create her own identity, a woman must first create her own autobiography. For Felman, a true feminine autobiography must be free of its "maleness"—that is, free of the influence of the male manner of thinking. Assia Djebar frees herself and the women of Algeria by writing her collective autobiography. Through the textualization of her own discourse, the author attempts to resist not only the male mold but the colonized Oriental one as well.

Pointing out the ways in which European historical accounts have reduced Algerians "to objects of a dominant gaze,"[16] Djebar seeks to restate the never-before-stated through her narrative, thus giving voice and presence back to the colonized Other.

Giving back power of presence to the colonized allows Djebar to furnish her character, the wife of Hussein, with the power to gaze back at her conqueror. Instead of having the reader witness the conquering of Algeria solely through the eyes of the French, Djebar hypothesizes a dialogue among the female residents of Algiers as they witness the encroaching French invasion: "I, myself, imagine that the wife of Hussein forgot about her morning prayer and went out onto the terrace. That the other women, for whom terraces were an end of the day haven, found themselves there also, in order to capture in the same gaze the imposing, dazzling French flotilla."[17] Reinstating and breaking the colonizing French gaze by giving presence in historical time to the view of the female Other, Djebar dismantles the despotic stereotypes in which the West has confined North African women throughout colonial history.

In general, Djebar strives to unmask the West's view of the Arab as a univocal, generalized Oriental stereotype, detached from the rest of the world as an isolated "living tableau of queerness."[18] Unmasking means empowerment, which in turn allows the isolated Other reintegration into history as an equal with his/her own identity, presence, and subjectivity. By documenting women's roles and writing of their historic presence, she provides a milieu in which all Algerian women, mute, veiled, and nonveiled, can speak:

> And here, the shrouded ones in the heart of the parade, those whose mute presence is tolerated, those who take pleasure in the sad privilege of staying veiled at the heart even of the harem! I understand at last and their condemnation, and their luck: these women who "scream" in everyday life, those whom the stout women spurn and scorn, personify without a doubt the necessity of a glance, of an audience![19]

Writing and Linguistic Duality

Writing and language for Djebar are central linking forces by which she penetrates her people's history as well as that of the former French colonizer's. Writing affords Djebar a means to explore the duality that two histories and two languages represent for her—the duality of a woman writing her own autobiography and of a researcher delving into the lost truth of a silenced female legacy. Djebar's split identity prevents her from fully embracing either the Arab or the French sphere; she is caught in an intersubjective field between these two worlds. Nevertheless, this split identity allows Djebar to work constantly both inside and outside her text. By being both inside and outside—inside as an Arab Algerian and outside as an author writing in French—Djebar is able to create a more global history that encompasses herself, the French colonials, and the forgotten stories of women who lived during the Franco-Algerian struggle.

Djebar's decision to carry out her research and to tell her stories using the French language is ironic. There are two principal reasons for employing French rather than Arabic. The author's first goal is to use the French language to interpret French archives concerning Algerian women and their representation in colonial, Algerian history. In a sense, the French language allows Djebar not only to see herself through the "eyes of the Other, but to draw on aspects of the colonizer's model in order to elaborate her own sense of subjectivity."[20] Through interpretation using the French language, Djebar corrects the oversights of French historic discourse as documented in colonial texts.

Djebar's second reason for using French extends much farther back in history. French colonialism deprived women of education and literacy during much of the colonial period, and because of this, female subjectivity remained purely oral.[21] Female identity, subjectivity, and history were primarily based on tribal and village stories handed down from one woman to the next. By writing in French, Djebar not only corrects French archival accounts, but also reinvests Algerian women with the literary voice of which they were deprived. In this way, the author once again displaces and subverts "the norms imposed by the colonizer upon the colonized."[22] Using French essentially affords Djebar the opportunity to turn around established oppressive norms and to institute new codes of subjectivity.

Providing the reader with information from her own sources as well as from French archives, Djebar uncovers the small, unnoticed events of the colonizing process and its affects on Algerian women. In one scene the author elaborates on an insignificant event of an archival document turning it into a short dialogue between French soldiers who comment on the massacre of seven Algerian women during an 1840 campaign: "A total of seven were executed by our soldiers, indicates one of the soldiers. The [women] welcomed us with insults."[23] Such a small incident becomes the symbolic representation for the universal, senseless suffering and death that was the fate of so many Algerian women.

Further drawing attention to France's banalization and frivolous documentation of the conquering of Algeria, the author focuses on the correspondence of French officers whose quasi-poetic discourses written up in newspapers and journals served to narrate the glorious, brutal, military campaigns of the 1830s and 1840s in Algeria. Djebar reappropriates the voice of the young French field marshal, Bousquet,[24] in 1840: "Our small army is in the midst of joy and festivity . . . there is something of everything in this conquest."[25] In these documentaries, Djebar notes how the officers' stories, letters, and eyewitness accounts generated sentiment in France for still more colonial endeavors that eventually aided in bringing about Algeria's total submission. These same documents helped found and shape the Civilizing Mission, the political goals that sustained colonization in Algeria for the next 132 years.[26]

Intertextual Parodies

Paradox is of primary importance in Djebar's recontextualization of Algerian history. Indeed, an historiographic metafictional text is predisposed to always lead to paradox because "while teasing us with the existence of the past as real . . . there is no direct access to that real which would be unmediated by the structures of our various discourses about it."[27] Paradoxical doubling in historiographic metafiction places all documents and histories on equal ground, freed to be interpreted by those who seek to reinscribe them. Furthermore, paradox is a catalyst by which all subjects gain access to reinscription as new equaled bodies of difference, each with his/her own story to tell.

Perhaps the most striking paradoxical intertext in Djebar's *L'amour, la fantasia* is the nineteenth-century painter Eugène Fromentin's encounter with a severed hand. Djebar appropriates Fromentin's travelogue, *Un été dans le Sahara* [*A Summer in the Sahara*] in which the artist recalls finding near the corpses of two dead Algerian women one of their severed hands. While in his narrative Fromentin discards it with disgust, Djebar picks up the hand in order to reinscribe the dismissed and unrecorded existence of that single, Algerian woman lost in French colonial history and in the nineteenth-century painter's banalization of the event[28]: "Eugène Fromentin extends to me an unexpected hand, that of an unknown woman who he was never able to paint. In June 1853, when he left the Sahel for the desert's edge. . . . Fromentin picks up from the dust, a severed hand of an unknown Algerian woman. He discards it along his path. Much later, I pick up this living hand, hand of mutilation and memory and I attempt to have it bear *qalam*."[29]

Djebar's use of *qalam* (the Arabic word for speech) in these last lines of her novel evokes, once again, her quest to bridge the gap between her divided French/Arab identity. The use of this single Arab word represents her own link to Arab history as well as to the speech that she must reinscribe for women who have had no voice in the past. The empowerment of speech finally affords all women a means by which to subjectivize their presence in history. Those who have existed in silence due to domination and colonization are at last able to reshape their own renditions of history.

Djebar's narrative is indicative of a new era of historic discourse, one that problematizes our reading of history and the domination of Western documentation on the "Orient." Problematizing established discourse exposes the Western marginalization of Arab women and Others whose voices were silenced. *L'amour, la fantasia* is a novel that "illuminate[s] the body, in order to lift up the forbidden, to unmask."[30]

Notes

1. Benjamin Stora, *La gangrène et l'oubli: La mémoire de la guerre d'Algérie* (Paris: La Découverte, 1991), 321.

2. Poststructuralist/Psychoanalytic term used to differentiate between self (Europe/France in this case) and other (Algeria, Algerian women), subject and object.

3. See Gerard Génette's *Palimpsestes: La littérature au second degré* (Paris: Seuil, 1982) for more description of palimpsest texts in modern literature.

4. Some of these stereotypical roles that come to mind are the "cut-throat" Arabs from Steven Spielberg's *Raiders of the Lost Ark* and the clichéd scenes in *Out of Africa* from the the mid-1980s.

5. Edward Saïd, *Orientalism* (New York: Vintage, 1979), 202.

6. Linda Hutcheon, *A Poetics of Postmodernism* (New York: Routledge, 1988), 96.

7. See Gilles Deleuze and Félix Guattari's *A Thousand Plateaus* (Minneapolis: University of Minnesota Press, 1987), for more detail on the concept of multiplicity and rhizomes of events.

8. Nada Turk, "*L'amour, la fantasia* d'Assia Djebar: Chronique de guerre, voix des femmes" in *Celfan Review* 7, 1–2 (1987–88): 21.

9. Roland Barthes, *Le dégre zéro de l'écriture* (Paris: Seuil, 1953), 14.

10. Assia Djebar, *L'amour, la fantasia* (Paris: ed. J.-C. Lattès, 1985), 11. All translations mine unless otherwise noted. All translated extracts from this text.

11. Djebar, *L'amour*, 48.

12. Djebar, *L'amour*, 236–237.

13. Djebar, *L'amour*, 237.

14. Shoshana Felman, *What Does a Woman Want?* (Baltimore: Johns Hopkins University Press, 1993), 18.

15. Felman, *What Does a Woman*, 18.

16. Mary Jean Green, "Dismantling the Colonizing Text," *The French Review* 66 (May 1993): 962.

17. Djebar, *L'amour*, 16.

18. Saïd, *Orientalism*, 103.

19. Djebar, *L'amour,* 230.

20. Adlai Murdoch, "Rewriting Writing: Identity, Exile and Renewal in Assia Djebar's *L'amour, la fantasia*," *Yale French Studies* 83 (1993): 74.

21. Although French government officials set up education programs as early as the 1880s, the masses of children needing education grew constantly, particularly in rural areas. Girls were allowed to attend school, but this was a rare phenomenon and usual only among the more wealthy families in the cities. Pierre Nora's book *Les Français d'Algérie* (Paris: Julliard, 1961) reported that in 1939 out of 1,230,000 children ages six to fourteen only 110,000 were in school. In the first year of the Algerian revolution (1954–55) only 15.5 percent of children in Algeria between the ages of six to fourteen were schooled (218).

22. Murdoch, "Rewriting," 71.

23. Djebar, *L'amour*, 66.

24. Pierre Bosquet, field marshal of France, was born in Mont-de-Marsan in 1810. He distinguished himself in military campaigns in Algeria and the Crimean. He died in 1861.

25. Djebar, *L'amour*, 67.

26. The Civilizing Mission in Algeria began immediately after Thomas Bugeaud (1784–1849), marshal of France and initial organizer of the colonization of Algeria, Bugeaud was responsible for the implementation of the first colonial settlements and their security. The Civilizing Mission, or those constituting the colonizing endeavor in Algeria, was made up of colonials, missionaries, and convicts exiled from France.

27. Hutcheon, *Poetics*, 146.

28. Anne Donadey, "Assia Djebar's Poetics of Subversion," *L'esprit créateur* 33 (1993): 116.

29. Djebar, *L'amour*, 255.

30. Djebar, *L'amour*, 75.

8

Contested Crossings: Identities, Gender, and Exile in *Le baobab fou*

Marjorie Salvodon

For us, it is not a question of exalting the "elsewhere," at the risk of losing oneself, nor is it about glorifying the "here," at the risk of confinement and sure death; it is a question of emerging from the fold without losing oneself in the elsewhere.

> —Yanick Lahens, *L'exil: entre l'ancrage et la fuite, l'écrivain haïtien*

Who is this exile? He is someone who interprets his life in a foreign country as an experience of non-belonging to his milieu, and who cherishes it for that very reason. The exile is interested in his own life, even in his own people; but he has observed that in order to protect this interest it would be best to live abroad, in a place where he does not "belong"; the status of foreigner is for him no longer temporary but permanent.

> —Tzetan Todorov, *On Human Diversity: Nationalism, Racism, and Exoticism in French Thought*

An exile is someone who inhabits one place and remembers or projects the reality of another.

> —Michael Seidel, *Exile and the Narrative Imagination*

Exile and the corresponding experience of immigration underscore the complex relationship between cultural identity and the reality of belonging to more than one country that, in many ways, parallels the concept of "double appartenance."[1] Geographic boundaries as well as linguistic, cultural, and social affiliations are destabilized and rendered obsolete by the exile's and the immigrant's adjustment to a "new world." As the epigraphs suggest, the situation engendered by exile and immigration exacts a dual responsibility, which involves mediating between the events of the past and the temporal immediacy of the present. The shifting between varying elements of time, location, and language situates both the exile and the immigrant in a particularly critical position. Whereas exile signifies "forced removal from one's native country" or "voluntary absence from one's country," immigration denotes the process by which one can "come into a country of which one is not a native for permanent residence."[2] That both meanings evoke the problem of inhabiting an "elsewhere" is essential; this distant "elsewhere" is always traversed by the temporal and geographical parameters of the present. While it is pertinent to clarify the differences between voluntary and forced exile, I am particularly interested in exploring the questions of gender and cultural identity that are amplified in the representations of exile in Ken Bugul's *Le baobab fou (The Abandoned Baobab)*.[3] In this text, it is through the experience of exile that the heroine articulates the interrelated issues of race, gender, and cultural identity. As a Black African woman, Ken's cross-cultural crossings produce an awareness of the simultaneity of her identities, each of which problematizes the notion of nonbelonging.

That exile evokes the fundamental problem of non-belonging is relevant. How does contemporary Francophone literature engage with the question of "nonbelonging," and specifically, how do the literary representations of exile and immigration characterize, in Todorov's words, "nonappartenance"? The experience of *nonappartenance* described by Todorov privileges the exile's choice of living in a foreign country. However, this important depiction does not specifically account for political exiles, or for exiles from formerly colonized countries. The former is subject to various forms of censorship imposed by state authority, while the latter is continually negotiating questions pertaining to language, cultural identity, and national autonomy.[4] The predicament of exilic existence is further problematized by Edward Saïd in the article "The Mind of Winter: Reflections on Life in Exile," in which he proposes to distinguish the geographical, historical, political, and psychological dimensions of the exile's particular situation by privileging the variety of locations from which the exile apprehends the world: "Most people are principally aware of one culture, one setting, one home; exiles are aware of at least two, and this plurality of vision gives rise to an awareness of simultaneous dimensions, an awareness that—to borrow a phrase from music—is contrapuntal."[5] By leading "life outside habitual order," the exile, in Saïd's perspective, inhabits provisional places without permanently settling in any singular location; this fluidity of geographical boundaries creates multiple positions from which the vagaries of exilic life are experienced.[6]

The physical passage experienced in exile drastically refigures the signification of space, both geographical and temporal, and calls into question polarized perspectives on movement between cultures, languages, and traditions. The "moving between" invokes the problem of migrancy that mediates ineluctably the representation of cross-cultural identities in contemporary Francophone literatures. The questions of identity and belonging, generated by the diverse instances of migrancy in the contemporary world, are aptly defined by Paul Carter in *Living in a New Country: History, Traveling, and Language:*

> An authentically migrant perspective would, perhaps, be based on an intuition that the opposition between here and there is itself a cultural construction, a consequence of thinking in terms of fixed entities and defining them oppositionally. It might begin by regarding movement, not as an awkward interval between fixed points of departure and arrival, but as a mode of being in the world. The question would be, then, not how to arrive, but how to move, how to identify convergent and divergent movements; and the challenge would be how to notate such events, how to give them a historical and social value.[7]

Carter's insistence on the importance of understanding the process, rather than the established points of arrival and departure in migrancy, reveals the extent to which migrant identities are constantly in the process of construction. An analysis of pre- and postmigratory identities must take into account the multiple mutations that occur before, during, and after the crossing. In reinventing their traditions, allegiances, and identities, immigrants problematize nostalgic notions of exile and *déracinement* through the disclosure of their particular lived experiences: "Migrancy . . . involves a movement in which neither the points of departure nor those of arrival are immutable or certain. It calls for a dwelling in language, in histories, in identities that are constantly subject to mutation. Always in transit, the promise of a homecoming—completing the story, domesticating the detour—becomes an impossibility."[8] These experiences, occurring via the passage from the formerly colonized country to the *métropole*, are sustained by the immigrant's ability to cross the border, both literally and figuratively, and adapt to the new territory. This adaptation to the "new world" represents neither a rejection of the traditions of the "old country," nor does it signify a comprehensive acceptance of all aspects of life in the chosen territory. Rather, the transition to the new world necessitates a continual process of defining and redefining one's national, linguistic, and cultural allegiances.[9]

To examine the particular condition of exile in light of the cultural and historical framework of colonialism and postcolonialism is to situate this particular "crossing" in a discussion on cultural identity and, most specifically, on the concept of cultural "communities." What is a community? Is it possible to define the exilic or immigrant community? What are the ramifications of this designation for these two communities?

In Benedict Anderson's important work on nationalism, he defines "community" in relation to the characterization of the nation as "an imagined political community": "It is imagined because the members of even the smallest nation will never know most of their fellow-members, meet them or even hear of them, yet in the minds of each lives the image of their communion."[10] The idea of community, then, is determined by the concept of unity, which in fact veils material differences such as class and gender privilege, that divide the various constituencies comprising the nation; the imagined unity of a community is founded on its own mythification. From Anderson's perspective, "the nation is limited because even the largest of them, encompassing perhaps a billion living human beings, has finite, if elastic boundaries, beyond which lie other nations."[11] The notion of an imagined community is especially interesting when discussed in conjunction with the representations of migratory experiences in Francophone literature.[12] How are communities "in flux," such as the one in exile, to be portrayed and understood? In this work, my definition of the concept of "community" encompasses a core of individuals whose shared history of experiences reflects points of commonality; nevertheless, this concept of community does not preclude the interrogation of the specificities of difference within the varied representations of exile. In examining the reinvention of postcolonial cultural communities in *Le baobab fou*, I will be especially interested in illustrating the ways in which the specific migratory experience of exile fosters and subtends a complex and liberating conceptualization of gender, racial, and cultural identities.

The Adventures of Exile

Published in French in 1984 under the pseudonym Ken Bugul, *Le baobab fou* has garnered moderate interest in North America.[13] This Senegalese autobiographical text explores the psychological, cultural, and geographic elements that hone the representations of exile. By situating *Le baobab fou* within the specific historical context of postcolonial crossings to the Western European métropoles in the twentieth century, I intend to define the parameters of the conflictual relationship between two languages, two cultures, and two distinct geographical locations as they are experienced by the female protagonist, Ken. In addition, I demonstrate the ways in which the interplay between the configurations of home and exile contribute to a complex representation of cultural identity. How does Ken Bugul, a young Senegalese woman writer, call into question dated notions of identity and migration? The examination of fundamental issues integral to the genre of autobiography, Bugul's own assertions concerning this text's genre, combined with a close textual analysis of the ramifications of exile in *Le baobab fou*, incorporate the structural framework of this journey.

In contemporary literary criticism, the genre of autobiography has inspired much debate, especially in relation to the hybrid and "autobiofictive" work of the French *Nouveau Roman* writers.[14] In referring to women writers' autobiographical projects in the twentieth century, Leah Hewitt recalls the two distinct, seemingly opposing, characteristics of autobiography: "autobiography as a mainstream literary genre (what is more canonical than Rousseau's *Confessions*)," and "as a marginal or inferior form."[15] While Hewitt's work primarily examines western European women writers, she also devotes a chapter to noted Guadeloupean writer Maryse Condé. Keenly aware of the confluence of "race" and autobiographical representations of the Caribbean and Africa in Condé's work, Hewitt asserts that "traditional autobiography's attention to factual accuracy concerning the individual's life data seems less of interest to her than the articulation of an open-ended, complex set of problems: readers must draw their own conclusions, provide their own interpretations."[16] In any given work, the reader must decipher and interpret the text as she/he chooses; the writer's role is not to impose any singular meaning on the work. Indeed, the interplay of race, gender, colonial histories, and migrancy is a salient feature in Condé's work that the reader must interpret; that a contemporary Senegalese woman writer explores similar issues in her work is of no small importance.[17] That the literary representations of migrancy in the form of exile, gender, and race explore, in autobiography as in other genres, the relationship between non-Western literatures and the legacy of postcolonial, imperialist, and capitalist entreprise in the contemporary world, is relevant.

In an interview with Bernard Magnier, Ken Bugul asserts the right to define the medium of her work: "I don't know the difference between a novel and a play. It's simply a way of writing. But it's the same writing process and the same intellectual development."[18] For Bugul, the boundaries of genre remain inconsequential; she states, "What is important is that one expresses oneself."[19] The writing process as "therapy" is Bugul's approach to writing. This approach privileges the writer's autonomy, and challenges the notion of writing as purely objective and neutral. Far from neutral, *Le baobab fou* critically interrogates the racist and colonialist implications of the character's interactions with Europeans. Described in minute detail, the trials and tribulations of Bugul's female protagonist, Ken, point to the interrelated questions of identity, migration, and exile, which are the cornerstone of the Senegalese heroine's experience in Brussels. The genre of autobiography prescribes the essential feature of authenticity that renders the text especially relevant and topical. The concerns with truth may represent an impulse to explain the text through actual events and experiences that can be historically confirmed.

If, as the following citation claims, migrancy is a salient feature of contemporary Francophone literature, what is the importance of this particular *topos*? Why do the vital questions of place, origin, and displacement recur in this body of literature? A critical examination of these questions will determine their place in *Le baobab fou*. The phrase "adventures of exile", then, encompasses the events detailed in the narrative that frame and are framed by situations of flight, migrancy, and departures: Journey and displacement are common motifs in the Francophone novel of Africa and the French Caribbean, and sum up the life experience of many a character. Journey embodies the quest of colonial and postcolonial subjects caught in epistemological ruptures and entangled multicultural contexts.[20] Not only are the characters' experiences reflective of thematic and theoretical concerns with migrancy in the form of exile, but so are those of the writers who create such characters.[21]

The adventures of exile are abundant in this text: the narrative weaves through sociological descriptions of a Senegalese village, the portrayal of modern city life in this West African country, and the flight from Senegal to Belgium. Indeed, the narrative is centered, to a great extent, around the events of departure and arrival. Divided into two main parts, "Ken's Prehistory" (*Pré-Histoire de Ken*) and "Ken's History" (*Histoire de Ken*), this autobiographical text unites the various focal points of the text.

In "Ken's Prehistory," Bugul details family life in the village where Ken is born. This preamble situates the social dynamics of family life in the village, and exposes the centrality of the baobab tree for the village of Ndoucoumane and its inhabitants. As the depiction of family life places Ken within a specific historical and familial heritage, the significance of the baobab tree extends beyond the history of Ken and the family to embrace the existential meanings of this tree in African tradition. The tree importantly occupies a powerful place in African history and life. Yet, it is not fixed in any eternal myth of Africa. The baobab tree's significance is not static. In fact, the symbol of the tree returns at the end of the narrative to mirror Ken's transformed sense of self through the mediation of her postexilic identity. In the article, "Innovation in Ken Bugul's *Le baob-*

ab fou," Susan Stringer describes the baobab's importance in the following way: "Thus, the baobab, a symbol for Africans of fertility, continuity and survival, is presented as the protector and provider of the family."[22] While the baobab does function as "protector" in its initial depiction in "Ken's Prehistory," its function is fundamentally transformed by Ken's migrancy. The baobab, depicted as dead and having gone mad at the end of the narrative, symbolizes a change but not an end. Because the death of the baobab tree coincides with Ken's postexilic return to Senegal, this auspicious parallelism proffers an end that reflects change and a new beginning.[23]

The second part of the narrative, "Ken's History," is structured by three concerns: physical and geographical displacement, school, and the debunking of a mythic and reified Africa. These three recurring motifs form, at the core of the narrative, an interlaced and complex questioning of cultural identity and exile. Ken's departure for "The Promised Land" (*La Terre Promise*) is initially described in this section. The poignant recounting of Ken's first voyage by airplane reinforces both her fears and the reasons for the departure from her native Senegal:

> When I opened my eyes again, I was still in the plane that seemed ignorant of all that was happening inside of me. Were we ever going to reach our destination or were we going to stay like this, but for how long? I was really at the end of my tether. I wasn't able to sleep as some passengers were, I wasn't able to concentrate as were others, reading newspapers. I was in the middle of a thousand tumultuous things. I was split, cut up into a thousand different me's.[24]

This suggestive excerpt privileges the psychological and cultural facets of the protagonist's experience with traveling; indeed, the "split" experienced by Ken will be echoed throughout the text as the confrontation and collision between two distinct cultures and traditions. Describing feelings of being torn and shattered in many pieces, Ken's narrative highlights the difficulty of reconciling her many selves. However painful this experience, it is only because of this departure that Ken can effectively negotiate her complex experience in Senegal and the desire to leave her native country.

The departures of Ken are multirooted and layered: she leaves the village of Ndoucoumane to attend high school in the city; upon obtaining her school diploma and a grant for study abroad in Belgium, she leaves Senegal for Europe. The departure for Europe signifies her confrontation with the myths fostered by her French education in Senegal: "In Paris I needed only to make a connection. We arrived at night. Everything was lit up. Europe at last, the West, the land of the white people, the land of the Gauls, the land of pine trees, of snow, the land of my 'ancestors.'"[25]

In pursuing her ancestors in Europe, Bugul confronts the colonialist myth of her lineage; this myth is subverted later when she realizes that the Gauls were not her ancestors. Through contacts with Europeans, and in day-to-day situations in which she feels doubly foreign—racially and culturally— Ken recognizes her "Africanness" and her "Blackness." As Stringer writes, "It is in Europe, however, that Bugul is forced to come face to face with herself as an African, as a woman and as a black woman. . . . She encounters little conventional racism, yet, among the people she frequents, Africa is fashionable and she is often treated as an exotic ornament rather than a human being."[26] Confronting the Gauls, her ancestors, Ken is confronted with the process of reconstituting her culturally and racially gendered identities as a Black African woman.

While Ken's departure for Belgium represents a "new world" in which stereotypes are shattered and the negotiations of cultural and racial identities inevitably emerge, the departure of Ken's mother remains a traumatic event in her life. This maternal abandonment is evoked throughout the text: "I had joined the mother one year after her departure. One year of weeping and bitterness and nobody to console me. . . . The void left by the mother's departure would not be filled. The father, old and wholly devoted to prayer, couldn't mind me. The first wife of the father couldn't replace the mother."[27] Interestingly, the mother's abandonment of Ken is explicitly framed by Ken's language. The obvious distance created in the use of the article "the" instead of "my" is a glaring display of Ken's internalization of this abandonment. As Susan Stringer argues, "This bereavement which obsesses the child and later the adult is expressed through prayer-like incantations which often appear without any apparent link to the context, as though the writer experiences an interminable void, an absence of love, from which she can never escape."[28] That the experience of abandonment is difficult remains irrefutable. In addition, it is also important to discern the ways in which leaving Senegal is emblematic of Ken's rewriting of this maternal abandonment, and of her eventual reappropriation of this experience. While each textual echo of this initial departure evokes Ken's suffering, it also renders the experience obsolete, rooted in a past that Ken must abandon. Both the mother's abandonment of her child and Ken's departure from Senegal reveal the fundamental sites of confrontation and negotiation that are deeply rooted/routed in the geographical displacements detailed in *Le baobab fou*.

Crossings: Forging New Cultural Identities

Another fundamental marker of difference in Ken's life is school. The narrator's description is telling: "The French school, our ancestors the

Gauls, cooperation, foreign exchanges, friendship between peoples had all created a new dimension: the foreigner, no longer able to recognize among one's own people the true bonds that used to shape and could guide destinies."[29] School transforms Ken into a foreigner. Her academic aspirations cause a rift between herself and her family. French school represents the Gauls and helps foster the stranger she becomes to her own environment and her people. Mudimbe-Boyi characterizes this alienation as an "internal exile":

> In going to the French school Bugul is severed from her own mother, and henceforth exiled from the world of childhood. Her years of schooling disconnect her from the indigeneous culture, and, on the other hand, from her kin: they do not understand her commitment to the new school and nobody is interested in her good grades. Solitude and books populated with images and representations of a foreign culture become her companions, her refuge, her locus of identification.[30]

That the French school, along with its attendant reification of all things French, including the Gauls and snow, delimits the contextual contradictions of Ken's existence is pertinent. The French school can be seen as subversive to the extent that even as it fragments Ken's imagination with the introduction of all things French, it also permits Ken to rediscover herself in the infinite play of her identities. Not only does school provide "her locus of identification," school is the conduit through which Ken articulates and comprehends her "selves." It is only because of her passage through school that Ken is able to debunk a mythic Europe as a "Promised Land," to reconceptualize Africa, and to articulate her identities as a Black African woman.

Ken's fluctuating relationship to Africa constitutes an essential component of the rewriting of exile in *Le baobab fou*. While in Europe, Ken encounters Africans with whom she does not connect, and from whom she receives little support. Particularly at the beginning, her sojourn in Brussels can be defined as the assimilation years in which she exclusively and consciously dated western European men and felt constantly "foreign," except with her friends who represented an international array of people. Although she is not surrounded by a large multitude of Africans, Ken reminisces frequently about an ideal Africa. As Mudimbe-Boyi notes: "For Bugul, alone, depressed, and disillusioned with her integration in the West, Africa as an 'over there' has taken an idyllic quality: it is the land where 'life is pure,' the land of 'poetry and rites' [143], where 'everyone is integrated, concerned, surrounded.'"[31] Ken's fragile condition in Brussels compels her to invoke a mythical Africa; however, this romanticization of Africa is transformed as Ken acknowledges the complexity of this image.

Toward the end of *Le baobab fou*, Ken's revelations of the mythic dimensions of Africa are exploded. In returning to Africa, Ken is confronted with the baobab's death, which signifies the end of her journey abroad and the beginning of a new life in Africa. The baobab tree, which is a witness and accomplice of the mother's departure, also undergoes its own transformation: ". . . The morning I arrived in the village, all the other baobab trees hid behind their trunks, folding their branches in on dense foliage. The sun was guarding the dead one as it stood fully lit. The birds were in mourning."[32] Africa as well as the baobab tree, then, are inflated with revelatory new meanings.

While the return to Africa signifies the end of exile, it also represents a transformed Ken; the past traumatic experience of the mother's departure shifts in meaning, as does the baobab tree, to represent a point of departure for new beginnings. Ken is fundamentally altered by her experience of exile. And this change is the symbol of a momentous passage through which cultural identities are rearticulated. The contested crossing of the geographical boundaries of Africa and western Europe compels Ken to confront her gendered cultural and exilic identities; this confrontation, then, spurs the negotiation of *all* her "warring" selves.

Notes

1. In this analysis, the term *double appartenance* is used to describe the plurality of positions that exiles and immigrants occupy; positions necessarily imply cultural, linguistic, and territorial allegiances to two or more places. See Abdelkébir Khatibi, *Amour bilingue* (Montpellier, France: Fata Morgana, 1983) and *Maghreb pluriel* (Paris: Denoel, 1983), in which Khatibi fully explores the tensions inherent in the concept of double appartenance with his theory of the *bi-langue*.

2. See Webster's Seventh New Collegiate Dictionary.

3. I am aware of collapsing the distinct cultural, economic, historical, and political implications of the terms, *exile* and *immigration*. I will be careful not to amalgamate these two specific experiences. My primary concern is to examine the ways in which exile raises questions that pertain to cultural identity, belonging, and gender in *Le baobab fou*. Indeed, many postcolonial critics have justly examined the varied economic, political, cultural catalysts for exile and immigration: Winifred Woodhull notes that "the economic and cultural marginality of immigrants makes the stakes of their struggle quite different" (from *émigrés* or expatriates, for instance) in *Transfigurations of the Maghreb: Feminism, Decolonization, and Literatures* (Minneapolis: University of Minnesota Press, 1993), 89. Also, all translations of Ken Bugul's *Le baobab fou* (Dakar: Les Nouvelles Éditions Africaines, 1984) are taken from Marjolijn de Jager's

translations *The Abandoned Baobab: The Autobiography of a Senegalese Woman* (Brooklyn, N.Y.: Lawrence Hill Books, 1991). A Baobab is a tree.

4. Political exile, although individual situations do vary greatly, represents the banishment of dissidents whose beliefs presumably threaten the authority and status of the state. One blatant contemporary example is Salman Rushdie; another is Taslimi Nasrin, while Wole Soyinka, whose passport has been recently confiscated, is undergoing an "inverted" exile whereby his mobility beyond the Nigerian border is dramatically curtailed. While the particular situation of confinement restricts mobility, it also parallels that of the banished individual because both conditions reveal the political repercussions of dissent for writers. Whether the exile is constrained to flee the country or is compelled to stay within the national boundaries of the country, her/his physical mobility is predicated by the state. Exiles from formerly colonized countries necessarily experience the *métropole*, the "chosen" territory, differently because of their distinct history with the colonizing power. Indeed, the imposition of a new language and territorial occupation are considered acts of colonist hegemony, which unequivocally engender internalized exile. The question of language choice—for example, Creole versus French, Arabic versus French, or Wolof versus French—is emblematic of the internalized exile that many "post"-colonial individuals undergo as they negotiate their linguistic identity.

5. Edward Saïd, "The Mind of Winter: Reflections on Life in Exile," *Harper's*, September 1984, 49–55.

6. Saïd, "The Mind," 55.

7. Paul Carter, *Living in a New Country: History, Traveling, and Language* (London: Faber & Faber, 1992), 101.

8. Ian Chambers, *Migrancy, Culture, Identity* (London: Routledge, 1994), 5.

9. As Azouz Begag writes, "Un immigré plus un autre immigré ne constituent pas automatiquement une communauté d'immigrés" [An immigrant plus another immigrant does not constitute a community of immigrants] in *Écarts d'indentité*, (Paris: Seuil, 1990), 59. This citation problematizes the concept of community, a concept that is not substantiated by sheer numbers, but rather by increased politicization and awareness of the members of a community.

10. Benedict Anderson, *Imagined Communities: Reflections on the Origin and Spread of Nationalism* (London: Verso, 1983 and 1991), 6.

11. Anderson, *Imagined Communities*, 7. Geographically demarcated and politically constructed, the nation then is determined by its insularity and presumed "unity." However, while the national boundaries remain "finite," the nations beyond its border also interact with and construct its identity. This imagined unity of a "national" community reveals, in fact the real divisions between members of the same "national" community.

12. Despite their shared "nationality," the citizens of a nation represent a broad range of interests and experiences; similiarly, communities in flux share the migratory circumstances of their lives, but the details of these circumstances vary greatly. Because Francophone literature is already traversed by questions of identity with respect to cultural and linguistic affiliations, the concept of

"imagined communities" enhances and expands the meaning of migrancy in this body of literature.

13. I am referring here to writers such as Alain Robbe-Grillet, who continually resist any facile categorization of their work. For a discussion on autobiofiction and autobiography see Ben Stolfus, "Lacan, Robbe-Grillet, and Autofiction," *Internations Fiction Review* 19, no. 1 (1992): 8–13 and Marie Miguet, Critique/autocritique/autofiction, *Les Lettres Romanes* 43, no. 3 (1989): 195–208.

14. Leah D. Hewitt, *Autobiographical Tightropes: Simone de Beauvoir, Nathalie Sarraute, Marguerite Duras, Monique Witting, and Maryse Condé* (Lincoln: University of Nebraska Press, 1990), 2.

15. Hewitt, *Autobiographical Tightropes*, 162

16. See Carole Boyce Davies, *Black Women, Writing, and Identity: Migrations of the Subject* (London: Routledge, 1994). This work aptly examines the interrelated issues of cultural crossings, migration, negotiation of identities, and gender in works by women of African descent. In particular, Boyce Davies's theoretical framework acknowledges the similarities in approach of women writers of the African diaspora, which she attributes to the interconnected experiences of colonialism, racism, and sexism.

17. Bernard Magnier, "Ken Bugul ou l'écriture thérapeutique," *Notre Librairie* 81 (1985): 154–155.

18. Magnier, "Ken Bugul," 154.

19. The importance and risks of writing an autobiographical text are abundant. Bugul, in an interview with Magnier, explains how the Senegalese publishing press, Nouvelles Éditions Africaines, refused to use her real name, and asked her to invent a pseudonym for *Le baobab fou*. Bugul agreed and chose the name "Ken Bugul," which in Wolof signifies "personne n'en veut" [No one wants it]. This expression is used to name a child so she/he can live: "When a woman who has had many stillbirths has a newborn child, she calls her/him Ken Bugul to help the infant escape the destiny of death." The self-chosen is a way to deflect any imminent danger from the newborn child; similarly, in choosing this pseudonym, Bugul has allowed her text to live.

20. Elisabeth Mudimbe-Boyi, "The Poetics of Exile and Errancy in *Le baobab fou* by Ken Bugul and *Ti Jean L'Horizon* by Simone Schwarz-Bart," *Yale French Studies* 83 (1993): 196.

21. Bugul states in the interview with Magnier that she had spent seven years in exile in Brussels, and several more in France.

22. Susan Stringer, "Innovation in Ken Bugul's *Le baobab fou*," *Cincinnati Romance Review* 10 (1991): 202.

23. It is interesting to note that the title of the English translation, *The Abandoned Baobab*, offers multiple meanings as to the function of the baobab tree. The word "abandoned" from the translation does not directly correspond to the original text's *fou* (crazy). This discrepancy reveals an important fact; while "abandoned" echoes the maternal abandonment suffered by Ken, a traumatic experience that is evoked throughout the narrative, its original French *fou*

correlates craziness with death. At the end of this autobiography, the baobab's craziness and death symbolize rebirth and a new beginning. Despite the usual negative associations of these terms, they are rewritten in Bugul's text and endowed with new meanings and possibilities.

24. Ken Bugul, *Le baobab fou* (Dakar: Les Nouvelles Éditions Africaines, 1984), 28.

25. Bugul, *Le baobab*, 28.

26. Susan Stringer, "Innnovations."

27. Bugul, *Le baobab*, 111–112.

28. Stringer, "Innovations," 203.

29. Bugul, *Le baobab*, 111.

30. Elisabeth Mudimbe-Boyi, "The Poetics of Exile, 83, 202"

31. Mudimbe-Boyi, "The Poetics," 205.

32. Bugul, *Le baobab*, 158–59.

9

Radical Ambiguities and the Chicana Lesbian: Body Topographies on Contested Lands

Jacqueline M. Martinez

The history of Americans of Mexican descent living in the southwestern United States is complex, diverse, and uneasily characterizable. Spanning a history that traces back nearly five hundred years to precolonial time, this land and the people born upon it can be said to have always been living in a state of war. Yet, the content and expression of this state of war—much like the people themselves—exists in multiple forms and to varying degrees. While events like the Mexican Revolution are markers for the people whose histories lie upon this land, there are other, less historically tangible and thus differently important markers signifying states of war. They are markers that tell us a great deal about human struggle, human liberation, and human transformation.

My interest in the work that follows is to examine the situation of war for the contemporary Chicana lesbian in light of the land and history of the southwestern United States. My general thesis is that the Chicana lesbian occupies a place of radical ambiguity that, when read through a history of the land of the southwestern United States, problematizes the "assimilationist versus nationalist" and "complicitous-traitor versus loyal-culturalist" binarisms. Indeed, the reading offered below intends to suggest how the emergence of the Chicana lesbian as a site of warring struggle demands a reconsideration of these binarisms; such a reading simultaneously creates different possibilities for understanding and achieving radical transformation for both the person and the social world.

The Emergence of "The Chicana Lesbian"

The Chicana lesbian[1] is, in one sense, a relatively recent phenomenon when

one considers the nearly five-hundred-year history of European domination in North America (that is, Mexico, Texas, New Mexico, Arizona, and
California).[2] It has only been since the 1960s that "Chicano," as an identity
designator, has existed at all. The contemporary construction of "lesbian"
(or "homosexual") is, likewise, quite specific to the latter half of this
century.[3] Though common knowledge today suggests that sexual relationships among people of the same sex have existed in all times and across
all cultures, the cultural meanings ascribed to such behavior vary widely.[4]
Considered in this way, the Chicana lesbian appears as a creation of this
time, occurring in a synchronicity of late twentieth century USA.

Yet, in another sense, the construction of the Chicana lesbian represents
the very struggle of the native peoples of North America against the heterogeneous forces of oppression sustained in the very history of this land—
a history that bears directly upon the meaningfulness of the life-
world-struggle for the self-declared Chicana lesbian today. The adoption of
"Chicano" as an identity designator is directly linked to the long history
of struggle of native and non-white (mestizo) people who have been the
objects of Spanish and American-European colonization. Its adoption signifies a consciously engaged resistance. When "lesbian" is adopted in
conjunction with "Chicana," we have a construction doubly laden with
consciously engaged resistance, which is posed against itself from within—
a consciousness at war.

Such a double engagement problematizes the normative conditions of
both the "nationalist" Chicano movement for its heterosexism and *machismo*, and feminist academic theory and practice for its racism and hegemony.[5] Even in the most obvious sense, the Chicana lesbian functions as
an exclusion across three sites: within the Chicano movement, within the
women's movement (and feminist academic practice), and within the dominant American culture.[6] Yet, in a much more subtle sense, the Chicana
lesbian embodies a radical ambiguity that demonstrates the insufficiency
of these more obvious sites as a basis for the Chicana lesbian to come to
have knowledge (*savoir*) of herself—a knowledge of self ontologically
contingent and going hand in hand with the condition of radical ambiguity.[7]
It is this more subtle sense of consciousness of self and world at war that
is therefore my primary focus for this work.

The construction of the Chicana lesbian, her situation as a warring situation, and her location within the heterogeneous forces of the dominant
discursive formations (white, European, colonial, heterosexual, capitalist),
is intricately intertwined with the histories, cultures, and lands from which
her production emerges. Given such a locatedness, the production of the
Chicana lesbian occurs as a struggle that is located within as it fights against
the multifarious deployment of colonial oppression. Within the meaning-

fulness of the life-world-struggle of the Chicana lesbian we have a site of discursive production whose interrogation suggests how radical transformations might obtain in the concrete practices of the academic-activist— a site of practice that can effectively serve the academy's own perpetuation of various forms of oppression and dominance.[8] Given my primary concern with *location* as an essential factor in the content and expression of the warring consciousness characteristic of the Chicana lesbian, it is important to emphasize three interrelated points that turn the focus back upon the location and situation of the production of this academic work itself.

First, the emergence of the Chicana lesbian as a self-declared identity is directly and necessarily linked to activism, intellectualism, and artistry of all kinds both inside and outside the academy. Chicano studies, for example, has never existed except as activist—the hegemony of the "American"[9] as ideology literally prohibits (excludes) its existence. Even a cursory look at the people and locations producing the Chicana lesbian as a site of resistance suggests that the boundary between inside and outside the academy, between activism, intellectualism, and artistry is virtually unintelligible.[10]

Second, as a site of activism and resistance, the production of the Chicana lesbian as a self-adopted label shares important points of commonality with other identities and communities produced in resistance to the domination of colonizing forces (e.g., African Americans, Asian Americans, Native Americans).[11] Chela Sandoval makes this point when she argues for a specific form of consciousness (a "differential" consciousness) common to "U.S. third world women" precisely because of their similar histories of oppression and the hegemony of feminist theory: "Both in spite of and yet because they represent varying internally colonized communities, U.S. third world feminists have generated a common speech, a theoretical structure which, however, remained outside the purview of the dominant feminist theory emerging in the 1970s, functioning within it— but only as the unimaginable."[12]

These points of commonality provide a basis upon which the hegemony of colonization, even in a "post"-colonial time and within the colonizing state, can be recognized for its implicit logic that governs the practices of dominant (First World) states and comes to presence in the hearts and minds of generations of the Others who are the targets of colonial powers.[13] Indeed, these commonalities across various communities have been crucial components of the best theorizing within feminist academic practice over the past fifteen years.

While these points of commonality across Othered communities help expose the perversity and legacy of colonial domination, an important caution also needs to be raised. The similar situations of various groups of people relative to the dominating force colonialism/postcolonialism, does not prevent the differences among and within these groups from themselves effecting the same logic of domination embodied by colonizers. Indeed, "divide and conquer" is alive and well as a strategy exacted by hegemonic forces precisely so as to continue domination.[14] Even a brief description of the situation of the Chicana lesbian illustrates this point: suspect in and suspecting of the European-American context, suspect in and suspecting of feminists, suspect in and suspecting of the Chicano community, and even within *la familia*, the Chicana lesbian has no clear direction in which she might fully resist the heterogeneous forces of oppression she faces. The Chicana lesbian finds forces of sexist and hetereosexist oppression working against her even in the midst of alliances built in the name of resistance against oppression. The experience of the Chicana lesbian thus situated suggests that activism and intellectualism that portends to radically subvert the conditions of domination must necessarily interrogate the condition and effects of its own practices within and across the various sites of its own production.

My third point, then, has to do exactly with the inseparability of the intellectual and activist from the concrete conditions in which she practices her intellectualism and activism, the inseparability of the (Chicana lesbian) theorist herself from that which she theorizes. An understanding of the situation of the Chicana lesbian as theorist, intellectual-activist, and academic demonstrates the imperative of a consciously engaged self-locatedness in one's practices where one takes on accountability for the effects of that locatedness, and thus engages in a self-reflexive critical and analytic methodology (a semiotic phenomenology) that allows for an interrogation of the conditions of production in the midst of its production.[15] This is a requirement also articulated by Judith Butler when she suggests that "it is important to resist that theoretical gesture of pathos in which exclusions are simply affirmed as sad necessities of signification."[16]

In taking the positionality of the Chicana lesbian as subject matter, I intend to suggest how particular past historical presences construct her as an exclusion and thus as a potential site of radical transformation. This effort is much akin to Spivak's description of the Subaltern Studies group:

It can be advanced that their work presupposes that the entire socius, at least in so far as it is the object of their study, is what Nietzsche would call a *fortgesetzte Zeichenkette*—a "continuous sign-chain." The possibility of action lies in the dynamics of the disruption of this object, the breaking and relinking of the chain. This line of argument does not set consciousness over against the socius, but sees it as itself also constituted as and on a semiotic chain. It is thus an instrument of study which participates in the nature of the object of study.[17]

As a multiply marginalized figure, the Chicana lesbian's exclusion is part and parcel of the dominant American-cultural meaning system (a continuous sign-chain) that makes her unintelligible. It is also, ironically, that very status as exclusion that offers the possibility of breaking that meaning system and bringing her to presence today. Describing the sites that produce her as an unintelligible by exclusion, however, also creates (is dependent upon) other exclusions. Those exclusions must also be engaged precisely because they create the circumstances for the realization of new possibilities even while they close off still other possibilities.[18]

In the sections that follow below, I begin with "Situating the Past," that is, with considering the presence of historical pasts in the production and construction of the contemporary Chicana lesbian. I use the work of contemporary Chicanas and Chicana lesbians to inform the selection of key figures and events from the history of the *mestizo* people in order to suggest how situations of radical ambiguity can create conditions for radical transformation. I then move to a "Self-Reflexive Interrogation" of the production of the discourse engaged in this academic work so as to engage the concrete reality present in its production. This self-reflexive turn necessarily emphasizes contingency.[19] The effort here is to disclose the functioning of difference in the construction of the Chicana lesbian. This discussion leads me to consider the "theoretical and methodological implications" of engaging the marginalized and excluded. Here, I attempt to articulate how an activism and intellectualism produced from the location of the Chicana lesbian might interrogate the conditions of its own practice within and across its various sites so as to radically subvert conditions of domination in an exertion of existential freedom.

Situating the Past: Mestizo Borderlands

In situating the historical past presences that produce and construct the Chicana lesbian, we abandon the notion of an "original" people or situation that existed prior to oppression and to which we might seek to return. In this way we also abandon the notion of an "originating experience"[20] that founds a subject that we call "Chicana lesbian." Rather, we are looking to the past to see how it lives in consciousness and the concrete practices of this moment. Recognizing that "discourse cannot restore the totality of its history within a strict framework," we set ourselves about the task of "replacing . . . the theme of becoming . . . by the analysis of the transformations in their specifics."[21]

Mother of the Mestizo People

The land of what is today the southwestern United States bears upon it a nearly five-hundred-year history of struggle against European colonization and its relentless and violent encroachments. The conquest of the Aztecs by Hernán Cortéz in 1521 resulted in the near-annihilation of the native peoples and initiated a proliferation of geographical and psychical "borderlands" that continues to this day.

> Before the Conquest, there were twenty-five million Indian people in Mexico and the Yucatán. Immediately after the Conquest, the Indian population had been reduced to under seven million. By 1650, only one-and-a-half-million pure-blooded Indians remained. The mestizos . . . founded a new hybrid race and inherited Central and South America. . . . Chicanos, Mexican-Americans, are the offspring of those first matings.[22]

These "borderlands" are first and foremost boundaries that serve the interests of the colonizing forces, but that also function to exacerbate sexism and heterosexism within what has become the Chicano/Mexican culture. In serving colonial interests, these borderlands have often divided the native peoples by setting up conditions for competing interests among themselves (particularly between women and men) and with other groups.[23]

There is perhaps no figure that more strongly represents this colonial-driven division than Malintzin Tenepal, also know as La Malinche. La Malinche,[24] the person and the myth, epitomizes the conflicting interests orchestrated by the forces of colonization that, not surprisingly, use women's sexuality for the construction of a *male* mythology that retains presence in the many generations of *mestizos* since the conquest. It is a mythology that, according to Cherríe Moraga, is "carved into the very bone of Mexican/Chicano collective psychology."[25] La Malinche's impact on Chicanas is stark: "The persuasiveness of the myth is unfathomable, often permeating and suffusing our very being without conscious awareness."[26]

As the interpreter, guide, and mistress for Cortez, La Malinche facilitated the conquest. For that, she is considered both the "mother of the Mexican people" (the mestizos), and "La Chingada," the fucked-one, a traitor to her people. As a myth, La Malinche exists precisely because of what she is taken to represent for women's sexuality. As Norma Alarcón describes it, "the male myth of Malintzin is made to see betrayal first of all in her very sexuality, which makes it nearly impossible at any given moment to go beyond the vagina as the supreme site of evil until proven innocent by way of virginity or virtue, the most pawnable commodities around."[27]

The omnipresence of the male myth of La Malinche creates a double bind for mestizo women. One strategy for survival under the force of the myth is to demonstrate obedience and devotion to men. The privileging of male perspectives, male desires, and male children all reflect the logic of the myth of La Malinche. To enact this strategy is for Chicanas to embrace a status as inherently unreliable (sexually) and in need of proving differently. It is, as Alarcón puts it, a circumstance in which one eventually comes to self-hate.

A second strategy is to assert one's existential freedom and refuse to make one's life meaningful according to the male myth of La Malinche. Yet, the persuasiveness of the myth within a conquered culture means that even in the assertion of one's existence in a "radical questioning of" the meaning system informing the socius, the Chicana/Chicana lesbian is taken as disobedient, nondevout, a traitor to her people. Alliances that might otherwise be built to fight a common enemy in the colonizing forces are doomed from the beginning. For the self-declared Chicana lesbian (and Chicanas generally), the myth of La Malinche functions as a barrier to alliances that would allow her to *both* pursue her existential freedom and form alliances with her Chicano brothers against the forces of colonialism.

The presence of the male myth of La Malinche constitutes a setup from the beginning. Recognizing this double bind of social circumstance, Chicanas and Chicana lesbian writers demonstrate a "pervasive preoccupation and influence of the myth" and the "need to demythify" it.[28] It is through just this kind of work, which so deeply challenges bedrock notions structuring the meaning systems of Chicano/Mexican culture, that Chicanas embody a radical ambiguity that comes to participate in radical transformation.

The terrain traveled in such radical transformation is, however, neither smooth nor imminently apparent. It occurs as a struggle with consciousness—a condition of war. Chicana lesbians today struggle across a variety of discursive contexts (as activists, academics, feminists, artists) out of necessity and precisely because of the social double binds in which she finds herself. As women, both heterosexual and lesbian Chicanas are subjected by the male myth of La Malinche; both seek to recover and demythify her in their work at least in part through feminism. Yet, to declare oneself feminist is also equated with disloyalty and hence acts of betrayal. The presence of the myth of La Malinche sets up circumstances in which coming to one's awareness of her lesbianism is prohibited; to openly declare oneself lesbian risks rejection of the most extreme sort. The effort to de-mythify La Malinche is an effort to create space where women can assert their own sexuality without stigmatization.

Having identified a mythological presence that is a key semiotic linkage in the meaning system of the Chicano/Mexican culture since the sixteenth-century conquest, I would like to turn briefly to a set of circumstances present for the people of the southwestern United States during the post-colonial period. My effort is to suggest that the double-bind out of which these Chicana writers discussed above seek to travel has certain circum-stances that resonate with the experiences of the people of the Southwest during the post-colonial time. From this brief discussion I shall return to the work of one contemporary Chicana lesbian and again identify what I see as common circumstances in all of the situations I discuss.

Historical Past Presences and the Contemporary Chicana Lesbian

While it is clear that the mythical presence of La Malinche plays an important role in the Chicana lesbian's coming to a consciously engaged resistance to oppression, there are many other circumstances that demon-strate how colonization creates divisions that serve the interests of the colonizers. A brief discussion of the colonial-created divisions also illustrates the workings of various forms of resistance that defy the "assimilationist versus nationalist" and "complicitous-traitor versus loyal-culturalist" binarisms. I refer specifically to the northward expansion by the Spanish, the early nineteenth-century Mexican Independence, and the 1848 Treaty of Guadalupe Hidalgo.

In their constant zeal for expansion, the Spanish-governed colonists of the late sixteenth and early seventeenth centuries forced their way north-ward and continued their effort to dominate other peoples native to those lands of what is today New Mexico, California, and Texas. The colonizing relationships proliferated along with new generations of mixed blood peo-ple situated within competing sets of interests (that is, in a negatively ambiguous way[29]) orchestrated by the forces of colonization. This geograph-ical expansion multiplies the psychical divisions among the various peo-ples subjected under colonization and creates layers upon layers of often conflicting identifications. Yet, even for Mexican/mestizo settlers who did not apprehend themselves to be working at conflicting interests, the forces of colonization still bore down upon their lives as the very conditions within which they etched out survival.

Between 1810 and 1825, Mexico freed itself from Spanish domination. In the northern frontier, the immediate effect of the fall of Spanish rule "was a laxity of control, as well as neglect, by Mexico." The new Spanish and mestizo settlers faced complex circumstances of association with other people. Some Native Americans had been bought and sold as slaves and remained under control of the Spanish-Mexican settlers after the ending of Spanish rule. But the absence of force that came with the vacated presidios and military outposts left the mestizo settlers open targets for depredations by Native American tribes who were *reacting* "to the pressures from Anglos pushing West," taking away their native hunting grounds and lands and generally threatening their very means of survival.[30] Mestizo and Native Americans become enemies, fighting against each other for their survival by virtue of colonial expansion from both the South and the East. The land of the southwestern United States becomes the field upon which these colonial-orchestrated conflicting interests get played out long after the departure of formal Spanish rule.

The Treaty of Guadalupe Hidalgo in 1848—an American annexation of the land of what is now the southwestern United States—added another layer of psychical and geographical conflict for the people living on this land. The treaty formally allowed Mexican citizens living in this territory to become American citizens with all the accompanying rights. But in reality, Mexicanos (mestizos) were marked against the Euro-American migrant, their ways of living and speaking taken as inferior; "Society became two-tiered, and racial and religious prejudice were evident."[31] Indeed, "racial slurs and derogatory comments about Mexicans appeared regularly in the *Congressional Record*, in newspapers, and . . . in travel accounts."[32]

"Belonging" to the United States, this land becomes a magnet for Euro-American migrants. The racism and socioeconomic pressures exacted with the westward expansion by Euro-Americans created circumstances where people of differently mixed blood simply knew that *how* they were identified ethnically made a difference.[33] Mexicanos were positioned to identify with the logic of racism as they pursued simple survival. The robbing of native lands and the destruction of established ways of life left native peoples and Mexicanos in the position of having to employ capitalism as a means of survival. The moment these already established communities engage in capitalist systems, they become entwined in the racism that informs the righteousness of white domination, a consequence that began developing well before the 1848 Treaty of Guadalupe Hidalgo. Within the context of pervasive ethnic discrimination governed by the socioeconomic and cultural domination of white Euro-Americans, the Mexicanos developed specific patterns of survival that they participated in while struggling against the forces of Euro-American expansion. The life of Doña Gertrudis Barceló, subject of the legend of "La Tules," illustrates this point well.

A prominent figure in the town of Santa Fé from the early 1800s until her death in 1852, Barceló was one of the town's most wealthy and well-respected citizens. She was revered in her community because of her continuous and generous support for others. She was a major figure and leader in a town that prospered despite difficult circumstances. There was, however, a double-edged sword to her success: while it helped create a vibrant and healthy community, it also created a place for Euro-American newcomers to become socialized, thus facilitating their eventual dominance. In this way, Barceló gave "herself to the conquest, but not to the conquerors."[34]

The parallel to Malintzin Tenepal seems all too obvious: woman facilitating conquest of her own people. But in writing about La Tules, González—like Alarcòn, Anzaldúa, Moraga, Rebolledo, Rivera, and many other Chicana writers (activists, artists, academics-intellectuals)—demand a rethinking of mestizo women in the (never having ceased) conquest. Consider, for example, the stark contrast between Barceló in Santa Fé and the Padre Antonio José Martínez in the sister city of Taos. Unlike Santa Fe, which was generally welcoming of newcomers, in Taos residents had killed newcomers. Padre Antonio José Martínez was "the famed resister to American encroachment . . . [who] opposed (in his separatist plans and principles) all that Barceló exemplified."[35] What sense do we make of these differences between Barceló and Martínez? Complicitor versus loyalist? What kind of "war" was each engaged in? What values are we to assign to each strategy? How does gender and sexuality play into the values we might come to assign to these different strategies? Would a revolution led by Martínez have done anything to challenge machismo or the taboos surrounding women's sexuality? The contrast between these two figures considered in the context of colonial expansion compels the recognition that the "complicitous-traitor versus loyal-culturalist" binarism is insufficient for understanding the war of consciousness engaged by the people of the southwestern United States.

As a marginal figure, Barceló's life and legend contradict orthodox notions of marginality in a situation of conquest.[36] Her very (and extraordinary) success as a businesswoman in fact gave her the economic achievement that allowed her to live outside of the oppressive force of the Malinche myth. Alarcòn reminds us that Malinche, the actual *historical* figure, was "doomed to live in chains."[37] The mythologization of her as traitor assumes that she lived in a context where she could have chosen not to be a slave to Cortéz. By the time of Barceló's great economic, personal, and community success the forces of colonialism had already doomed the southwestern United States to Euro-American dominance. Barceló's strategy for survival and prosperity could be read as an exertion of existential freedom that benefited greatly the immediate life and well-being of her community.

This is not to suggest that Martínez should have adopted Barceló's strategies or vice versa. But it is to suggest that simply juxtaposing the two as loyal-nationalist versus complicitous-assimilator hinders our ability to comprehend the totality of circumstances in which each of these figures engaged in their circumstances of war. Upon what criteria should we judge the choices of these two figures? In describing the historical circumstances in which Barceló and Martínez came to live and struggle in the southwestern United States, I wish to emphasize certain patterns that can also be identified with the emergence of the contemporary Chicana lesbian. I turn now to this discussion.

Cherríe Moraga: A Contemporary Chicana Lesbian

In the same way that the male myth of La Malinche serves the interests of men by making women's sexuality inherently suspect (ready to serve the interests of the conquerors), so too do descriptions of Barceló that quickly dismiss her as a "complicitous-assimilator" prohibit our understanding of her own powerfulness as a woman; it also prohibits our understanding of the ways in which she might very well have created the conditions for a more sustained survival of her community and culture.

It is just this accusation of assimilation that functions in many debates in the contemporary struggle for racial and ethnic freedom in the United States today. The situation of the contemporary Chicana lesbian problematizes the notion that "assimilation" toward the dominant culture is *de facto* complicitous. The experiences of Cherríe Moraga, a contemporary self-declared Chicana lesbian, illustrates this point.

The sexism and heterosexism within her mestizo/Chicano community are precisely what led her away from identifications with that community: "I gradually became anglocized because I thought it was the only option available to me toward gaining autonomy as a person without being sexually stigmatized. I can't say it was conscious at the time, only that at each juncture in my development, I instinctively made choices which I thought would allow me greater freedom of movement in the future."[38] Situated between cultures, recognizing the dangers for the self entailed in the heterosexism of her most intimate groups of association, the Chicana lesbian moves toward the dominant culture with all of its racism. The conditions for this movement toward dominant culture are in fact set up by racism.[39] Taught to hide her Mexican heritage, to speak English, to become educated in white-dominated schools, and that her light skin was an advantage for her, all signified a moving up in socioeconomic class from the struggles of her parents (and mother especially).[40] Recognizing her sexual attraction to women and the dangers of that expression within her family and the Chicano community simply impels her in directions already set up as (racist) normative despite the known risks. Moraga the person exists in a state of war for her conscious recognition that all her choices put her at risk.

Consider, for example, the divided desires expressed by Moraga in the following:

> During the late 60s and early 70s, I was not an active part of la causa. I never managed to get myself to walk in the marches in East Los Angeles (I merely watched from the sidelines); I never went to one meeting of MECHA on campus. No soy tonta. I would have been murdered in El Movimiento—light skinned, unable to speak Spanish well enough to hang; miserably attracted to women and fighting it; and constantly questioning all authority, including men's. I felt I did not belong there.[41]

In order to decide that one does "not belong there," one must have necessarily been considering whether one *could* belong there. Watching "from the sidelines," anticipating how one would be received, and noticing the differences between the self and this group of identification—these are precisely the conditions of a "borderland" existence in which competing interests are at work irrespective of which position one consciously chooses to take at any given moment. This is why the simple binarism that poses "assimilation" versus "loyalty" is insufficient for understanding the deployment of racism or the assertion of existential freedom in this context.[42]

This condition of marginal positionality, then, is exactly what makes it possible for Moraga to offer a different understanding of the meaning of *la causa, la familia* and the terms of commitment to one's people. Within such an understanding it is possible that "to be critical of one's culture is not to betray that culture."[43] It is also from this position that Moraga takes feminism to task both for its heterosexism and its racism: "In failing . . . to take race, ethnicity, class into account in determining where women are sexually, many feminists have created an analysis of sexual oppression (often confused with sexuality itself) which is a political dead-end."[44]

Thus we can see how one contemporary Chicana lesbian takes account of her own concrete practices and life-choices through the intricately textured presence of historical pasts as she identifies them in her conscious experience, something that is also a common feature in contemporary Chicana literature.[45] For the Chicana lesbian, such a taking up of these life-choices emerges from her understanding of how her sexuality positions her as an outsider (if not traitor) to her people. While sexuality becomes a key factor in the understanding of her outsider position, the racism and classism that situate her prior to her understanding of heterosexism create a natural move toward white culture (revealing its inherent racism, the bleaching effect of the "melting pot"). The Chicana lesbian is posed against herself from within and thus comes to occupy borderlands where she is neither here nor there, where she is nowhere.[46]

Beginning a Self-Reflexive Interrogation

How are we to read the legacy of Malintzin Tenepal, Barceló, and others like them? What is "their" presence in the hearts and minds of "their" descendants?[47] If success within a socioeconomic world or safety for the expression of one's lesbianism requires a homogenization of cultural differences, then how are we to judge decisions by Mexican-Americans like Moraga (and my father), to become "anglocized"? As a collusion? As a sellout? As a commitment to survival for oneself and one's family?

I have been attempting to engage these very questions through a consideration of the experiences of consciousness and moments of conscious experience traced by Chicana lesbian (and Chicana) writers. That I have made the selections of figures and circumstances for consideration above is not arbitrary, but reflexive with my own experiences of consciousness. In tracing the histories of female figures in the history of the land upon which they struggle, Chicana lesbians reveal these struggles as lived upon their bodies and especially in their sexuality. Standing outside looking in, considering the possibilities and hoping against and within the conflicts of complex situations, the Chicana lesbian moves haltingly, freezes, breaks away to make a small movement here or there. These are bodily lived-experiences that are entirely connected to the communities and histories upon which Chicana lesbians live. They portend possibilities of radical transformation for both the self and the socius (resistant though the socius is). Yet, this portention of radical transformation occurs precisely because Chicana lesbians occupy a place of radical ambiguity where they recognize their participation in systems of domination even as they struggle against domination. Chicana lesbians trace a history that is inscribed upon their own bodies as those who have been the geographical and psychical objects of colonization—a circumstance that continues to this day.

The discursive sites that produce the Chicana lesbian therefore necessarily involve self-alienation for the person located in such sites. In the midst of this self-alienation, the Chicana lesbian embraces this identity precisely because it prevents her from being fully situated here or there. Such a move creates the possibilities for new kinds of self-consciousness—a strategic move that seems consistent with those of the "Subaltern" described by Spivak: "It is within the framework of a strategic interest in the self-alienating displacing move of and by a consciousness of collectivity, then, that self-determination and an unalienated self-consciousness can be broached."[48]

Considered according to the work and experiences of Chicana lesbians, such a broaching of unalienated self-consciousness seems to be always that, a *broaching*. This position of movement that remains a broaching thus appears as an essential location that produces the Chicana lesbian; it is, then, a position of radical ambiguity lived in the body. Jane Gallop similarly embraces the situation of an unalienated self-consciousness as always broached but never fully achieved when she says, "Identity must be continually assumed and immediately called into question."[49] What Gallop embraces as practice, Chicana lesbians demonstrate by their existence. These considerations of the construction of the Chicana lesbian focus our attention on consciousness in the narrow and situated (*not* the transcendental) sense in which the assumption and immediate questioning of identity occurs simultaneously.[50]

Theoretical and Methodological Implications

Given my own situation as a Chicana lesbian academic who has come to academic practice and feminist theorizing *precisely because* it offers me the opportunity to consider these issues as I have encountered them throughout my life, the *only* way I can engage the work of Chicana lesbians is through a very particular kind of identification.[51] It is an identification of living within conflicting interests, an identification of difference and alienation emanating from a number of (apparent) sources and locations; it is an identification made possible through the reversibility of human perception and expression—that is, through human communication.[52]

The move to foreground "personal experience" in considering my work here is not part of an effort to privilege personal experience as definitive of some "identity" (Chicana lesbian) that occupies me as subject-matter deserving of exploration.[53] Rather, I use my "personal experiences"—as all (good) theorists and researchers do—as offering moments of initial insight, glimpses that then require sustained attention beyond the situation and circumstances in which those glimpses appeared. As I engage this sustained attention, "glimpses" continue to appear. It is this inherently reflexive interrogation and reinterrogation of moments of experiences of consciousness, which allows the theorist to *realize* the ways in which an engagement in human communication allows one to *actualize* the forces and functions of discourse as situator of subject/author.[54] But one should not understand these movements of self-reflexivity as occurring within a consciousness that is separate from a world. To the contrary, the situated historical consciousness we are interested in cannot make these moves *except* as it exists in an intensional-extensional relationship to the world. As an essential feature of the location that produces the Chicana lesbian, the condition of self-reflexivity seems to entail within it certain dispositions useful for theory and methodology that is interested in transformations beyond oppression. Because consciousness does not exist separate from the socius, a reflexive interrogation of it necessarily involves the specification of location. The location from which the self comes to adopt the label of Chicana lesbian is an inherently contradictory one that creates a radical and ontologically contingent ambiguity.

Such an insistence on self-reflexivity constitutes a "repetition of method" consistent with what Merleau-Ponty calls "the *radical cogito* and what Heidegger . . . has in mind with his *daeseinsmässig*. Simply put, the process is one of reversibility, of converting consciousness into experience and vice versa."[55] Spivak's comments about "the greatest gift of deconstruction" convey very much the same meaning as Merleau-Ponty's "repetition of method": "This is the greatest gift of deconstruction: to question the authority of the investigating subject without paralyzing [her or] him, persistently transforming conditions of impossibility into possibility.[56] The persistent "transforming of conditions of impossibility into possibility" might be another way of describing the movement of consciousness engaged by Sandoval in her description of a common "U.S. third world feminist" consciousness that has emerged precisely because of its exclusion from the discourse of feminist theory. The location and production of the Chicana lesbian are consistent with Sandoval's theorizations.[57] Sandoval describes "U.S. third world feminism" as representing "a form of historical consciousness whose very structure lies outside the conditions of possibility which regulate the oppositional expressions of dominant feminism." Sandoval delineates this historical consciousness *topographically*, as a surface that the "U.S. third world feminist" negotiates *differentially*, shifting from one position to another as she move in and out of feminist contexts that display varying degrees of white hegemony.[58] In this differential consciousness, the Chicana lesbian, like Sandoval's "U.S. third world feminist," lives a radical ambiguity where she is always posed as never fully here nor there. An interrogation of the location of the production of the Chicana lesbian therefore provides a means by which this radical ambiguity might in fact provide the impetus for radical transformations precisely because of the essential undecidability of her positionality. Such a position requires the kind of theoretical movements described by Butler:

> The task is to refigure this necessary "outside" as a future horizon, one in which the violence of exclusion is perpetually in the process of being overcome. But of equal importance is the preservation of the outside,

the site where discourse meets its limits, where the opacity of what is is not included in a given regime of truth acts as a disruptive set of linguistic impropriety and unrepresentability, illuminating the violent and contingent boundaries of that normative regime precisely through the inability of that regime to represent that which might pose a fundamental threat to its continuity.[59]

Enacting these theoretical movements is not simply an abstract theoretical endeavor; rather, it is always already lived—and must be engaged as—on the bodies of those occupying the topographies of contested lands where the material (geographical) and psychical struggles entail radical shifts in apprehension and understanding of one's circumstance so that one broaches, but never achieves, an unalienated self-consciousness.

Conclusion

The presence of historical pasts through which I have considered the production of the Chicana lesbian has involved a focus on ambiguous figures who have been refigured by Chicana lesbian (and Chicana) writers so as to create space for transformations in meaning and practice *for themselves*. In their work, Chicana lesbians like Cherríe Moraga reveal themselves also as ambiguous figures *to themselves*. Deeply entwined within racist, sexist, heterosexist, and classist formations that pit them against themselves, other women, and their ethnic/racial communities, these Chicana lesbians attain agency by engaging these conflicting forces, yet always in a contingent way.

It is this condition of contingency that challenges static notions of "assimiliationist versus nationalist" and "complicitous-traitor versus loyal-culturalist" binarisms. It also suggests the necessity of self-reflexivity in academic work that purports to challenge the oppression and hegemony entailed in academic institutions. By her very existence, the Chicana lesbian embodies a radical ambiguity which requires a continual reengagement in subject position—borderland. I have suggested that it is precisely the contingency of her borderland subjectivity that creates the possibilities for radical transformation.

The question remains to be asked: What exclusions are produced in the work performed here? Writing is necessarily, it seems, a solitary endeavor that when performed within an academic institution is disciplined, constrained, governed by the institution. The Chicana lesbians (and radical women of color generally) who have been excluded from academic practice have, ironically, provided a means by which they may come to presence in radically new ways. The institution, however, is resistant to change.

Its "letting-in" of "difference" often functions simply to reinforce its constraints. Still, despite such resistance, perhaps it is possible to glimpse at and pursue new possibilities—the place of another beginning.

I could not have produced this work were it not for communities of lesbians, Chicanas, women of color, feminists, and other allies in the struggle against oppression. Though produced in a "solitary space," this work is nonetheless part of ongoing conversations about, and active struggles against, the forces and functions of domination as we face them both inside and outside our mutual location in the academy. It is to these ongoing conversations that I, finally, look to discover those other exclusions that are necessarily here, in this work—it is of "the community" that the possibility to realize radical transformations must ultimately be located.

Notes

1. Although I use the language "the Chicana lesbian," I do not intend to suggest that there is such a thing as *the* Chicana lesbian—presumably a person or group of persons who share a common ancestry and same-sex sexual orientation. Rather, I focus on "the Chicana lesbian" as a site of discursive production. I do not intend this focus to represent itself as exhaustive or exclusive to itself. There are, clearly, many other ways of talking about or representing "Chicana lesbian." Indeed, Trujillo's work (1991) reveals a great diversity among those who identify themselves as Chicana lesbians. My work here does not intend to homogenize this group. I am interested, however, in tracing through the work of contemporary Chicanas and Chicana lesbians in order to evocate histories and circumstances that participate in one kind of emergence for the Chicana lesbian today; there needs to be many works that take up this effort.

2. I use "North America" to refer to the land that today is Mexico and the southwestern United States (Texas, New Mexico, Arizona, California).

3. See Michel Foucault, *The History of Sexuality,* vol. 1 (New York: Vintage, 1980); L. Faderman, *Surpassing the Love of Men: Romantic Friendship and Love between Women from the Renaissance to the Present* (New York: William Morrow, 1981).

4. See E. Blackwood, "Sexuality and Gender in Certain Native American Tribes: The Case of Cross-Gender Females," *Signs* 10 (1984): 27–42, for an anthropological discussion of the meaning and practices of "cross-gender females" in certain North American tribes. Blackwood illustrates how European-Western categories that rely on stringent dichotomies are insufficient for understanding the experience and social meaning of these "cross-gendered" females. See also E. Blackwood, "Cross-Cultural Lesbian Studies: Problems and Possibilities," in *The New Lesbian Studies: Into the Twenty-First Century,* ed. B. Zimmerman and T. McNaron (New York: Feminist Press, 1996).

5. See Y. Yarbro-Bejarano, "The Female Subject in Chicano Theatre: Sexuality, Race, and Class," in *Performing Feminisms: Feminist Critial Theory*

and Theatre, ed. Sue Ellen Case (Baltimore: Johns Hopkins University Press, 1990) for a discussion of the Chicano theater movement, which illustrates how the *teatros* emphasized a cultural (Mexican) nationalism that "also led to the reinscriptions of heterosexual hierarchization of the male/female relationship" (132). For additional discussion of women in the Chicano theater movement, see Yolanda Julia Broyles, "Women in El Teatro Campensino: '?Apoco Estaba Molacha La Virgen de Guadalupe?'" in *Chicano Voices: Instersections of Class, Race, and Gender,* ed. Teresa Cordova et al. (Austin, Texas: Center for Mexican American Studies, 1986). The term *machismo* should be understood as a particular form of masculine bravado emergent in the Mexican/Mexican-American culture; Ana Castillo traces its roots back to the Catholic heritage brought by the Spanish, whose culture was deeply influenced by the cultures of North Africa. Its emergence in more contemporary terms is directly linked to the fact of the Mexican people being descendants of conquered people. Angie Chabram Deneresian ("And Yes . . . The Earth Did Part: On the Splitting of Chicana/o Subjectivity," in *Building with Our Hands* [Berkeley: University of California Press, 1993], 40) cites Armando Rendon's *Chicano Manifesto* for its discussion of *machismo.* In this text, *machismo* "is synonymous with revolutionary struggle, commitment and progress." As Rendon formulates it, *machismo* is coupled with its female counterpart, *malinchismo,* which designates "retrocession, betrayal, and conquest" (40–41). Deneresian points out that,

> by [Rendón's] pen, (Chicana) female *malinches* are in effect banished from the political movement itself, cast over to the other side with the heinous Tío Tacos (Chicano Uncle Toms) and Anglo oppressors. But female betrayal is much worse than the male version, since *malinches* betray not only a political principle but also male dignity and manhood as well. Ultimately, for Rendón, (Chicanas) *malinches* obstruct social progress, collective identity, and reconciliation with oneself, the family, and the nation (41).

See also Chela Sandova., "U.S. third World Feminism: The Theory and method of Oppositional Consciousness in the Postmodern World," *Genders* 10 (1991): 1–24, for an important discussion of racism within U.S. feminist theory during the 1980s.

6. See P. Giddings, *When and Where I Enter: The Impact of Black Women on Race and Sex in America* (New York: Bantam, 1984), and N. Cott, *The Grounding of Modern Feminism* (New Haven: Yale University Press, 1987) for discussions of the history of antiblack racism within the women's movement since the late nineteenth century. Both texts expose racist practices among white women that continue to exist today. See A. Garcia, "The Development of Chicana Feminist Discourse," *Gender and Society* 3 (1989): 217–238, for a discussion of the common expressions of racism encountered by Chicana, Asian, and Black American women in feminist academic work during the 1970s.

I do not mean to suggest that any of these three sites are static or by some essential condition necessarily a site of exclusion for the chicana lesbian. To the contrary, certainly within the Chicano movement, the work of the National

Association of chicano Studies has, over the past several years, engaged issues of sexism directly; the establishment of Mujeres Activas en Letras y Cambio Social (MALCS) in 1983 draws "from a tradition of political struggle" and is "dedicated to the documentation, analysis, and interpretation of the Chicana/ Latina experience in the United States" (A. de la Torre and B. Pesquera, eds., "Introduction" in *Building with Our Hands: New Directions in Chicana Studies* [Berkeley: University of California Press, 1993], 5). But the actual effects of these changes, the extent to which they are precursors for transformations in discursive formations, is unknowable as yet. Regardless, the history that allows us to see the discursive formations that situate the Chicana lesbian as an exclusion is clear and therefore also present even as processes of transformation may be enacting.

7. It is important to emphasize that I am *not* engaged in a project to find the "true" site where the Chicana lesbian comes to "know herself." Rather, I am attempting to demonstrate that it is the insufficiency of these "obvious" sites that *is* the production of the Chicana lesbian. In this way, "self-knowledge" is not posited as achievable in the colloquial sense of knowing oneself, but as a consciously engaged situation in which one's knowledge of what there is to know of the self and socius always exceeds one's ability to fully know. See M. Merleau-Ponty, *Signs* (Chicago: Northwestern University Press, 1964), 369, for a discussion of the *Radical Cogito*.

8. This is a point bell hooks makes when she says, "It is sadly ironic that the contemporary discourse [postmodernism] which talks the most about heterogeneity, the decentered subject, declaring breakthroughs that allow recognition of Otherness, still directs its critical voice primarily to a specialized audience that shares a common language rooted in the very master narratives it claims to challenge" (*Yearning: Race, Gender, and Cultural Politics* [Boston: South End Press, 1990], 25). hooks cautions that "without adequate concrete knowledge of and contact with the non-white 'Other,' white theorists may move in discursive theoretical directions that are threatening and potentially disruptive of that critical practice which would support radical liberation struggle" 26.

9. With respect to the diversity of the people living in the United States, the notion of being an "American" has often been characterized (particularly in the Southwest) as living in a "melting pot," which is, of course, not a melting together of differences, but a coercive bleaching of differences such that to be white is to be good and to be dark is to be not as good (if not wholly bad). Hence, we have the notion of a "successful Mexican-American" as one who embodies all the signifiers of white-middle-class-heterosexual-American—one who can be understood entirely within the "American" ideology and thus poses no threat to the white-dominance structure that is America.

10. Cherríe Moraga makes this point about her own work: "So these are not essays as much as they are poems and these are not poems so much as they are essays. Possibly the distinction no longer matters—between the poem and the essay, between my art and my activism" (*The Last Generation: Poetry and Prose* [Boston: South End Press, 1993], 4).

11.   See also Garcia, "The Development of Chicana Feminist Discourse"; G. Andzaldua and C. Moraga, eds., *This Bridge Called My Back: Writings by Radical Women of Color* (New York: Kitchen Table/Women of Color, 1983); and G. Anzaldua, ed., *Making Face: Making Soul/Haciendo Caras: Creative and Critical Perspectives by Women of Color* (San Francisco: Aunt Lute, 1990).

12.   Sandoval, "U.S. Third World Feminism," 1.

13.   See V. Ruiz, "'Star Struck': Acculturation, Adolescence, and the Mexican American Woman, 1920–1950," in *Building with Our Hands* (Berkeley: University of California Press, 1993) for an excellent discussion of the pressures of Americanization faced by young Mexican-American women in the Southwest between 1920 and 1950. While aspirations for economic success were often embraced by these young people, such success *required* Americanization. Even while these young women retained strong senses of their own ethnic heritage, their efforts to move up the social-economic ladder was so besieged with racism and their life-world so besieged with "American Images," that despite their own sense of cultural self they were forced to adopt the outward signs of "white-American" as prerequisites for success. Ruiz's essay offers examples that especially "hit home" for me given that my father, who was born into deep poverty in 1928 in McAllen, Texas (in the southern tip of Texas), grew up during this time and faced many of the same circumstances described by Ruiz. His own stories told to me about his childhood resonate in the stories told by Ruiz.

14.   See Norma Alarcòn, "The Theoretical Subject(s) of *This Bridge Called My Back* and Anglo-American Feminism," in *Making Face, Making Soul/Haciendo Caras*, ed. Gloria Anzaldúa (San Francisco: Aunt Lute, 1990). Sandoval (1990) illustrates this point specifically within feminist academic theorizing since the late 1970s.

15.   Following Lanigan, I use the words "self-reflexive," "critical," and "analytic" to denote theoretical movements that take the researcher/theorist in situ as problematic, and thus engages in a turning back upon the conditions of production (self-reflexive) by using criteria that are alternatively determined as necessary or sufficient for those conditions; these are the first steps of an eidetic application of semiotic phenomenology (see R. Lanigan, *Speaking and Semiology: Maurice Merleau-Ponty's Phenomonological Theory of Existential Communication* [Berlin: Mouton de Gruyter, 1991]; *Phenomenology of Communication: Merleau-Ponty's thematics in Communicology and Semiology* [Pittsburgh: Duquesnes University Press, 1988]; *The Human Science of Communicology: A Phenomenology of Discourse in Foucault and Merleau-Ponty* [Pittsburgh: Duquesnes University Press, 1992], appendix). See also Linda Alcoff, "The Problem of Speaking for Others," *Cultural Critique* 20 (Winter 1992): 5–32.

16.   Judith Butler, *Bodies That Matter: On the Discursive Limits of Sex* (New York: Routledge, 1993), 53.

17.   Gayatri Spivak, *In Other Worlds: Essays in Cultural Politics* (New York: Routledge, 1988), 198.

18.   One should not conclude, however, that all exclusions are created equally. The system of racism in American culture that produces whiteness as

norm and nonwhiteness as different from (less than) that norm, operates with a level of force and dominance that simply cannot be paralleled to or equated with the productions of exclusions that happen *within* the exclusions produced by the deployment of racism and heterosexism that is the dominant American culture. A specification of the locations (and the presence of historical pasts) from which identities and practices are produced should highlight these differences as well. A similar point is made by Butler when she says, "Even if every discursive formation is produced through an exclusion, that is not to claim that all exclusions are equivalent: what is needed is a way to assess politically how the production of cultural unintelligibility is mobilized variably to regulate a political field, i.e., who will count as a 'subject,' who will be required not to count" (*Bodies That Matter*, 207). My effort here is to focus on the situation of consciousness when a subject is unintelligible (Chicana lesbian) and suggest how this situation offers the possibilities of radical transformation.

19. I use "contingency" in the sense of Merleau-Ponty's "logic in contingency—an oriented system which nevertheless always elaborates random factors, taking what was fortuitous up again into a meaningful whole—an incarnate logic" (Merleau-Ponty, *Signs*, 88).

20. See Michel Foucault, *The Archaeology of Knowledge and the Discourse on Language* (New York: Irvington), esp. "The Discourse on Language."

21. Foucault, *The Archaeology of Knowledge*, 227, 230.

22. Anzaldúa (1987, 5).

23. In the case of intercultural domination, the forces of colonial powers, in the actual deployment of that power, situate different groups as *mediums* for that power. There is some sense in which simply being an object of colonialism entails a carrying through of that power and its interests. In the context I am describing here, the colonized people become mediums of colonial power and thus assist in its deployment. This creates fractures *within* a previously self-identified group as it recognizes the interests it serves. The same dynamics occur *between* previously identified groups who both become objects of colonial power. For discussions regarding this particular function of groups, see Lanigan, *Phenomenology of Communication*, 203–222; *The Human Science of Communicology*, appendix D; T. McFeat, *Small Group Cultures* (New York: Pergamon, 1974); and J. Reusch and G. Bateson, *Communication* (New York: W. W. Norton, 1987).

24. "She is known by different names. . . . La Malinche is called Malinal, Malintzin, Malinche, or Doña Marina. Malintzin is formed from her Nahuatl birth name; La Malinche is the syncretic, mestizo form" (S. Cypress, *La Malinche in Mexican Literature* [Austin: University of Texas Press, 1991], 2).).

25. Cherríe Moraga, "From a Long Line of Vendidas: Chicanas and Feminism," in *Feminist Studies/Critical Studies,* ed. Teresa de Laurentis (Bloomington: Indiana University Press, 1986), 176.

26. N. Alarcón, "Chicana's Feminist Literature: A Re-vision Through Malintzin/or Malintzin: Putting Fless Back on the Object," in *This Bridge Called My Back,* ed. Cherríe Moraga and Gloria Anzaldua (New York: Kitchen Table Press/Women of Color Press, 1983), 184.

27. Alarcon, "Chicana's Feminist Literature," 183.

28. Alarcon, "Chicana's Feminist Literature," 185–186.

29. For a discussion of the difference between "good" and "bad" ambiguity, see Lanigan, *Phenomenology of Communication*, 3–18. See also Bateson's work on the double-bind (G. Bateson, *Steps to an Ecology of Mind* [new York: Ballantine, 1972], 271–278).

30. T. Rebolledo and E. Rivera, *Infinite Divisions: An Anthology of Chicana Literature* (Tucson: University of Arizona Press, 1993), 7.

31. Rebolledo and Rivera, *Infinite Divisions*, 9.

32. D. Gonzalezs, "La Tules of Image and Reality: Euro-American Attitudes and Legend Formation on a Spanish American Frontier," in *Building with Our Hands* (Berkeley: University of California Press, 1993), 81.

33. Gonzalez, "La Tules of Image and Reality," 81.

34. Gonzalez, "La Tules of Image and Reality," 80.

35. Gonzalez, "La Tules of Image and Reality," 86.

36. Gonzalez, "La Tules of Image and Reality," 79.

37. Alarcon, "Chicana's Feminist Literature," 187.

38. Moraga, "From a Long Line of Vendidas," 174.

39. See L. Gordon, *Bad Faith and Antiblack Racism* (Atlantic Highlands, N.J.: Humanities Press, 1995) for an analysis of bad faith as it informs the racist minds and practices that produce the systems and structures that maintain cultural racisms. Such an analysis demands a shift from considering racism on an individual level to its very situation in the social world: "The task, in short, is to address the problems between society and the self, the problem of socially situated existence under the force of institutional sites of power or terror. This is precisely the point of examining racism from the standpoint of bad faith: one must address the transcendent and factical dimensions of human reality as a situated reality" (72).

40. See Cherrie Moraga, "La Guera," in *This Bridge Called My Back* (New York: Kitchen Table/Women of Color Press, 1983).

41. Moraga, "From a Long Line of Vendidas," 183; Ana Castillo makes a similar point, though she did participate in El Movimiento: "As a political activist from El Movimiento Chicano/Latino, I had come away from it with a great sense of despair as a woman. Inherent to my despaire, I felt, was my physiology that was demeaned, misunderstood, objectified, and excluded by the politic of those men with whom I had aligned myself on the basis of our mutual subjugation as Latinos in the United States" ("LaMacha: Toward a Beautiful Whole Self," in *Chicana Lesbians*, ed. Carla Trujillo [Berkeley: Third World Woman Press, 1991], 24.

42. bell hooks(*Yearning*, 29) makes a similar point in the context of the essentialism/constructivism debate in Black academic and nonacademic worlds.

43. Moraga, "From a Long Line of Vendidas," 180. Thus Moraga offers a revisioning of the family:

Family is not by definition the man in a dominant position over women and children. Familia is cross-generational bonding, deep emotional ties between opposite sexes, and within our own sex. It is our sexuality, which involves, but is not limited to, intercourse or orgasm. It springs forth from touch, constant and daily. The ritual of kissing and the sign of the cross with every coming and going from the home. It is finding familia among friends where blood ties are formed through suffering and celebration shared (1983b,182).

See Audre Lorde (1984) for a similar revisioning of the possibilities for the place of erotic-emotional bonds as they relate to spiritual and political transformation.

44. Moraga, "From a Long Line of Vendidas," 187.

45. See Rebolledo and Rivero, *Infinite Divisions.*

46. Note that the word "nowhere" is both "no-where" and "now-here." For an informative discussion of the methodological implications of Foucault's "rhetoric of the person situated in discourse," see Lanigan, "Somebody Is Nowhere: Michel Foucault on Rhetoric and the Discourse of Subjectivity in the Human Sciences," *The Human Science of Communicology*, 81–113.

47. It is very important to *not* make generalizations about some group of people arbitrarily designated "Mexican-Americans." Migration to the United States from Mexico has been and continues to be an always present phenomenon. First, second, third (etc.) generation migrants have widely differing experiences. The socioeconomic class of immigrants also makes profound differences. My effort in this work is to focus on those "Americans" who have never been "immigrants," whose ancestry on the land of the southwestern United States predates 1848. Yet, this is not to claim some sort of "authenticity" based on this equally arbitrary designation. It does, however, situate me (this is heritage of my father) relative to this academic-activist effort, and begins to lay the ground for directing my interrogations precisely upon the conditions of its production.

48. Spivak, *In Other Worlds*, 206.

49. Cited in Fuss, *Essentially Speaking* (New York: Routledge, 1989), 104.

50. Spivak, *In Other Worlds*, 204.

51. For a very interesting discussion of precisely how race and (lesbian) sexuality function both oppositionally and complicitously within an academic environment, see Dhairyam, "Racing the Lesbian, Dodging White Critics," in *The Lesbian Postmodern*, ed. Laura Doan (New York: Columbia University Press, 1994).

52. See Lanigan, *Phenomenology of Communication*; C. Schrag, *Communicative Praxis and the Space of Subjectivity* (Bloomington: Indiana University Press, 1986).

53. See Fuss, *Essentially Speaking,* 97–112, for an informative discussion of "identity politics."

54. Lanigan (*The Human Science of Communicology,* appendix B), in his "Communicology: An Encyclopedic Dictionary of the Human Sciences," defines realization as "*capability; consciousness of experience*; the process of constituting a subject/object of consciousness; what can be thought by a person."

Actualization is defined as *"ability; experience of consciousness*; the process of constituting a subject/object of experience; what can be lived by a person."

55. Cited in Lanigan, *Phenomenology of Communication*, 14.
56. Spivak, *In Other Worlds*, 201.
57. Sandoval, "U.S. Third World Feminism," 1.
58. Sandoval, "U.S. Third World Feminism," 11.
59. Butler, *Bodies That Matter*, 53.

Afterword

Berenice A. Carroll

The title of this volume, *Spoils of War: Women of Color, Cultures, and Revolutions*, appears in one aspect as an allusion to the treatment and representation of women, especially women of color, as objects of appropriation and victimization in wars and revolutions across cultures. But in another aspect, as professors T. Denean Sharpley-Whiting and Renée T. White make clear in their preface, it calls to mind a contrasting image of women of color as active agents against their own reduction to "spoils of war." Thus, women become not spoils but rather spoilers, or disrupters, of the hideous games and rituals of war.

From that perspective, the papers collected here break new ground and offer many challenging and provocative insights in the complex issues of women and war. The literature on these issues today is substantial, yet it is marred by egregious neglect of the *intersections* of gender with race and class. Despite frequent complaints from the political right about the alleged domination of academia by the "politically correct" proponents of feminism and multiculturalism, studies that recognize and give proportionate weight to race, ethnicity, class, and gender together are nearly nonexistent. Many works that focus on race and class tend to neglect women and gender, while most of the works that focus on gender give at best token representation to women of color.

This volume is the first to address the issues through foregrounding the experience of women of color in diverse contexts. It is also unique in bringing together studies on the multiple dimensions and forms of war faced by women of color in the workplace, the academy, the "private" realms of personal and sexual violence, the "public" realms of international war and theocratic politics, and the arenas of struggle over contested identities in literature and practice. As such, it greatly enlarges the prevailing conceptualizations of how gender influences war, revolutions, and resistance to oppressive systems.

It is a particular pleasure for me to see this volume come to fruition, having had a small hand in supporting the conference on the topic organized by the editors in 1995. As noted in the preface, both the conference and this volume were proposed in the context of a discussion about the responsibilities of a women's studies program. As we engaged this discussion in 1994, we were acutely conscious of the severe crises taking place beyond the academy, in our own society, and around the globe. The genocidal conflicts in Bosnia and Rwanda, the neocolonial oppression and violence in Haiti, and many other places, the intolerable poverty and denial of rights in our own communities, demanded that we consider how women's studies should relate to such critical events and struggles of our time.

The philosophical perspective that emerged from that discussion affirmed the premise that scholarship and action are tied to each other inextricably, in ways that are now always acknowledged, understood, and respected in the academy. Women's studies scholars have responsibilities to the movements from which our intellectual work emerged and our scholarship continues to draw ideas and challenges from those movements. Women's studies from its beginnings has woven activists commitments together with our scholarship in ways that have strengthened and nourished our endeavors in both arenas. As we continue to build this fruitful interaction, women's studies must expand the recognition of its multiple and multicultural roots, for it is not only the "women's movement" (in itself too monolithic a concept) but also the movements for racial, economic, and sexual justice to which we owe the impetus and vitality of our work.

This volume is a superb example of that integration of scholarship and action, theory and practice, which are necessary to carry forward that work. Above all, it is itself a model and offers a positive frame of cross-cultural and international feminist action to resist the construction of women as "spoils of war."

Bibliography

Abbas, A. A. 1991. "The National Islamic Front and the Politics of Education." *MERIP* (September-October): 22–26.

Abu Odeh, L. 1993. "Post-Colonial Feminism and the Veil: Thinking the Difference." *Feminist Review* 43 (Spring): 26–103.

Abu-Lughod, L. 1995. "Movie Stars and Islamic Moralism in Egypt." *Social Text* 42 (Spring): 53–67.

Ahmed, L. 1992. *Women and Gender in Islam: Historical Roots of a Modern Debate*. New Haven: Yale University Press.

al-Khalil, S. 1990. *Republic of Fear: The Inside Story of Saddam's Iraq*. New York: Pantheon Books.

Alarcòn, N. 1983. "Chicana's Feminist Literature: A Re-vision Through Malintzin/or Malintzin: Putting Flesh Back on the Object." In *This Bridge Called My Back: Writings by Radical Women of Color*, ed. Cherrìe Moraga and Gloria Anzaldùa. New York: Kitchen Table Press/ Women of Color Press.

———. 1990. "The Theoretical Subject(s) of *This Bridge Called My Back* and Anglo-American Feminism." In *Making Face, Making Soul/ Haciendo Caras: Creative and Critical Perspectives by Women of Color*, ed. Gloria Anzaldùa. San Francisco: Aunt Lute Foundation.

Alcoff, L. 1992. "The Problem of Speaking for Others." *Cultural Critique* 20 (Winter): 5–32.

Anderson, B. 1983. *Imagined Communities: Reflections on the Origin and Spread of Nationalism*. London: Verso.

Anderson, E. 1990. *Streetwise: Race, Class, and Change in an Urban City*. Chicago: University of Chicago Press.

Anzaldúa, G., and C. Moraga, eds. 1983. *This Bridge Called My Back: Writings by Radical Women of Color*. New York: Kitchen Table/ Women of Color.

Anzaldúa, G. 1987. *Borderlands: The New Mestiza, La Frontera*. San Francisco: Spinsters/Aunt Lute.

Anzaldúa, G., ed. 1990. *Making Face, Making Soul/Haciendo Caras: Creative and Critical Perspectives by Women of Color*. San Francisco: Aunt Lute.

Bachman, R., and A. Coker. 1995. "Police Involvement in Domestic Violence: The Interactive Effects of Victim Injury, Offender's History of Violence, and Race." *Violence and Victims* 10(2): 94–106.

Baker, E., and M. Cooke. 1935. "The Bronx Slave Market." *The Crisis: A Record of the Darker Races* 42 (November): 330–340.

Barbee, E. 1992. "Ethnicity and Woman Abuse in the United States." In *Violence against Women*, ed. Carolyn M. Sampselle. New York: Hemisphere Publishing Corporation.

Barthes, R. 1953. *Le degré zéro de l'écriture*. Paris: Seuil.

Bateson, G. 1972. *Steps to an Ecology of Mind*. New York: Ballantine Books.

Begag, A., and A. Chaouite. 1990. *Ecarts d'identité*. Paris: Seuil.

Bennoune, K. 1994. "Algerian Women Confront Fundamentalism." *Monthly Review* 46, 4 (November): 26–39.

Bergner, G. 1995. "Who Is That Masked Woman?: or, The Role of Gender in Fanon's *Black Skin, White Masks*." *PMLA* 110 (January): 75–88.

Bernstein, N. 1991. "Women Soldiers. Mothers of Amazons?" *Propaganda Review*, 8 (Fall): 16–17, 53.

Bhabba, H. 1994. *The Location of Culture*. New York: Routledge.

Bhatia, B., M. Kawat, M. Shahin. 1992. *Unheard Voices: Iraqi Women on War and Sanctions*. London: Change.

Blackwood, E. 1984. "Sexuality and Gender in Certain Native American Tribes: The Case of Cross-Gender Females." *Signs: Journal of Women in Culture and Society* 10: 27–42.

———. 1996. "Cross-Cultural Lesbian Studies; Problems and Possibilities." In *The New Lesbian Studies: Into the Twenty-First Century*, ed. B. Zimmerman and T. McNaron. New York: The Feminist Press.

Bonn, C. 1995. *Le roman algérien de langue française*. Paris: L'Harmattan Books.

Branch, T. 1988. *Parting the Waters: America in the King Years, 1954–63*. New York: Simon and Schuster.

Britton, J. 19 June 1968. Interview with Ella Baker, Civil Rights Oral History Documentation Project. Moorland-Spingarn Library, Howard University, Washington, D.C.

Brooks, G. 1991. "Please Do Not Offend the Saudis." *Esquire* 115 (April): 94–96.

Broyles, Y. 1986. "'Women in El Teatro Campensino: '¿Apoco Estaba Molacha La Virgen de Guadalupe?'" In *Chicana Voices: Intersections of Class, Race, and Gender*, ed. Teresa Córdova et al. Austin, Tex.: Center for Mexican American Studies.

Buchwald, E., P. Fletcher, and M. Roth, eds. 1993. *Transforming a Rape Culture*. Minneapolis: Milkweed Editions.

Buckley, M. I. 1990. "Encounter with Asian Poverty and Women's Invisible Work." *RNEW Update*, no. 11 (Winter).

Bugul, K. 1984. *Le baobab fou*. Dakar: Les Nouvelles Éditions Africaines.

Butler, J. 1993. *Bodies That Matter: On the Discursive Limits of Sex*. New York: Routledge.

Butler, J., and J. Scott, eds. 1992. *Feminists Theorize the Political*. New York: Routledge.

Cairns, R., and B. Cairns. 1994. *Lifelines and Risks: Pathways of Youth in Our Time*. London: University of Cambridge.

Cantarow, E., with S. O'Malley. 1980. *Moving the Mountain: Women Working for Social Change*. Old Westbury, N.Y.: The Feminist Press.

Carter, P. 1992. *Living in a New Country: History, Traveling, and Language*. London: Faber & Faber.

Castillo, A. 1991. "La Macha: Toward a Beautiful Whole Self." In *Chicana Lesbians: The Girls Our Mothers Warned Us About*, ed. Carla Trujillo. Berkeley: Third World Woman Press.

Chambers, I. 1994. *Migrancy, Culture, Identity*. London: Routledge.

Chomsky, N. 1989. *Necessary Illusions: Thought Control in Democratic Societies*. Toronto: CBC Enterprises.

———. 1991. "Force and Opinion." *Z Magazine* (July-August), 10–24.

Clark, R., et al. 1992. *War Crimes: A Report on United States War Crimes against Iraq*. Washington, D.C.: Maisonneuve Press.

Clark-Hine, D. 1989. "Rape and the Inner Lives of Black Women in the Middle West." *Signs* 14(4): 912–920.

Cleaver, E. 1992. *Soul on Ice*. New York: Dell.

Cobbett, D. 1986. "Women in Iraq." In *Saddam's Iraq: Revolution or Reaction?*, ed. The Committee against Repression and for Democratic Rights in Iraq. London: Zed Books.

Collins, P. H. 1990. *Black Feminist Thought*. New York: Routledge.

Collins, R. 1991. "Women Want Canada To Be the Peacemaker." *Calgary Herald*, 19 January, B5.

Costello, C., and A. Stone. 1994. *The American Woman, 1994–95: Where We Stand*. New York: W. W. Norton.

Cott, N. 1987. *The Grounding of Modern Feminism*. New Haven: Yale University Press.

Cypress, S. 1991. *La Malinche in Mexican Literature: From History to Myth.* Austin: University of Texas Press.

Davies, Carole Boyce. 1994. *Black Women, Writing, and Identity: Migrations of the Subject.* London: Routledge.

Davis, A. 1983. *Women, Race, and Class.* New York: Random House.

De la Torre, A., and B. Pesquera, eds. 1993. "Introduction." In *Building with Our Hands: New Directions in Chicana Studies.* Berkeley: University of California Press.

Deleuze, G. and F. Guattari. 1987. *A Thousand Plateaus.* Minneapolis: University of Minnesota Press.

DeMaris, A. 1992. "Male Versus Female Initiation of Aggression: The Case of Courtship Violence." In *Intimate Violence*, ed. Emilio Viano. New York: Hemisphere Publishing Corporation.

Denersesian, A. 1993. "And Yes . . . The Earth Did Part: On the Splitting of Chicana/o Subjectivity." In *Building with Our Hands.* Berkeley: University California Press.

Dhairyam, S. 1994. "Racing the Lesbian, Dodging White Critics." In *The Lesbian Postmodern*, ed. Laura Doan. New York: Columbia University Press.

Djebar, A. 1985. *L'amour, la fantasia.* Paris: J.-C.Lattès.

Donadey, A. 1993. "Assia Djebar's Poetics of Subversion." *L'Esprit Createur* 33, 9: 107–117.

Donnelly, E. "What Did You Do in the Gulf, Mommy? (Debate on Women in Combat)." *National Review*, 43 (18 November): 41–44.

Doumato, E. A. 1991. "Women and the stability of Saudi Arabia." *Middle East Report* 171 (July/August): 34–37.

Eickelman, D. 1993. "Islamic Liberalism Strikes Back," *Middle East Studies Association Bulletin* 27, 2 (December): 163–67.

el-Saadawi, N. 1992a. "Speaking at Point Zero: Oob Talks with Nawal El-Saadawi." *Off Our Backs*, March, 1.

———. 1992b. "Patriarchs and Petroculture." *New Internationalist*, October, 8–9.

Elshtain, J. 1987. *Women and War.* Brighton, U.K.: Harvester Press.

Enloe, C. 1991. "Does Khaki Become You? Are Women Pawns or Players in the War Game?" *New Internationalist*, July, 18–19.

———. 1989. *Making Feminist Sense of International Politics: Bananas, Beaches, and Bases.* Berkeley: University of California Press.

Esposito, J. 1993. "Secular Bias and Islamic Revivalism," *Chronicle of Higher Education*, May 26, A44.

Faderman, L. 1981. *Surpassing the Love of Men: Romantic Friendship and Love between Women from the Renaissance to the Present.* New York: William Morrow & Co.

Fairstein, L. 1993. *Sexual Violence: Our War against Rape.* New York: Berkeley Books.

Fanon, F. 1965. *A Dying Colonialism.* New York: Grove Press.

———. 1967. *Black Skin, White Masks.* New York: Grove Press.

Farah, N. 1991. "The Egyptian Women's Health Book Collective." *Middle East Report,* 173 (November-December): 16–17, 25.

Farmanfarmaian, R. 1991. "Should Women Fight? Even as the Gulf War Raged, You Said Yes." *McCall's,* 118 (May): 50.

Farmer, Ruth. 1993. "Places But No Importance: The Race for Inclusion in Academe." In *Spirit, Space, and Survival: Black Women in (White) Academe,* ed. Joy James and Ruth Farmer (New York: Routledge).

Farouk-Sluglett, M., and P. Sluglett. 1990. *Iraq Since 1958: From Revolution to Dictatorship.* London: I. B. Tauris and Co., Ltd.

Federal Bureau of Investigation. 1994. *Uniform Crime Reports.* Washington, D.C.: U.S. Government Printing Office.

Feldman, D., ed. 1990. *Culture and AIDS.* New York: Praeger.

Felman, S. 1993. *What Does Woman Want?: Reading and Sexual Difference.* Baltimore: Johns Hopkins University Press.

Fisher, M. 1991. "Bandits and Furballs Parts of Military Jargon." *The Globe and Mail,* January, A10.

Follingstad, D., L. Rutledge, K. McNeill-Herkins, and D. Polek. 1992. "Factors Related to Physical Violence in Dating Relationships." In *Intimate Violence,* ed. Emilio Viano. New York: Hemisphere Publishing Corporation.

Foucault, M. 1972a. *The Archaelogy of Knowledge and the Discourse on Language.* New York: Irvington Foundation.

———. 1972b. "History, Discourse and Discontinuity." *Salmagundi* 20 (Summer-Fall): 225–248.

———. 1980. *The History of Sexuality, Volume 1.* New York: Vintage.

Fromentin, E. 1893. *Une Année dans le Sahel.* Paris: Plon.

———. 1896. *Un été dans le Sahara.* Paris: Plon.

Fuss, D. 1989. *Essentially Speaking: Feminism, Nature, and Difference.* New York: Routledge.

Garber, J., and R. Turner, eds. 1995. *Gender in Urban Research.* Thousand Oaks, Calif.: Sage Publications.

Garcia, A. 1989. "The Development of Chicana Feminist Discourse." *Gender and Society* 3: 217–238.

Garrison, J. 1994. *Heavy Justice: The State of Indiana v. Michael G. Tyson.* Reading, Mass.: Addison-Wesley.

Garrett, D. 1995. "Violent Behaviors Among African-American Adolescents." *Adolescence* 30(117): 215–216.

Garrow, D. 1986. *Bearing the Cross: MLK, Jr. and the SCLC.* New York: William Morrow and Company.

Génette, Gerard. 1982. *Palimpsestes: La littérature au second degré.* Paris: Seuil.

George L., I. Winfield, and D. Blazer. 1992. "Sociocultural Factors in Sexual Assault: Comparisons of 2 Representative Samples of Women." *Journal of Social Issues* 48(1): 105–125.

Ghoussoub, M. 1987. "Feminism—or the Eternal Masculine—in the Arab World." *New Left Review* 161 (January-February): 3–18.

Giacaman, R., and P. Johnson. 1989. "Palestinian Women: Building Barricades and Breaking Barriers." In *Intifada: The Palestinian Uprising against Israeli Occupation,* ed. Zachary Lochman and Joel Beinin. Boston: South End Press.

Giddings, P. 1984. *When and Where I Enter: The Impact of Black Women on Race and Sex in America.* New York: William Morrow.

Gilliam, A. 1991. "Women's Equality and National Liberation." In *Third World Women and the Politics of Feminism,* ed. Chandra Mohanty, Ann Russo, and Lourdes Torres. Bloomington: Indiana University Press.

González, D. 1993. "La Tules of Image and Reality: Euro-American Attitudes and Legend Formation on a Spanish-Mexican Frontier." In *Building with Our Hands.* Berkeley: University of California Press.

Gordon, L. 1995. *Bad Faith and Antiblack Racism.* Atlantic Highlands, N.J.: Humanities Press.

———. ed. 1996. *Existence in Black: An Anthology of Black Existential Philosophy.* New York: Routledge.

———. 1997. *Her Majesty's Other Children: Philosophical Sketches from a Neocolonial Age.* Lanham, Md.: Rowman & Littlefield.

Gordon, L., and R. White, eds. 1998. *Black Texts and Textuality: Constructing and De-Constructing Blackness.* Lanham, Md.: Rowman & Littlefield.

Gramsci, A. 1971. *Selections from the "Prison Notebooks,"* trans. and ed. Quintin Hoare and Geoffrey Nowell Smith. New York: International Publishers.

Grant, J. 1981. *Fundi: The Story of Ella Baker.* New York: First Run Films.

Grant, J., ed. 1968. *Black Protest: History, Documents and Analyses, 1619 to the Present.* New York: Ballantine Books.

Green, M. J. 1993. "Dismantling the Colonizing Text." *The French Review,* 66 (May).

Greenberg, S. 1991. "The War on Women." The [*Montreal*] *Gazette,* 19 August, B3 [reprinted from *New York Times* and *Newsweek*].

Gross, A. 1990. "Women under Fire." *Ladies' Home Journal*, 107, (December): 93.

———. 1991. "Our Women at War." *Ladies Home Journal*, 108 (April): 51–52.

Gulf Committee, The. 1975. *Women and the Revolution in Oman*. London: The Gulf Committee & Leeds, Oman Solidarity Campaign.

Hackett, R. 1991. *News and Dissent: The Press and the Politics of Peace in Canada*. Norwood, N.J.: Ablex Publishing Corporation.

Hackworth, Col. D. 1991. "War and the Second Sex" *Newsweek*, 5 August, 24–29.

Haeri, S. 1993. "Obedience versus Autonomy: Women and Fundamentalism in Iran and Pakistan." In *The Fundamentalist Project: Fundamentalisms and Society*, vol. 2., eds. Martin E. Marty and R. Scott Appleby. Chicago: University of Chicago Press.

Hale, S. 1994. "Gender, Religious Identity, and Political Mobilization in Sudan." In *Identity Politics and Women: Cultural Reassertions and Feminisms in International Perspective*, ed. Valentine M. Moghadam. Boulder: Westview Press.

Halliday, F. 1974. *Arabia without Sultans*. Middlesex, U.K.: Penguin Books.

Hammami, R., and M. Rieker. 1988. "Feminist Orientalism and Orientalist Marxism. *New Left Review* 170 (July-August): 93–109.

Hampton, R. 1987. *Violence in the Black Community*. Lexington, Mass.: Lexington.

Herman, E. 1992. "Democratic media." *Z Papers*, January/March, 23–30.

Hewitt, L. 1990. *Autobiographical Tightropes: Simone de Beauvoir, Nathalie Sarraute, Marguerite Duras, Monique Witting, and Maryse Condé*. Lincoln: University of Nebraska Press.

Hill, A., and E. Coleman-Jordan, eds. 1995. *The Legacy of the Hill-Thomas Hearings: Race, Gender, and Power in America*. New York: Oxford University Press.

Hill, H., S. Hawkins, M. Raposo, and P. Carr. 1995. "Relationship between Multiple Exposures to Violence and Coping Strategies among African-American Mothers." *Violence and Victims* 10(1): 55–71.

hooks, b. 1990. *Yearning: Race, Gender, and Cultural Politics*. Boston: South End Press.

———. 1992. *Black Looks: Race and Representation*. Boston: South End Press.

Hughes, P., and N. Buermeyer. "Women in the Military." *National NOW Times*, March/April, 6–7.

Hull, G., P. Bell-Scott, and B. Smith, eds. 1982. *All the Women Are White, All the Blacks Are Men, But Some of Us Are Brave: Black Women's Studies.* New York: The Feminist Press.

Hutcheon, L. 1988. *A Poetics of Postmodernism.* New York: Routledge.

————. 1989. *The Politics of Postmodernism.* New York: Routledge.

Hutchinson, E. 1996. *Beyond OJ: Race, Sex and Class Lessons for America.* Los Angeles, Calif.: Middle Passage Press.

Ibrahim, S. E. 1980. "Anatomy of Egypt's Militant Islamic Groups." *International Journal of Middle East Studies* 12, no. 4: 423–53.

Ingersoll, J. 1995. "Which Tradition, Which Values? 'Traditional Family Values' in American Protestant Fundamentalism," *Contention* 4, no. 2 (Winter): 91–103.

Jad, I. 1990. "From the Salons to the Popular Committees, Palestinian Women, 1919–1989." In *Intifada: Palestine at the Crossroads,* ed. Jamal R. Nassar and Roger Heacock. New York: Praeger.

James, J. 1996. *Resisting State Violence in US Culture.* Minneapolis: University of Minnesota Press.

————. 1996. *Transcending the Talented Tenth.* New York and London: Routledge.

James, J., and R. Farmer, eds. 1993. *Spirit, Space, and Survival: African American Women in (White) Academe.* New York: Routledge.

————. 1993. "Paradigms of Exclusion and 'Integration' of Multiculturalism." *The Black Scholar* 23, nos. 3 and 4.

————. 1987. Interview with Dottie Miller. New York City.

Johnson, D. 1992. "Survey Shows Number of Rapes Far Higher than Official Figures." *New York Times,* 24 April, A-14.

Jones, J. 1985. *Labor of Love, Labor of Sorrow: Black Women, Work, and the Family: From Slavery to Present.* New York: Vintage.

Kabeer, N. 1991. "The Quest for National Identity: Women, Islam and the State of Bangladesh." In *Women, Islam and the State,* ed. Deniz Kandiyoti. Philadelphia: Temple University Press.

Kandiyoti, D. 1988. "Bargaining with Patriarchy," *Gender and Society* 2, no. 3: 274–90.

————. ed. 1991. *Women, Islam and the State.* Philadelphia: Temple University Press.

Krupp, C., and M. Weissinger. 1991. "Newswomen at War." *Glamour,* 89 (May): 172.

Kuhn, A. and A. Wolpe, eds. 1986. *Feminism and Materialism: Women and Modes of Production.* London: Routledge and Kegan Paul.

Kulp, K. 1981. "Acquaintance Rape." *WOARpath* 7 (Fall): 2–3.

Lahens, Y. 1990. *L'exil: entre l'ancrage et la fuite, l'ecrivain haïtien.* Port-au-Prince, Haiti: Editions Henri Deschamps.

Lakoff, G. 1991. "Metaphors of War." *Propaganda Review*, 8 (Fall), 18–21, 54–57.

Lanigan, R. 1991. *Speaking and Semiology: Maurice Merleau-Ponty's Phenomenological Theory of Existential Communication.* Berlin: Mouton de Gruyter.

————. 1988. *Phenomenology of Communication: Merleau-Ponty's Thematics in Communicology and Semiology.* Pittsburgh: Duquesne University Press.

————. 1992. *The Human Science of Communicology: A Phenomenology of Discourse in Foucault and Merleau-Ponty.* Pittsburgh: Duquesne University Press.

Lerner, G., ed. 1973. *Black Women in White America.* New York: Vintage.

Lindsey, K. 1970. "The Black Woman As Woman." In *The Black Woman: An Anthology*, ed. Toni Cade. New York: Mentor.

Lionnet, F. 1989. *Autobiographical Voices: Race, Gender, Self Portraiture.* Ithaca, N.Y.: Cornell University Press.

Lorde, A. 1984. "Uses of the Erotic: The Erotic as Power." *Sister Outsider: Essays and Speeches.* Trumansburg, N.Y.: The Crossing Press.

MacBride, S. 1980. *Many Voices, One World.* Report by the International Commission for the Study of Communication Problems. London: Kogan Page.

MacLeod, A. 1992. "Hegemonic Relations and Gender Resistance: The New Veiling as Accommodating Protest in Cairo." *Signs* 17: 3, (Spring): 533–57.

Magnier, B. 1985. "Ken Bugul ou l'écriture thérapeutique." *Notre Librairie* 81.

Maguire, K. et al. 1995. *Sourcebook of Criminal Justice Statistics, 1994.* U.S. Department of Justice, Bureau of Justice Statistics. Washington, D.C.: U.S. Government Printing Office.

Maguire, K., A. Pastore, and T. Flanagan, eds. 1993. *Sourcebook of Criminal Justice Statistics, 1992.* U.S. Department of Justice, Bureau of Justice Statistics. Washington, D.C.: U.S. Government Printing Office.

Mahony, R. 1991. "Voices of Dissent: Taking on the Pentagon." *Ms.* March/April, 86.

Makiya, K. 1992. "The Anfal: Uncovering an Iraqi Campaign to Exterminate the Kurds." *Harper's Magazine*, May, 53–61.

Marks, C. 1990. "Limits to the Decline of White Supremacy." Unpublished paper presented at the University of California-Santa Barbara. April.

Marty, M. 1995. "Comparing Fundamentalisms," *Contention* 4, no. 2, (Winter): 19–39.

Marty, M., and R. Scott Appleby, eds. 1991. *The Fundamentalism Project: Fundamentalisms Observed*, vol. 1. Chicago: University of Chicago Press.

————, eds. 1993. *The Fundamentalist Project: Fundamentalism and Society*, vol. 2. Chicago: Chicago University Press.

McFeat, T. 1974. *Small Group Cultures*. New York: Pergamon Press.

Merleau-Ponty, M. 1964. *Signs*. Chicago: Northwestern University Press.

————. 1981. *Phenomenology of Perception*. Trans. Colin Smith [trans. revisions by Forrest Williams and David Guerrière]. Atlantic Highlands, N.J.: Humanities Press.

Merlo, A., and J. Pollock, eds. 1995. *Women, Law, and Social Control*. Boston: Allyn and Bacon.

Merton, R. 1968. *Social Theory and Social Structures*. New York: Free Press.

Mernissi, F. 1987. *Beyond the Veil: Male-Female Dynamics in Modern Muslim Society*. Bloomington: Indiana University Press.

————. 1987. *Le harem politique*. Paris: Albin Michel.

————. 1989. *Doing Daily Battle: Interviews with Moroccan Women*. New Brunswick, N.J.: Rutgers University Press.

————. 1992. *Islam and Democracy: Fear of the Modern World*. Reading, Mass.: Addison-Wesley Publishing Co.

Middle East Watch. 1990. *Human Rights in Iraq*. New Haven: Yale University Press.

————. 1992. *Punishing the Victim: Rape and Mistreatment of Asian Maids in Kuwait*. New York: MEW and Women's Rights Project.

Miller, J. 1991. "Saudi Arabia: The Struggle Within." The *New York Times Magazine*, 10 March, 26–31, 38–39, 46.

Moghadam, V. M. 1993. *Modernizing Women: Gender and Social Change in the Middle East*. Boulder: Lynne Rienner Publishers.

Mohamad, M. 1989. "Islam, The Secular State, and Muslim Women in Malaysia." In *Women Living Under Muslim Laws*. Grabels, France: Dossier.

Mohanty, C., A. Russo, and L. Torres, eds. 1991. *Third World Women and the Politics of Feminism*. Bloomington: Indiana University Press.

Mojab, S. 1987. "Women in Politics and War: the Case of Kurdistan." Women in International Development. Working Paper #145, Michigan State University.

Moraga, C. 1983. "La Güera." In *This Bridge Called My Back*. New York: Kitchen Table/Women of Color Press.

————. 1983. *Loving in the War Years: Lo Que Nunca Pasó Sus Labios.* Boston: South End Press.

————. 1986. "From a Long Line of Vendidas: Chicanas and Feminism." In *Feminist Studies/Critical Studies,* ed. Teresa de Lauretis. Bloomington: Indiana University Press.

————. 1993. *The Last Generation: Poetry and Prose.* Boston: South End Press.

Morrison, T., ed. 1992. *Race-ing Justice, En-gendering Power: Essays on Anita Hill, Clarence Thomas, and Construction of Social Reality.* New York: Pantheon.

Mortimer, M. 1988. "Language and Space in the Fiction of Assia Djebar and Leila Sebbar." *Research in African Literatures* 19: 3: 301–11.

Mudimbe-Boyi, E. 1993. "The Poetics of Exile and Errancy in *Le baobab fou* by Ken Bugul and *Ti Jean L'Horizon* by Simone Schwarz-Bart," *Yale French Studies* 83: 196–212.

Mueller, C. 1990. "Ella Baker and the Origins of Participatory Democracy." In *Women in the Civil Rights Movement,*" ed. Vicki Crawford et al. Brooklyn, N.Y.: Carlson Publishing.

Munson, H. 1988. *Islam and Revolution in the Middle East.* New Haven: Yale University Press.

Murdoch, A. 1993. "Rewriting Writing: Identity, Exile, and Renewal in Assia Djebar's *L'amour, la fantasia.*" *Yale French Studies* 83: 71–92.

Musallam, B. F. 1989. *Sex and Society in Islam.* Cambridge: Cambridge University Press.

Naison, M. 1983. *Communists in Harlem during the Depression.* Urbana: University of Illinois Press.

Nicholson, L., ed. 1990. *Feminism/Postmodernism.* New York: Routledge.

Oates, J. 1992. "Rape and the Boxing Ring." *Newsweek*: (24 February), 60–61.

Ong, A. 1990. "State Versus Islam: Malay Families, Women's Bodies, and the Body Politic in Malaysia." *American Ethnologist* 17, no. 2 (May).

Page, C. 1991. "Gulf War Blitzkrieg Pulverizes Language." *Toronto Star,* 11 February, A15 (reprinted from *Chicago Tribune*).

Painter, N. 1992. "Hill, Thomas, and the Use of Racial Stereotype." In *Race-ing Justice, En-gendering Power: Essays on Anita Hill, Clarence Thomas, and the Social Construction of Reality,* ed., T. Morrison. New York: Pantheon.

Pape, K., and I. Arias. 1995. "Control, Coping, and Victimization in Dating Relationships. *Violence and Victims* 10(1): 43–54.

Payne, C. 1989. "Ella Baker and Models of Social Change." *Signs* 14, 4 (Summer): 885–899.

Peled, G. 1992. "Birth and the Gulf War." *Mothering*, Spring, 63, 90–93.

Pigg, S. 1991. "Women, Children Protest for Peace." *Toronto Star*, 19 January, A14.

Pirog-Good, M. 1992. "Sexual Abuse in Dating Relationships." In *Intimate Violence*, ed. Emilio Viano. New York: Hemisphere Publishing Company.

Pollitt, K. 1992. "Are Women Morally Superior to Men." *The Nation*, 28 December, 799–807.

Ramazani, N. 1993. "Women in Iran: The Revolutionary Ebb and Flow." *U.S.-Iran Review: Forum on American-Iranian Relations* 1, no. 7 (October): 8–9.

Ramazanoglu, C., ed. 1993. *Up Against Foucault: Explorations of Some Tensions Between Foucault and Feminism.* New York: Routledge.

Randolph, L. 1991. "The Untold Story of Black Women in the Gulf War." *Ebony*, September, 46, 100–102.

Rebolledo, T., and E. Rivera. 1993. *Infinite Divisions: An Anthology of Chicana Literature.* Tucson: The University of Arizona Press.

Reeves-Sanday, P. 1996. *A Woman Scorned: Acquaintance Rape on Trial.* New York: Doubleday.

Reusch, J., and G. Bateson. 1987. *Communication: The Social Matrix of Psychiatry.* New York: W. W. Norton.

Roach, C. 1991. "Feminist Peace Researchers, Culture and Communication." *Media Development* [London], 38, 2: 3–6.

Rodinson, M. 1978. *Islam and Capitalism.* Austin: University of Texas Press.

Rollins, J. 1985. *Between Women: Domestics and Their Employers.* Philadelphia: Temple University Press.

RSC (Revolutionary Sisters of Color). 1991. "Women of Color Speak Out Against the War in the Persian Gulf." *Off Our Backs*, April, 11.

Ruiz, V. 1993. "'Star Struck': Acculturation, Adolescence, and the Mexican American Woman, 1920–1950." In *Building with Our Hands.* Berkeley: University of California Press.

Rushing, A. 1993. "Surviving Rape: A Morning/Mourning Ritual." In *Theorizing Black Feminisms*, ed. Stanlie M. James and Abena P. A. Busia. New York: Routledge.

Saïd, E. 1993. *Culture and Imperialism.* New York: Alfred A. Knopf.

———. 1979. *Orientalism.* New York: Vintage.

Sampselle, C., L. Bernhard, R. Kerr, N. Opie, M. Perly, and M. Pitzer. 1992. "Violence Against Women: The Scope and Significance of the Problem." In *Violence Against Women*, ed. Carolyn M. Sampselle. New York: Hemisphere Publishing Corporation.

Sandoval, C. 1991. "U.S. Third World Feminism: The Theory and Method of Oppositional Consciousness in the Postmodern World." *Genders* 10: 1–24.

Sanghatana, S. S. 1989. *'We Were Making History. . . ': Life Stories of Women in the Telangana People's Struggle.* London: Zed Books.

Sargent, L., ed. 1986. *The Unhappy Marriage of Marxism and Feminism: A Debate on Class and Patriarchy.* London: Pluto Press.

Sayigh, R. 1989. "Palestinian Women: Triple Burden, Single Struggle." *Palestine: Profile of an Occupation.* London: Zed Books Ltd.

Schrag, C. 1986. *Communicative Praxis and the Space of Subjectivity.* Bloomington: Indiana University Press.

Seidel, M. 1986. *Exile and the Narrative Imagination.* New Haven, Conn.: Yale University Press.

Shaaban, B. 1991. *Both Right and Left Handed: Arab Women Talk About Their Lives.* Bloomington: Indiana University Press.

Shapiro, B. 1992. "The High Price of Conscience." *The Nation,* 20 January, 50, 53–54.

Shapiro, H. 1988. *White Violence and Black Response: From Reconstruction to Montgomery.* Amherst: University of Massachusetts Press.

Shepherd, H. 1991. "Women and War the Issue for Moral Thinker." The *Montreal Gazette,* 2 March, K8.

Sirman, N. 1989. "Feminism in Turkey: A Short History." *New Perspectives on Turkey* 3, no. 1, (Fall): 1–34.

Sluglett, P. 1976. *Britain in Iraq 1914–1932.* London: Ithaca Press.

Small, S., and D. Kerns. 1993. "Unwanted Sexual Activity among Peers during Early and Middle Adolescence: Incidence and Risk Factors." *Journal of Marriage and the Family* 55: 941–952.

Sorenson, S., and J. Siegal. 1992. "Gender, Ethnicity, and Sexual Assault: Findings from a Los Angeles Study." *Journal of Social Issues* 48(1): 93–104.

Spivak, G. 1988. *In Other Worlds: Essays in Cultural Politics.* New York: Routledge.

Statistical Abstracts of the United States 1994. Washington, D.C.: Government Printing Office.

Stora, B. 1991. *La gangrène et l'oubli: la mémoire de la guerre d'Algérie.* Paris: La Découverte.

Stringer, S. 1991. "Innovations in Ken Bugul's *Le baobab fou,*" *Cincinnati Romance Review* 10: 200–207.

Todorov, T. 1993. *On Human Diversity: Nationalism, Racism, and Exoticism in French Thought.* Cambridge, Mass.: Harvard University Press.

Trujillo, C., ed. 1991. *Chicana Lesbians: The Girls Our Mother Warned Us About.* Berkeley: Third World Woman Press.

Turk, N. 1987-88. *"L'amour, la fantasia* d'Assia Djebar: Chronique de guerre, voix des femmes." *Celfan Review* 7, 1–2: 21–24

U.S. Bureau of the Census. 1993. *Fifteenth Census of the United States 1930*, Population, vol. 2, General Report. Washington, D.C.: Government Printing Office.

U.S. House of Representatives, Select Committee of Children Youth and Families. 1990. "Victims of Rape." Washington, D.C.: U.S. Government Printing Office.

Urguizo, A., and B. Goodlin-Jones. 1994. "Child Sexual Abuse and Adult with Women of Color." *Violence and Victims* 9(3): 223–232.

Walzer, M. 1977. *Just and UnJust Wars: A Moral Argument with Historical Illustrations*. New York: Basic Books.

White, J., and S. Sorenson. 1992. "A Sociocultural View of Sexual Assault: From Discrepancy to Diversity." *Journal of Social Issues* 48(1): 181–195.

Williams, E. 1992. "The Attack on the Women's Peace Ship." In *War Crimes: A Report on United States War Crimes against Iraq*, ed. Ramsey Clark et al. Washington, D.C.: Maisonneuve Press.

Williams, P. 1994. *The Alchemy of Race and Rights*. Cambridge, Mass.: Harvard University Press.

Wilson, K. 1991. "'We Were Making History. . .' by Stree Shakti Sanghatana, Zed Books." *Off Our Backs*, January, 22. (review)

Wilson, W. J. 1987. *The Truly Disadvantaged*. Chicago: University of Chicago Press.

Woodhull, W. 1993. *Transfigurations of the Maghreb*. Minneapolis: University of Minnesota Press.

Wyatt, G. 1992. "The Sociocultural Context of African American and White American Women's Rape." *Journal of Social Issues* 48 (1): 77–91.

Wyatt, G., and M. Reiderle. 1994. "Sexual Harassment and Prior Sexual Trauma among White America." *Violence and Victims* 9(3): 233–249.

Yarbro-Bejarano, Y. 1990. "The Female Subject in Chicano Theatre: Sexuality, Race, and Class." In *Performing Feminisms: Feminist Critical Theory and Theatre*, ed. Sue Ellen Case. Baltimore: Johns Hopkins University Press.

Index

abortion, 85
Abu-Lughod, Lila, 95
academia, 21–23
activism, 7, 13; in Saudi America, 64; and women, 4–18
adolescence, developmental stages of, 41
Afary, Janet, xv, 83–100
Afghanistan, 85
Africa: mythology of, 121–22. *See also* North Africa
African American. *See* black
African American studies, 19, 20
African American Studies and Research Center (AASRC), xi
Ahmed, Leila, 94–95
Algeria, xv, 61, 66–67, 85–86, 103–12
American women, 65–66; and identity, 148n47
Anderson, Benedict, 116
anger, 39–40
anomie, 39, 44n24
Appelby, R. Scott, 84
Arab: identity, 108–11
Arab Women's Solidarity Association (AWSA), 69, 86
Asian women: exploitation of, 62

assassination, of women, 86, 109
assault, 47, 62, 86
assimilation, 138; and Chicanas, 145n13
autobiography, 105, 116–17, 124n19

Baker, Ella, 3–18
Bambara, Toni Cade, xiii
Bangladesh, 86, 90
baobab, symbolic meaning of, 118–19, 122, 124n23
Barceló, Gertrudis (La Tules), 135–36
battered woman syndrome, 36
belonging, cultural, 114. *See also* culture
black Americans: and economic determinism, 6; intellectuals, 14; liberation struggles of, 13; northern migration of, 5; political activism of, 4–5
black American men: and sexual assault, 46; social status of, 39
black American women: and domestic labor, 17n34; exploitation of, 7, 8; and identity, 42; labor, 19; sexual assault of, 27–56; stereotyping of, 50; wages of, 17n36

About the Contributors

Janet Afary teaches history and women's studies at Purdue University. She is the author of several articles on Arab women and critical theory. Her book, *The Iranian Constitutional Revolution, 1906–1911: Grassroots Democracy, Social Democracy, and the Origins of Feminism*, was published by Columbia University Press.

Berenice A. Carroll teaches political science and women's studies at Purdue University. Her works include *Design for Total War: Arms and Economics in the Third Reich* (Mouton) and *Liberating Women's History: Theoretical and Critical Essays* (University of Illinois Press).

Lewis R. Gordon teaches religion and African American studies at Brown University. He was formerly at Purdue University, where he taught African American studies and philosophy. He is author of *Bad Faith and Anti-Black Racism* (Humanities Press), *Fanon and the Crisis of European Man* (Routledge), *Her Majesty's Other Children* (Rowman & Littlefield); coeditor of *Black Texts and Black Textuality* (Rowman & Littlefield) and *Fanon: A Critical Reader* (Blackwell); and editor of *Existence in Black* (Routledge).

Joy James teaches ethnic studies at the University of Colorado at Boulder. She is author of *Transcending the Talented Tenth* (Routledge*), Resisting State Violence* (University of Minnesota Press), and coeditor of *Spirit, Space and Survival: African American Women in (White) Academe* (Routledge), winner of the Gustave Myers Award for Human Rights. She is editor of the forthcoming *Angela Davis Reader* and *Angela Davis: A Critical Reader* (Blackwell) and author of a forthcoming biography of Ella Baker (Rowman & Littlefield).

Jacqueline M. Martinez teaches Communication and Women's Studies at Purdue University. Her published works include, "Speaking as a Chicana: Tracing Cultural Heritage Through Silence and Betrayal" in *Chicanas and Language: Reflection, Reconstruction and Innovation* (University of Arizona Press), "Chicana y Chicana: Dialogue on Race, Race, and Chicana Identity" (co-authored with Dorothy Leland) in *Readings in Cultural Contexts* (Mayfield Publishing) and "Signifying Harassment: Communication, Ambiguity, and Power" (co-authored with Andrew Smith) in *Human Studies*.

Shahrzad Mojab teaches adult education, community development, and counseling psychology in the Ontario Institute for Studies in Education at the University of Toronto. Her areas of research include minority women's access to education, antiracism education, Islam and women's rights, and gender, ethnicity, and nationalism.

Valérie Orlando teaches French and critical theory and philosophy at Eastern Mediterranean University. She has published articles in *Women in French* and the *Romance Review*. She is the author of the forthcoming *Beyond Postcolonial Rhetoric: Feminine Identity in the Contemporary Francophone Text* (Ohio State University Press).

Marjorie Salvodon teaches French at Connecticut College. She is currently completing a book on Caribbean literature and the experience of exile entitled *Cross-Cultural Crossings*.

Chela Sandoval teaches feminist and cultural theory and Chicano studies at the University of California at Santa Barbara. The author of *The Theory and Method of Oppositional Consciousness in the Postmodern World*, she has published and lectured widely on "U.S. Third World Feminism" and feminist theory and activism. Her work has appeared in *Genders*, *Disposition*.

T. Denean Sharpley-Whiting teaches French and African American studies at Purdue University. She is the author *Frantz Fanon, Conflicts and Feminisms* (Rowman & Littlefield), *Black Venus: Sexualized Savages, Primal Fears, and Primitive Narratives in French* (Duke University Press, forthcoming), and coeditor of *Fanon: A Critical Reader* (Blackwell).

Renée T. White teaches sociology at Central Connecticut State University. She formerly taught sociology and African American studies at Purdue University. She is coeditor of *Fanon: A Critical Reader* (Blackwell) and *Black Texts and Black Textuality* (Rowman & Littlefield), and author of *Putting Risk in Perspective: Black Teenagers in the Era of AIDS* (Rowman & Littlefield).